INTERZONES

POPULAR CULTURES, EVERYDAY LIVES

Robin D.G. Kelley and Janice Radway, Editors

INTERZONES

*Black/White Sex Districts in Chicago and
New York in the Early Twentieth Century*

Kevin J. Mumford

COLUMBIA UNIVERSITY PRESS
New York

Columbia University Press
Publishers Since 1893
New York   Chichester, West Sussex
Copyright © 1997 Columbia University Press
All Rights Reserved

Columbia University Press wishes to express its appreciation to
the National Urban League for permission to reprint four drawings for
Mullattoes by Richard Bruce, which appeared originally in *Ebony and
Topaz: A Collectanea*, edited by Charles Spurgeon Johnson, 1927.

Library of Congress Cataloging-in-Publication Data
Mumford, Kevin J.
Interzones : Black/White sex districts in Chicago and New York
in the early twentieth century / Kevin J. Mumford.
p. cm—(Popular Cultures, Everyday Lives)
Includes bibliographical references and index.
ISBN 0-231-10492-8 (cloth : alk. paper); 0-231-10493-6 (pbk : alk. paper)
1. Miscegenation—Illinois—Chicago—History. 2. Miscegenation—New York
(State)—New York—History. 3. Prostitution—Illinois—Chicago—History.
4. Prostitution—New York (State)—New York—History. 5. Sex customs—Illinois—
Chicago—History. 6. Sex customs—New York (State)—New York—History.
7. Chicago (Ill.)—Race relations. 8. Chicago (Ill.)— Moral conditions.
9. New York (N.Y.)—Race relations. 10. New York (N.Y.)— Moral conditions.
I. Title
F548.9.N4.M86   1996
306.84'6—dc20   96-26945

To my mother, Karen,
and for the lost

★

CONTENTS

★

ACKNOWLEDGMENTS

The first thing I do when I open a book is read the acknowledgments. Where did the author attend school—who are his friends—who supported her? I find myself surprised to have reached the point, finally, of writing my own brief statement, divulging some professional and personal gossip. There are in fact many friends and institutions that helped me to bring my research project to publication. I wish first to thank the staffs of the libraries, particularly at the Beineke Rare Book and Manuscript Library at Yale University, the Lesbian Herstory Archives, the Library of Congress, the New York Public Library, the Schomburg Center for Research in Black Culture, the Special Collections at Stanford University Archives, the Regenstein Special Collections at the University of Chicago, the Wisconsin Historical Society, the Iowa State Historical Society, and the Kansas Historical Society. In particular, I wish to thank Melanie Yolles, Jim Popp, Jim Knox, Joan Nestle, and Jim Hansen.

I benefited from the financial assistance of numerous institutions and individuals. I wish to thank the Department of History at Stanford University, the Danforth-Compton Foundation, and the

Stanford Humanities Center. This book would not have been possible without the financial support of the University of California President's Postdoctoral Fellowship for minority scholars. I also thank Karen Mumford, my mother, for financial support without which this book would not have been possible.

A number of scholars and friends provided scholarly advice and support as I made my way toward publishing a book of history. As an undergraduate, I became interested in the historical profession through my admiration for several among the faculty at the University of Wisconsin. Stanley Kutler was a model and an enthusiastic supporter. As a graduate student, I learned much from my adviser, Estelle Freedman. Throughout those years, I benefited from conversations with George Fredrickson, Lou Roberts, Bliss Carnochan, Carl Degler, Bill Tobin, Daryl Scott, and Mark Ventreska. My counselor, Fred Coleman, helped me make sense. I was awarded a fellowship at the Stanford Humanities Center that helped me change the way I think about my discipline. Randy Rodriguez was a meticulous research assistant. I wish to thank John D'Emilio, Michael Cowan, Alden Reimonenq, Herman Gray, and audiences at the University of California — Berkeley, University of California — Santa Cruz, and the University of Amsterdam for their helpful comments. My editor, Ann Miller, helped me enormously at every stage of the way.

For a number of complicated reasons, much of this book was written in relative isolation, without much human contact. At various moments I reached back into my own personal history and found sustenance from some queer memories. I never wavered from my desire to complete my study, though I don't know why. When I walked the streets of Santa Cruz or Minneapolis or Madison or Toronto and glimpsed an interracial couple, and especially a racially mixed child, I felt a renewed sense of purpose. I believed that my story might make life somehow better for people who crossed the color line, and that their children's difficult predicament might somehow be made less painful because they would understand its origins.

★

★

INTRODUCTION

In our culture, when a black person has sexual relations with a white person, the act is often controversial and always extraordinary. Because of history—slavery, racism, gender relations, sexual repression, power politics—sex across the color line always represents more than just sex. *Interzones* interprets some of the central events in the history of black/white sexual relations in the early twentieth century. It is not a traditional story of miscegenation—nor a chronicle of the conflicted experiences of racially mixed children. To employ some theoretical jargon that actually signifies a meaningful analytical process: *Interzones* is an attempt to excavate a genealogy and map a geography of black/white sexuality. Throughout the study I employ interracial sex as a category of analysis and then, with an eye for phenomena related to intercultural or interracial relations, move the interpretive lens across the historical landscape. From boxing scandals, speakeasies, and prostitutes to dance halls, bohemians, and the Harlem Renaissance, *Interzones* recounts the story of how interracial vice districts were formed and reconstructs the social experiences of the people who inhabited them.

To argue that black/white sexual relations will always be con-flicted or controversial is not to posit a kind of inevitability in the his-torical record. At no point do I suggest that people are born racist, but I do conclude that black/white sexual intimacy will always be influenced by the American past, and that we cannot escape the contours (or cages) of a distorted, sexually racist history. To that extent, sexual racism can seem inevitable.

If *Interzones* demonstrates any single historical thesis, it is that underlying the major events in the history of black/white sexual rela-tions—the famous marriage, the sexual scandal—there lies a rich history of black/white sexuality. *Interzones* proposes that these inter-racial relations on the margins remain central to understanding the character of modern American culture. At first glance many histori-ans would take this claim to be overstatement, a bold exaggeration, but from a historical perspective, it should be obvious. The fact is that black/white sexual relations are at the center of crucially impor-tant events in American history: slavery in the nineteenth century and African-American urbanization in the twentieth. Indeed, this book covers the traditional or so-called canonical events of the era—Progressive reform, commercialized leisure, populist politics—but it begins from a unique perspective, in the forgotten pasts of the despised and dispossessed. In my study the margin is at the center. For some time now, historians have argued for a methodology known as history from the bottom up, but the problem is that too many studies of common people ignored uncommon—and pro-foundly important—episodes in the past. We lost the connection between everyday lives and the big events at the center of traditional historical writing. *Interzones* privileges subcultural history, to be sure, but it also encroaches on the terrain usually staked out by his-torians writing from the "top down." The chapters on Progressivism are a case in point. In conceptualizing this section of the study, I was interested principally in learning about sexual relations in dance halls and speakeasies. Soon, however, I found myself wondering about how the speakeasy districts were formed. To answer that ques-tion required research into the history of urban reform and antivice politics. Thus, while attempting to excavate a microsocial history of speakeasies, I learned that antiprostitution reformers were responsi-ble for the creation of modern black/white vice districts and, more significant, that Progressivism ought to be understood as a deeply racial movement. Likewise, in a chapter on the commercialization of leisure, I explore the intricate rituals between dance hall patrons and hostesses, but the conclusions drawn ultimately address such historic concerns as the making of racial identities and the nature of American citizenship.

Still, *Interzones* is a study in social history—and the findings presented here stand on their own as historically significant. A chapter on black/white homosexuality explores the furtive participation of black and white homosexuals in the vice districts. There, in the most stigmatized of saloons and underground dance halls, men and women who desired people of their own sex experienced moments of pleasure and affirmation. Like other relations on the margins, these same-sex liaisons were increasingly commercialized, shaped by cultural contexts of illicit leisure institutions. If in a taxi-dance hall a Filipino man exchanged a token for a dance, further into the center of the sex districts people exchanged money for sexual intercourse. The movement of vice into African-American neighborhoods, and the influx of more and more African-American women into sex work, dramatically reshaped prostitution in the modern era. The chapter on prostitution builds on current work dealing with African-American women's labor history, while introducing for the first time the topic of migration and sex work.

The final chapters of *Interzones* try to keep the promise of providing a new and unique perspective on more traditional themes and topics. This section works toward a new conception of modernism, offering a social-historical interpretation of the Harlem Renaissance and then linking it to conservative reaction. When we place the sex districts at the center of American modernity— by citing them as original sources of modernism—the Harlem Renaissance novels seem less the products of "high" culture and more the fictional memoir of sophisticated, if displaced, bohemians reporting on sexual life in the urban trenches. The final, more familiar chapter on the moral conservatism of the 1920s, as understood from the perspective of black/white sexual relations, furthers a revisionist interpretation. Not all of the cultural conservatism of the 1920s concerned racial mixture or black/white sexuality, but an analysis of the restriction of intermarriage reveals the extent to which white anxiety over interracial sexuality influenced the social backlash of the 1920s.

For those who might be interested in theories of historical interpretation or in the craft of history writing, I will say something simple about my use of evidence. I do not believe that historians can write anything about anyone at any time. As a work of history, my narrative is structured by the availability and content of documentary sources—organization archives, newspapers, commission reports, sociological manuscripts, investigator reports, novels. Throughout, theoretical discussions help to open modes of analysis, but the basic themes of the story are defined by my experiences in archival research, transcribing and theorizing historical documents. At the same time, I believe in the value of the historical imagination.

The research for this project occupied many years, and frequently a single endnote represents hours of historical research. My interpretations are careful and considered, but in some instances I was confronted with but a few chards of evidence and was forced to choose between sharing the images and thoughts they inspired, and silence.

Some of my most important insights emerge from strategic readings of informal vice investigator reports that were produced by private detectives who were hired to go undercover into the brothels and speakeasies. Vice investigators were not neutral reporters of facts, obviously, but they were keen observers of detail. As I pored over the documents, I tried to apply a historian's skepticism to the materials, making great effort to distinguish between biased statements, full of moralizing and prejudice, and the statements that could be corroborated by other testimonies or at least seemed to me plausible. In the first case, when bias appeared, I did not merely discard the information, but rather used the material as evidence of the general system of morality operating in 1920s urban America. At the same time, I believed that some of the material was legitimate and truthful. Certain events and circumstances—investigator's conversations, their descriptions of speakeasies, the quoted prices of specific sexual acts—were not perfectly remembered and precisely transcribed, and that is an issue with which I have continuously struggled. But I cannot think of a good reason why highly trained professional investigators would intentionally misrepresent their observations in the reports that they filed. Throughout this study, when the information strikes me as highly judgmental, it is taken as evidence of the dominant moral system. When the information seems relatively "neutral," the evidence is accepted as contingent descriptions of historical reality.

Interzones covers a relatively narrow period in U.S. history, in two cities, but it does, I believe, pioneer new historiographical terrain. Scholars recently have become interested in the topic of intercultural relations—and something of a renaissance is emerging in the study of black/white sexuality. Until recently, however, the historical literature did not address the issue—and probably could not because of the volatility of the subject. Within the existing scholarship two trends can be identified. Historians have tended to focus on miscegenation in the South, principally in the context of early American or slave society. They have explored the extent to which demography, property relations, and prejudice determined patterns of mixture and systems of social classification. They also have explored racial mixture in comparative perspective, interrogating the unique features of the U.S. system. Almost all the scholarship begins with this point: in world history, the United States stands virtually alone in its strict regulation of black/white marriage and its generalized relegation of the progeny of intermarriage to the status of the subordinate group. The origins of this facet of the American character can be located in slavery, and yet I argue for historical discontinuity between the southern and northern modes of racial/sexual regulation.[1] Nobody wishes to downplay the significance of slavery in the historical—or, for that matter, the contemporary—construction of black/white sexual relations, but I should say that *Interzones* is very much a study of social change. It is premised on the proposition that the shift from rural to urban America, from southern agricultural economies to modern commercial infrastructures, from communal to modern anonymous social relations represented a historic watershed—that modernization reconstituted the meaning and regulation of black/white sexuality in America.

Even given my challenge to the older scholarship on interracial relations, it should be noted that my study is indebted to two classic works on race relations. One is, of course, St. Clair Drake's and Horace Cayton's *Black Metropolis: A Study of Negro Life in a Northern City*, which guides my analysis of urban ethnography throughout the central and, in some sense, most important chapters. The second study, which I wish to discuss briefly, is Gunnar Myrdal's *An American Dilemma*.[2] In his study Myrdal argued that the so-called anti-

amalgamation doctrine—the taboo against black/white sexual relations—provided the fundamental ideological basis for social segregation in the South. Southerners could justify Jim Crow by invoking
the necessity of sexual separation of the races. Although Myrdal
focused on the South, he suggested that the antiamalgamation doctrine also defined northern society, but he never fully explored or
explained the social taboo against interracial sex in the North. To that
extent my study takes up the challenge of bringing Myrdal's work
north, to help us more clearly understand contemporary urban relations between African-American and white people.

Moreover, even though Myrdal did not deeply analyze the
North, his work did have implications for race relations more generally. Myrdal argued that the southern antiamalgamation doctrine, particularly the interracial sexual taboo, served to maintain
the exclusion of black people from the polity and to stratify racially
the labor market. The taboo represented an ideological justification for material inequality: "The announced concern about racial
purity is, when the economic motive is taken into account, no
longer awarded the exclusive role as the basic cause in the psychology of the race problem." Yet Myrdal explicitly rejected a
reductionist economic argument: "Though the popular theory of
color caste turns out to be a rationalization, this does not destroy it.
For among the forces in the minds of white people are certainly
not only economic interests, but also sexual urges, inhibitions, and
jealousies."[3] Indeed, at least since 1933, when the black novelist
James Weldon Johnson argued that "in the core of the heart of
American race problems the sex factor is rooted," several genera-
tions of scholars explained the connection between sexuality and
racism by focusing on individual psyches. In a now famous volume
of psychoanalytic theory, the African anticolonialist writer Franz
Fanon explored the extent to which interracial sexual relations
recapitulated colonial relations, focusing particularly on the black
male psyche. Although it has come under heavy attack, Myrdal's
insistence on the psychological—and the social—basis and power
of racism continues to be an argument with which all serious
scholars must grapple. My findings can certainly be interpreted to
suggest the power of the psyche in racial matters.

Much of the recent theorizing, however, has moved away from
these "idealist" interpretations of sexual racism because they tended

★

to essentialize race and racism.[4] Instead of examining "racial attitudes" and locating a monolithic and static racism, these scholars have posed a different set of questions: How does the construction of race, as a culturally defined category of difference, change over time?[5] The issue of the changing nature of race and sexuality recurs throughout my study, but the questions of social constructionism, so hotly debated a few years ago, are less pressing today because most scholars simply reject essentialism.[6] Now the challenge is to specify poststructuralist theoretical claims, to make concrete applications, to provide conceptual details. If race and sexuality are constructions, then what precisely are the phenomena of their creation? As is demonstrated throughout my study, race is more than a matter of money and more than a cluster of ideas or discourses.

Race is made up of many phenomena, and I focus on three: ideology, institutions, and human interactions. As the study progresses, the significance of each of these three concepts should become clarified, both through theoretical elaboration and through historical example. Here let me suggest that by ideology, I refer to the more or less official realm of dominant culture—of symbols, popular cultural apparatus, mechanisms of cultural control, technologies of generalized discipline. Race and, more specifically, sexual racism is more than a matter of the legal or national cultural commitments of social inequality—it is also constructed into the infrastructure of our cities and everyday lives, not only in bureaucracies and schools, but also saloons, brothels, even sidewalks and alleyways. Finally, race, sexuality, and particularly their historical intersection cannot become traceable artifacts of history unless they are constantly produced and reproduced. Their reproduction is accomplished through the intricate, intimate encounters between people designated as different. By focusing on black/white contact, then, this study proposes to document not only discrete historic social phenomena, but also the historical creation of race and sexuality in the United States.

Interzones is situated, appropriately enough, at the intersection of two historic trends that shaped the period between 1900 and 1930. The first is the Great Migration. In response to wartime economy, and in protest of outrageous repression, African-Americans picked up, left their southern roots, and commenced a movement that would transform American life. The population movement of black people from the South to the North represented concrete, social structural change. This book centers on Chicago and New York, though some of its conclusions could be applied to other major urban areas. In 1890 in Chicago only 14,000 of the city's more than 1 million residents were black; by 1930 nearly 240,000 black people lived in Chicago. Between 1910 and 1920 the black population of New York increased by 66 percent, and from 1920 to 1930 it expanded by 115 percent, from roughly 153,000 to more than 327,000 black residents. Although black immigrants represented a relatively small percentage of the total northern urban population, what remains significant was the "event" of the sudden surge in their numbers, a development coded or made highly visible by color difference.[7]

At the same time that more African-Americans migrated to the North, a decisive transformation in the history of sexuality was taking place, a transformation emanating from the city. Beginning at the turn of the century and culminating in the so-called revolution in manners of the 1920s, gender roles, standards of sexuality, and ideals of marriage were transformed. These changes have been characterized by historians as a sexual revolution, but a new generation of scholars now emphasizes the counterrevolutionary nature of this paradigmatic shift in the sex/gender system. Liberation from Victorianism imposed a whole new set of modern constraints. During the modern era, roughly between 1900 and 1930, American urbanites turned from their homes into the dance halls, speakeasies, and amusement parks. The new forms of sociability reflected the rise of a more public consumer culture—a phenomenon linked to the shift from a production-based economy to a public sphere grounded on the anonymous, competitive social relations of mass consumption. As the scholarly literature on other capitalist countries has demonstrated, particularly the important work on leisure culture in Britain, social modernization had the profound effect of blurring the boundaries between the so-called private and public spheres, reshaping not only how urbanites spent their hours off the job but how they organized and perceived the most intimate aspects of their lives.[8]

This study begins with the proposition that black/white sexuality frequently extends beyond the interpersonal and into the political realm, variously signifying political change or social inversion or moral decline. The miscegenation taboo remained so central to American culture, I believe, because intermarriage reflected, in a particularly visible and dramatic fashion, the realities of the Great Migration—racial diversification. In turn, the changing face, and faces, of the city seemed to signal all that was changing about America. The historical thesis that the early twentieth century represented an era characterized by the decline of a communal, agrarian, traditional society and the rise of the modern still captures a central trend of the era, but we now know that race and sexuality must have played a more central role in that historic social transformation.

In the end, *Interzones* returns to a particularistic, localized view of American cultural history. There was, I believe, something unique about the Jazz Age. Any study of the 1920s that centers on the Great Migration must ultimately conclude that the rise of consumption and the consequent transformation of sexuality did not proceed in a similar fashion in every modern global context, the same, for instance, in London as in Chicago. As black people crossed state borders and white people crossed the borders of urban neighborhoods, black and white people crossed the sexual color line. These crossings were historic. When placed under a historical, analytical lens, these cultural interactions, hidden away in the vice zones, reveal some of what was indeed unique about modern America.

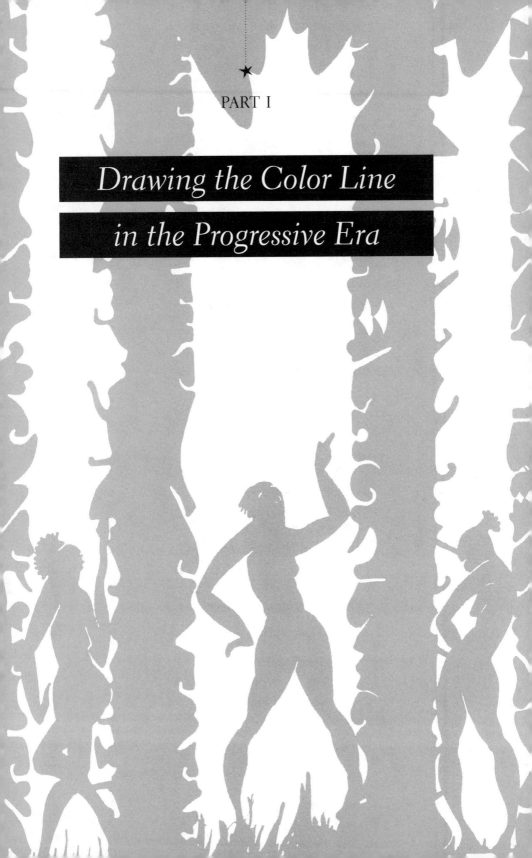

★

PART I

Drawing the Color Line
in the Progressive Era

★

1

JACK JOHNSON AND THE ABOLITION OF WHITE SLAVERY

In 1913 the Wisconsin Teasdale Commission, a Progressive-era reform organization, hired a black woman to work undercover as an investigator in Milwaukee. Posing as a prostitute, she reported her observations in dance halls and recounted her conversations with male patrons. In one case, she noted that a patron had asked her to dance but that she had refused, saying, "What would the girls say if you should be my beau?" Responding to the points implicit in her rhetorical question—that the patron was white, that she was black, and that together they could incite controversy—the white man smoothly replied: "Look at Jack Johnson and lots of other colored men with white wives."[1] Jack Johnson was the first African-American boxing champion to achieve international stardom. The patron's reply to the undercover investigator refers to Johnson's reputation for dating white women. The white customer's attempt to justify his proposition to the black woman by invoking Jack Johnson's interracial liaisons represented a peculiar estimation of Johnson's fortunes. Rather than a figure who might serve to encourage interracial intimacy, Jack Johnson was an example of the opposite. As were many black men who dared to become involved with white women, he was brought down swiftly by the forces of prejudice and repression. More than a victim, Jack Johnson was the central sexual and racial scapegoat of his era.

The story of Jack Johnson remains familiar to many, either through history books, the popular drama *The Great White Hope*, or racial folklore. His persecution has become a national legend, symbolizing the injustice of white supremacy. Even in its retelling, the story serves as a kind of ideological reinforcement of the sexual color line. Johnson was a popular boxer who defeated a formidable white opponent in a match that came to be known around the world. After Johnson's victory, white Americans tried in vain to find a white fighter capable of defeating Johnson, commencing the search for the fabled American "Great White Hope." As the futility of this search became apparent, Americans sought to defeat Johnson outside the ring through symbolic and quasi-legal repression, an effort that in the end proved successful. And yet the myth of Jack Johnson and the Great White Hope is not a complete, historically accurate story of the champion's trials. For the Johnson episode was more than an event in the annals of boxing history, and more than an example of white supremacist politics. If there were lessons to be drawn from the Johnson story, certainly one was that racism was alive and well in Progressive-era America. But as will become clearer in the following reinterpretation of the controversy, changing gender relations and particularly anxiety about female sexual excess made Johnson's persecution possible. Through the harassment and persecution of Johnson—and his lover and eventual wife—the beginnings of a new gender/sexuality system were symbolically or ideologically installed. In the process, white male sexual prerogative was also reinforced. Black men involved with white women were severely punished, while white men's sexual crossings of the color line continued to be tacitly approved.

The origins of this racial/sexual system can be located in the slave South. In general, black/white sexual relations were discouraged, because racial mixture threatened to erode the distinctions between white yeoman and free blacks, which were vital to the maintenance of slave democracy. Another significant tenet of American slave society held that white male access to slave women

★

was not uncommon; in some instances, it was considered a rite of passage for young white men.

It is often forgotten, however, that the antimiscegenation taboo also shaped northern society, where it served additional social purposes. Certainly the commitment to slavery was a national one, and to that extent northerners were as invested as southerners in stopping interracial relations. In the North, however, the interracial taboo took on a set of political meanings and became part of political discourse to an extent that, oddly enough, was not really true of the South (perhaps because in the South interracial sex was a fact of life and a source of embarrassment, and therefore should not be matter of public record). In the antebellum North, however, discussion of black/white sexual relations intermittently entered the fray of urban politics. In the 1830s, local citizens' groups opposed to the abolition of slavery accused antislavery activists of promoting "amalgamation of the races." In New York, for instance, the charge that antislavery activists were in reality proposing the amalgamation of white and black people resulted in a riot. It should be noted that the charges were in fact wrong, since only the so-called radical abolitionists, such as William Lloyd Garrison, advocated the repeal of intermarriage laws and, ultimately, the disintegration of the color line. In the 1860s, the charge of amalgamation was again leveled against the advocates of abolition and emancipation. Democratic politicians tried to smear Republicans in the election of 1864 by claiming that Lincoln's policy on slavery was intended not only to rid the country of slavery but to foster the amalgamation of the races, and they coined the term "miscegenation" to describe the impending racial disaster. It is true, then, that northerners supported the restriction of black/white sexual relations, reflecting a national commitment to slavery. But it was in the North where the racial mixture issue was brought out as a political weapon to use against movements for racial equality.

In the end, of course, Lincoln was reelected and the abolitionists triumphed. The political strategy of antimiscegenation was not seemingly successful. Indeed, it would be fair to say that the various and sporadic eruptions of antiamalgamation sentiment did not necessarily produce an enduring, deeply structured historical legacy. In the era of Reconstruction, many northern states repealed laws against intermarriage, a movement that, according to David Fowler, indicated the rise of a kind of northern liberalism. In Boston, once the site of intense conflict over the future of slavery, Garrison's dream of repealing the anti-intermarriage law was realized, and the number of black/white marriages increased dramatically. On the level of national politics, as well, the taboo seemed to possess less currency than earlier in the century. Frederick Douglass is a case in point. In the 1880s Douglass, the most famous black man of the nineteenth century, married a white woman, Helen Pitts.[2] In a now famous public address, Douglass claimed that, after having married a black woman, it was time to honor the other side of his ancestry by marrying a white woman. As a symbolic act, Douglass's marriage seemed a gesture of reconciliation, perhaps even a proposed method for ameliorating racial conflict. But the fact was that Douglass's intermarriage was hardly welcome, and few believed that racial mixture represented a feasible solution to American racial troubles. It is true that there was less protest against Douglass's intermarriage than against, say, the reputed "amalgamationist" abolitionists. Compared with the first half of the nineteenth century, the 1880s represented an era of relative racial calm — and Douglass was therefore able to intermarry without suffering the consequences of a major racial backlash. In any case, it seems true that the symbolic power or political salience of the miscegenation taboo declined over the course of the nineteenth century, paralleling the decreasing salience or significance of racial conflict in northern political life.[3]

All of that changed as America entered the twentieth century. If Douglass was the most famous black man of the nineteenth century, Jack Johnson was the most visible black celebrity of his era.[4] There are many significant differences between a leader born in slavery who became the foremost black intellectual and a national hero who gained stardom by winning boxing matches against white men. Yet each in their own way tried to challenge white supremacy in America. In a famous Fourth of July speech, Douglass challenged Americans to live up to the ideals of democracy and pointed to the hypocrisy of segregation and racism. On the Fourth of July over a decade later, Jack Johnson knocked out a white opponent, symbolizing the potential of black Americans to resist racial oppression and, perhaps, inspiring some to fight for racial justice.

After Johnson defeated Jim Jeffries, news of his victory spread across the country. More than ever before in his career, Johnson was perceived as a danger, a threat to the prevailing racial order; his victory sparked riots and led to a major campaign of repression and harassment. Johnson was not the first black boxer to rise to stardom. In the early 1900s, Herbert Gans, a lightweight, reigned as undefeated. Famous for his victory over white opponents, Gans also married a white woman.[5] Yet Gans did not achieve the notoriety, or infamy, of Johnson, in part because within the boxing world lightweights were less prominent than heavyweights. There is more to the matter than sporting history, however. If the historian Al-Tony Gilmore is correct that Johnson's victory "had sparked the first nationwide conflict between blacks and whites," then the depth and intensity of the reaction against Johnson requires an explanation. The difference in the response accorded Gans, or Douglass for that matter, and the response to Johnson was a matter of timing—a matter, that is, of history.[6]

To return to the sport: boxing was popular and dramatic—the matches provided an easy metaphor for the intensity of racial conflict in American culture. But the reaction to Johnson can only be understood as, first, a prelude to the generalized reaction against the influx of African-Americans from the South, and, second, as a surge of anxiety over the safety of white women in the city. To an observant urban dweller, even as early as 1910 the racial geography was changing. African-American neighborhoods were growing and new areas forming, and more black southerners were likely to follow. Moreover, as with most national dramas, the Johnson episode was given coherence only to the extent that it resonated with coincidental developments. In this case, the increasing visibility of single white women in the city, along with emergence of an antiprostitution movement, meant that the issue of white female sexuality just beneath the surface in the Johnson saga would become explicit and, in the end, as significant as the issue of white supremacy and early black migration.

By literally knocking out a white man, Johnson challenged fundamental ideological assumptions of white superiority; soon thereafter the search for a Great White Hope proceeded. A boxing defeat, no matter how controversial and in whatever racial context, does not logically lead to government intervention. Before and after his victory against Jeffries, state and federal authorities initiated various quasi-legal efforts to hassle or entrap Johnson. In 1910, one newspaper headline reported that Johnson could "not shake the habit of get-ting arrested." To be more precise, he could not elude official harass-ment. Less than three weeks before the Jeffries match, police arrested Johnson for speeding. According to reports, "three police officers battered down a training camp door of Johnson after chasing him for refusing to stop after police officers hailed him." Then the officers accused Johnson of resisting arrest, but eventually these charges were dropped, probably because of insufficient evidence.[7] After the fight, as well, officials harassed Johnson and his supporters. When, for example, Johnson was scheduled to appear in New York, police officers entered the racially mixed Tenderloin area—some-times referred to as Black Bohemia—and raided the clubs that tol-erated black/white socializing. They harassed the local patrons, warning them against open support for the black boxer. Well before his victory, as Johnson ascended to the status of world champion, state officials were already engaged in a program of calculated per-secution and personal injury. In several instances, Johnson was arrested for assaulting white men and in one case for assaulting a white woman, a showgirl named Annette Cooper. In these cases, the charges were dropped and Johnson was released.[8]

Johnson was a boxing victor but, in the end, a defeated cham-pion. It is hardly a matter of historical accident that Johnson met defeat in the public arena of sexual discourse. He was a brilliant ath-lete—with a fierce personality and a sleek, heavily muscled body—charged with African-American sex appeal. Cavalier and arrogant, he exploited his considerable erotic attraction. During sparring ses-sions, the champion reportedly wrapped gauze around his penis to enlarge its size. In boxing circles, Johnson was considered a rogue, known for his attraction to white women. And according to reports, the attraction was mutual. One paper declared that "Jack Johnson has actually been hounded by women in nearly every city he vis-ited."[9] Johnson's sexual predicament reflected the long-standing paradox of black male sexuality, in which the black figure is both feared and desired. Johnson was admired for his strength, boldness, and beauty, but also feared because of them. White women—and white men—must have glimpsed something alluring, perhaps even erotic, in Johnson's brash demeanor and ostentatious lifestyle. At least in part, it was the unsettling combination of sexual desire and racial fear that shaped the white social response to Johnson.

Johnson's sexuality, and his preference for white women, strained his relations with black America. Indeed, many African-Americans voiced opposition to Johnson's intermarriage. Johnson's first wife, Etta Johnson, was unhappy in her marriage, perhaps because of the pressures she experienced as the white wife of a black man. In 1911 she committed suicide. The next week the black newspaper, the *Chicago Defender*, ran a telling headline: "Mrs Johnson Was Not Hated by Negroes."[10] The *Defender* revealed the guilt produced by denying something with which one is never charged. Johnson's decision to marry white women estranged him from the African-American community. He was caught in between, with neither a white nor a black constituency to support him in a time of crisis. According to Gilmore, "much of the [black] anti-Johnson rhetoric was similar to that of whites." One black reporter, summarizing his view of Johnson's tendency to intermarry, plainly stated that, "From a racial point, we in this country would be better off if Jack Johnson would quit the United States, burning the bridges as he leaves."[11]

After the death of his first wife, Johnson began a relationship with another white woman, Lucille Cameron. Cameron was born in Minnesota and worked as a prostitute in Minneapolis until she met Johnson and moved to Chicago. When Cameron's mother learned of the relationship between her daughter and Johnson, she filed charges of abduction. Like many white women who consorted with black men, Cameron was accused of insanity. Indeed, her mother, Mrs. Cameron-Falconet, proclaimed, "I would rather see my daughter spend the rest of her life in an insane asylum than see her the plaything of a nigger." In fact, to support her case against Johnson, she "swore to a formal complaint that Lucille was insane." Soon Cameron was arrested and placed in "protective custody."[12] In this instance, as with Johnson's first wife, the African-American response was equivocal. One reporter's opinion probably summarized the black viewpoint: "He had a right to choose a wife of his own liking, but that it would have been much better and easily acceptable to both whites and blacks if he had chosen some worthy black woman." Johnson had few supporters and many detractors. Even before his successful prosecution under the Mann Act, Johnson's situation was precarious. The attempt to imprison the boxer for marrying his fiancée was a clear warning. As one reporter put it, in response to Johnson's marriage "the public streets were the scene of demonstrations which should have convinced Johnson to leave Chicago."[13] Despite the controversy, Johnson and Cameron were married in their home less than three weeks after the charges were dropped.

Johnson's interracial marriages were made the more visible, and to some offensive, by his proprietorship of a cafe called, appropriately enough, the Cafe de Champion. Catering to a wealthy clique of Chicago sophisticates, plushly furnished and richly appointed, the cafe was a polite, upscale version of the underworld clubs where black/white couples socialized. According to Johnson, the Cafe de Champion from time to time attracted patrons who "caused trouble," drawing unwanted attention from police. Moreover, as Johnson put it, "prejudice also played a part, for in my cabaret [there was] the practice of the races coming into contact."[14] Johnson was as controversial among African-Americans as among whites. The *Baltimore Afro-American* writer summarized one view when he stated, "I do not look upon Jack Johnson as a race leader nor do I in any way endorse his life and mannerism for it will not pay any one to follow it."[15]

Johnson's boxing champion status, his marriage to Cameron, and his proprietorship of a racially mixed club combined to move him to the center of national attention. Johnson was feared and persecuted as a symbol. The fear stemmed from his ability to "knock out" white men and symbolically defeat white supremacy. To maintain legitimacy—the appearance of neutrality and integrity—boxing authorities could not simply bar the victor from the ring. As the search for a white boxer capable of defeating Johnson continued, white authorities worked to persecute Johnson within the symbolic realm of sexuality. Under the guise of morality and the protection of virtue, white Americans could rid themselves of a major threat to the prevailing social order. And there was little to help protect Johnson, because the system organizing black/white sexual relations was so convoluted that, initially, black Americans reacted more to Johnson's sexual relations than to his racial persecution. In response to Johnson's intermarriage, both the black and white press printed negative stories. A United States congressman introduced a constitutional amendment to prohibit black/white marriage. In at least ten northern states, where the African-American populations

remained negligible, legislatures introduced bills to outlaw black/
white marriages.[16] Combine the explosive power of sexuality with
the deep wounds of racial conflict, and the result is an emotional,
impassioned, deeply irrational response of repression. The controversy surrounding an intermarriage in Chicago had spread across
the upper Midwest and into the East, from Nebraska and Wisconsin into Pennsylvania.[17]

In June, Congress proposed and passed the "White Slave Traffic
Act," written by Representative James R. Mann, which represented
an attempt to regulate prostitution by prohibiting the transportation
of women across state lines for immoral sexual relations.[18] Federal
authorities alleged that Johnson traveled across state lines for the
purpose of prostitution with his former girlfriend, Belle Schreiber.[19]
The charges included not only prostitution, but also the peculiar
legal categories of "debauchery," "crimes against nature," and
"unlawful sexual intercourse."[20] According to contemporary
accounts, Belle was "strikingly beautiful," an elite prostitute
employed at the Everleigh Club, on Dearborn Street in Chicago.
Authorities alleged that Johnson had transported Schreiber from
Pittsburgh to have "immoral" relations with her. Unlike Cameron,
Schreiber volunteered to testify against Johnson, revealing the jealousies of a jilted lover. Throughout her testimony, doubts were
raised as to her integrity because of her tainted past as a prostitute,
but her testimony nonetheless prevailed against Johnson. Though
she was believed, Schreiber was sometimes vilified for her statements. One black newspaper characterized her as the kind of
woman who was "not fit to wipe your feet upon."[21] But perhaps the
most damaging moment in the trial came when Johnson admitted
that he and Schreiber had engaged in sexual relations. Even though
followers of the trial must have guessed as much, Johnson's well-
publicized testimony shocked both black and white Americans.[22]
Black Americans certainly were disturbed and highly critical, but
they believed that Johnson should be chastised and warned in some
fashion. Indeed, the *Chicago Defender* predicted that in the "sentimental" case, Johnson would only be fined. They were wrong.
Johnson was found guilty and sentenced to a year in prison. He fled
to Paris rather than serve his sentence, and did not return to do his
time until 1920.[23]

As news of Johnson's conviction spread, African-Americans began to protest that he was a victim of race prejudice. One paper reported that "Johnson is in trouble. The whole world is upon him today. Behind it all you can see a large degree of race prejudice." Another paper argued that Johnson had been "crucified for his race."[24] Pointing up the racism, *Chicago Defender* reporters and editors noted that "if Johnson had been a white man and had made the display of honorable intention all of the court procedure would have terminated." According to Johnson, the Mann act was a "rank frame-up." "The charges were based upon a law that was not in effect at the time Belle and I had been together." Of course, Johnson was right.[25]

Groups protested on Johnson's behalf, and eventually most African-Americans supported him — and denounced his persecution as an example of white supremacy. But the [white] Progressive response to black/white sexual relations was clear and unequivocal: black men who consorted with white women would suffer serious punishment. Johnson's case may have been emblematic, but it was not unique. Throughout the Midwest and the North, despite the fact that only Indiana had passed a law prohibiting black/white intimate relations, black men and white women were stigmatized and often punished for engaging in interracial intimacy. Like Johnson, they were charged with either abduction or violation of the Mann Act.[26] In one case, for example, the press reported that a "white mother of five elope[d] with a negro Chauffeur." On the day the couple eloped, the woman told her husband that she was going to town to buy shoes. When a train conductor saw the interracial couple together, he alerted local authorities. According to one press report, Baltimore County authorities [tried] to have the black man "indicted on a white slave charge."[27] In another case, a couple from Kentucky, which prohibited intermarriage, decided to elope to Chicago. According to the *Defender*, however, "telegrams sent ahead of the couple resulted in their arrest." Thomas, the black man, was "being kept in jail on a charge of violating the Mann Act."[28] When the Mann Act could not be applied, local authorities relied on age of consent laws or morality charges.[29]

Black men were not only convicted of miscegenation, but, like Johnson, also sentenced to prison. In one case in Green Bay, Wisconsin, police arrested a black man, Olin Caver, whose only offense was that he intended to marry a white woman. Wisconsin did

★

not prohibit intermarriage by law. In addition to accusing him of intending to marry a white woman, the complaint charged him with having sexual relations with her. According to the press, Olin Caver and his fiancée, Elsie, had traveled to Michigan to obtain a marriage license, but the county clerk refused to issue it, again despite the fact that Michigan had no "antimiscegenation" statutes. In a letter to the NAACP, a sympathetic observer explained that "there is no law prohibiting intermarriage between the races, nor were they breaking age of consent laws."[30] The court also interrogated the mother of the young woman. According to testimony, she had consented to the marriage. The judge pronounced her to be an unfit mother, and removed the remainder of the children from her custody.[31] Writing to the NAACP, an attorney, Charles Bentley, stated that the charges against Caver were "subterfuge to get him out of the way and prevent his marrying the white girl."[32] Another source added that "he was not tried by a jury."[33] Olin Caver was sentenced to fifteen years at Waupan State Prison.

If in general there was a kind of continuity between the southern mode of regulating black male sexuality and the northern persecution of Jack Johnson or Olin Caver, there are important elements of discontinuity between the southern and northern ideological conceptions of white women who transgressed the color line. While some evidence suggests that lower-class southern women caught consorting with black men were seen as possessing "bad character"—and were sometimes punished for their immoral behavior—the ostensible purpose of Ku Klux Klan action against black/white sexual relations was to circumvent the political rights of black men. The effects of sexual lynchings on white women were secondary.[34] By the end of the Progressive era, the case of white women involved with black men was more complicated, reflecting complex shifts in gender and class ideology. In the North, white women who voluntarily married black men were viewed as depraved, insane, or prostitutes. As will become clearer in the following chapters, the status of white women involved with black men was historically contingent on changing conceptions of prostitution. During the nineteenth century, in the North it was widely believed that prostitutes were depraved fallen women—and only a few groups of female reformers believed in the possibility of their social redemption.[35] By the 1900s, prostitution was conceived of as white slavery, and white slavery discourse held that prostitutes had been trapped into prostitution, or, to use the language of the era, sold into sexual slavery. Since they did not *voluntarily* enter this trade, former prostitutes were worthy of uplift.[36]

It is worth highlighting the racial dimension of the white slavery discourse, because it remains connected to the racial trends of the era and, ultimately, to the fate of Jack Johnson. In describing the phenomenon of white slavery, Clifford Roe, a Chicago district attorney, proclaimed that "the white slave of Chicago is as much a slave as the Negro was before the Civil War."[37] Between 1909 and 1913, twenty-two major white slave novels—in which innocent white women are lured into sexual bondage by sinister, dark men—were published. Across the country vice commissions released annual reports on the traffic in young women. The ideology of white slavery was in fact a staple of early-twentieth century American culture.[38] Against this ideological backdrop, the fate of Lucille Cameron becomes all the more striking. In an era when moralists, reformers, and the federal government invested their resources in "rescuing" white women "enslaved" in prostitution, Lucille Cameron was not the beneficiary of social uplift but rather the target of state-sponsored persecution, imprisoned in a Rockford penitentiary. The contrast itself remains historic. As we shall see, by the 1920s white female prostitutes who accepted black male customers were highly stigmatized, both within and outside vice districts. In a sense, Cameron's imprisonment and eventual exile set the urban symbolic precedent for the generalized stigmatization of white women who consorted with black men that would gain hegemony in the 1920s. As will become clearer in the following chapters, when white women attempted to marry black men, judges frequently declared them to be morally degenerate or insane.[39]

Perhaps the least studied aspect of the white slavery ideology is its effect not on black men or white women, but on black women. The historical reality is that white slavery did not seem to extend to a concern with "black sexual slavery." African-American women entered the ranks of prostitutes in the greatest numbers after World War I. But the fact is that beginning in the late nineteenth century, black women were a visible presence in Chicago and New York vice districts. A few antivice reform movements briefly acknowledged the racial dimensions of vice, particularly its location in black neighborhoods.[40] But the prevailing policies of white slavery diverted attention, and resources, away from the social issue of black female prostitution.

Black reformers criticized white reformers for the diversionary effects of white slavery discourse. In 1896, for example, the leading black female reformer, Mrs. Frances E. W. Harper, addressed a convention of the National Purity Congress. There Harper reminded her audience that she belonged to "a race which more than thirty years ago stood on the threshold of a new era." Although black women were once in a degraded condition, Harper tried to emphasize the extent to which, in general, they had worked to uplift themselves. She also tried to connect that project of uplift to the self-interest of her primarily white, middle-class audience. Harper pointed out that "in your homes to-day are women in whose arms your babes are nestling . . . who are leaving the impress of their hands upon your children during the impressible and formative period of their young lives."[41] Simply put, to include the concerns of black women was to protect not only their virtue but also the virtue of their charges—the white children of the middle class.

Harper concluded her address by underscoring the racial contradictions embedded in vice reform. She recounted a recent experience at a rescue home: "I went to a midnight Mission and asked if a colored girl could be admitted, and was answered 'no'; and yet I do not think there was a Charity in our city that talked more religion in its advertisement than this one." She then pointed up the counterexample: "At another time I went to that same Mission with a degraded white girl whom I had found with more colored persons; for her the door was opened and a ready admittance given." As she concluded: "Black and white could sin together, but they could not be rescued in that home together."[42]

In another speech, a white woman introduced the topic of white male access to black women. In opening her address, Martha Schofield Aiken recounted her work experience as a reformer in the South: "Thirty years of missionary work in the South that forced the conviction that the blackest shadow lies on the white race."[43] In appealing to social purity reformers, Aiken held up examples of interracial sex as proof of the kinds of degradation that black women had faced. "We stood by the coffin of a beautiful girl of twenty years, whose rich English father had died suddenly and the property he left her colored mother, since dead, lessened in the lawyers' hands. Her boarding school knowledge and inherited refinement (father and grandfather white) added to her attractiveness." Then, pausing for effect, she queried: "Did these things end with slavery? No! No! No!" she answered. Near the end of her address, Aiken drew attention to the vulnerability of black women. "One cannot conceive of the feelings of modest, retiring, educated and refined colored women who know they are never safe from the insults of white men." Aiken made the argument that the sins of interracial sex had not remained confined to the past, in the history of slavery. Employing the parlance of the era, Aiken observed that "the social evil is written everywhere in the color of the children born since the war."[44]

Social scientific studies of white slavery also revealed, through their elision of blackness, that the worthy fallen woman was coded as white. For example, on several occasions, in his influential study of prostitutes in New York City, George Kneeland gives examples of "colored" women who solicited white men. Yet he never includes a discussion of black vice conditions, black neighborhoods, or the unique problems faced by black prostitutes.[45] Likewise, in her pioneering investigation of inmates at Bedford Hills Reformatory, Katharine Bement Davis provided perhaps the most precise data on the social backgrounds of prostitutes ever assembled. In one study of 647 prostitutes, 13 percent were black women, and yet African-American women represented approximately 2 percent of New York City's population. Additionally, Davis examined 2,363 prostitutes, of which 4.78 percent were black. While Davis carefully analyzed the statistics for native-born white women and theorized about the disproportionate representation of immigrant white women, she did not utilize her data on black women; instead, she buried it in a graph in an appendix. Like Kneeland, Davis was confronted with clear evidence of the impact of race on prostitution, but she overlooked the statistics and furthered an exclusively white analysis.[46] Likewise, Maude Miner, in her study *The Slavery of Prostitution*, found evidence of black participation in prostitution. Miner dealt with a similar group of New York prostitutes, but, again, discusses only white native-born and immigrant women, not black women.

Although black reformers were critical of the racial politics of Progressive reform, many did support the Mann Act.[47] But they crit-

★

icized the racial coding of the white slavery discourse because it constricted the scope of the implementation of the Mann Act, which was, after all, also named the "White Slavery Act." Thus black leaders indicated that they "would welcome any movement for safeguarding society by protecting women, but we think it should be broad enough to reach the colored woman as well as the white."[48] As one black newspaper reported, "white slavery seemed to suggest that black women were not worthy of legal protection" from the government.[49] According to black critics, the conduct of prostitution reform served to make "black women the legitimate prey of white men."[50] As another commentator on this double standard pointed out, a "white man had never been convicted of the same charges when a black woman was involved." These voices of criticism were faint, and often muted, but they provide an astute series of criticisms of the extent to which early Progressive reform was a deeply racial movement—for white women only. The fact remains that, at this stage of research, there is not one case of Mann Act prosecution in which the defendant is a white man charged with endangering the morals of a black woman.[51]

The case of Jack Johnson in the context of the white slavery scare had multiple and contradictory effects. First and foremost, the consecutive prosecutions of perhaps the most famous black man in America signaled that white supremacy and the maintenance of the color line was not merely a southern folkway but had become a national commitment. More specifically, the persecution of Johnson put all black men on notice: the North could be seen as less repressive than the South, but there were enforced and unequivocal limits on black male autonomy. White power holders could with relative impunity curtail black freedom; sexuality represented the symbolic arena in which this could be demonstrated. The prosecution of black men under the Mann Act also signaled the extent to which, on the symbolic level, racial ideologies remained connected to sexual matters and gender matters. It would be wrong to romanticize the white slavery scare, since it can be seen as an effort to shore up and control female sexuality, but it remains true that the scare activated a movement willing to expend energy and resources on women usually left behind as degenerate and permanently fallen. As an ideology, white slavery made it possible to restore females to white womanhood. Perhaps the most important legacy of white slavery, however, is a negative one. As the next chapter will show, the racial basis of the movement—the exclusion of black women from the category of the deserving and redeemable—created a social policy that effectively relocated vice in less policed areas and, ultimately, led to the abandonment of black prostitutes.

★

2

Transforming Urban Geography

When Jack Johnson fled the country, an exiled national scapegoat, he left behind him a profound cultural legacy. Johnson had effectively challenged white supremacy—in the realms of masculinity and sexuality—and exacerbated fears among some Americans of the potential of black male power. After his conviction, however, Americans could deny or dismiss the threat that Johnson symbolized. By the mid-1910s the Johnson panic had to a great extent subsided, and the national anxieties over gender security and racial control turned toward international politics and ultimately toward World War I. Instead of a full-blown national legacy, then, in the years immediately following Johnson's escape, the effects of his persecution were focused and localized. The new miscegenation taboo filtered downward, reshaping the experiences of the people who actually crossed the sexual color line. Life within the black/white vice districts would never be the same. By the beginning of the 1920s the process initiated by the ideological conflicts of the Johnson era would find completion, as antiprostitution reform transformed the sexual and institutional geography of Chicago and

New York, and consequently sexual relations between black and white people.

Vice reform, the effort to rid the cities of prostitution, should be understood as a definitive aspect of American social Progressivism. By 1913 vice reformers mounted a mass movement to close red-light districts across the country. The movement was astonishingly successful—for a brief time vice districts disappeared—and reformers believed that with their disappearance, prostitution too was eradicated. Indeed, in the 1920s white social reformers gradually retreated from the investigation and analysis of prostitution. Their untimely withdrawal helped to create a series of areas, neighborhoods, or zones in which "vice" resettled and then significantly changed.

I wish to designate these black/white sex districts, termed vice districts by urban authorities, as interzones, in part to specify their spatial and ideological definition. Simultaneously marginal and central, interzones were located in African-American neighborhoods, unique because their (often transient) inhabitants were black and white, heterosexual and homosexual, prostitute and customer. In a sense the zones might be conceptualized as a series of concentric circles, with the most stigmatized vice located in the center. In this imaginary conceptual map, interzones should be understood foremost as areas of cultural, sexual, and social interchange. After the passage of the Volstead Act and enforcement of Prohibition, these interzones became more deeply marginalized—their borders more pronounced—but also, in a sense, subculturally invigorated. In response to the restriction of alcohol, clubs known as speakeasies spread throughout the cities, and those considered most immoral and sexualized emerged in the zones. The following chapters will reconstruct everyday life in the interzones to shed historical light on the rituals of interracial sexual relations. Before this ethnographic reconstruction becomes plausible, we must understand the historical processes and, more concretely, the social policies that laid the foundations for the new sexual geographies of Chicago and New York. We must understand, in other words, the making and remaking of urban space before analyzing the changing constructions of black/white sexuality.

Historians have long debated the significance of Progressive social reform, continuously searching for ways to classify the various ideological factions and to periodize the decline of Progressivism. Vice reform—in many ways a quintessential but overlooked aspect of that

★

flowering of social reform activity—can be divided into two parts, early and late Progressivism. In my view, then, Progressivism persisted and informed the rise of the New Deal, but it changed ideologically somewhere in the mid-1910s. To an extent not usually acknowledged, the sources suggest that the ideological division between early and late Progressive reform can best be understood through reference to race or, more precisely, to the social impact of the Great Migration.

The implicit divisions in vice reform—temporal and ideological—come to the surface when attempting to understand the changing social agenda of Progressive vice reformers. Throughout the nineteenth century many city governments tolerated prostitution within segregated areas. In response to the lax policy, the first phase of Progressive vice reform prosecuted pimps, rescued fallen women, and closed red-light districts. The second phase has had scant study and remains little understood, but I would argue that it amounted to an ironic return to the older policy of tacit approval that allowed prostitution to flourish in the first place. The problem was that in urban America of the 1920s, tolerating prostitution in the interzones served to create a new complex of racial and gendered politics. Because the urban geographies of Chicago and New York were increasingly shaped by race, almost any reform effort directed at reorganizing city spaces inevitably became involved not merely in sexual reform but in racial politics.

The most influential policy makers in the antiprostitution movement were the vice commissions; of these, the New York Committee of Fourteen was the country's widely acknowledged reform leader. In 1905 the City Club of New York and the Anti-Saloon League (a key proponent of Prohibition) founded the Committee of Fourteen. The committee's first mission was to close the so-called Raines Law hotels, a type of saloon that had emerged as part of an effort to elude legislation prohibiting the sale of alcohol on Sunday. The law did not apply to hotels. Thus the proprietors added ten beds to their establishments, effectively complying with the definition of a hotel; in reality they were "houses of assignation," or houses of prostitution. In its first five years, the committee vastly reduced the number of Raines Law hotels but then became "conscious of the need of a much larger work which must be done." With that discovery, Progressive antiprostitution reform was born.[1] In Chicago the leading vice organization was the Committee of Fifteen, which was formed by the city council. Chicago's Juvenile Protective Agency also was active in antiprostitution, though they worked more on the problem of youth who patronized the dance halls than on prostitution in brothels. The commissions represented the "new" liberal social reform impulse, just emerging in the early twentieth century. Rather than old-style religious moralists, wealthy white philanthropists presided over the organizations—figures such as John D. Rockefeller, Julius Rosenwald, and George Foster Peabody. The advisory board of the Chicago Committee of Fifteen consisted of forty-three members. More than half the members were social service reformers, but the remainder were "corporate presidents, entrepreneurs, or executives." In general, a new generation of professional social scientists organized the programs, interpreted the data, and formulated much of the policy. The commissions attacked vice from several directions. The committees secured the passage of Injunction and Abatement Laws, authorizing the prosecution of landlords who knowingly rented buildings to tenants involved in prostitution. They initiated the investigation of prostitution in department stores.[2] Most important, "they attacked the semi-public, unofficial toleration of prostitution by the municipal governments."[3] The committees did not conduct direct rescue efforts, however; that remained the work of neighborhood missions and settlements. Instead, the committees employed undercover investigators to pose as customers, observe events within the clubs and brothels, and then deliver detailed written reports. These reports provided the data on which Committee of Fourteen policy was formulated. Commissions across the country emulated the New York Committee of Fourteen. Churches, high school libraries, and civic organizations wrote letters requesting copies of the committee's annual reports.[4] The New York Committee of Fourteen and, to a lesser extent, the Chicago Committee of Fifteen profoundly influenced the repression, geography, and regulation of urban prostitution throughout the United States.[5]

From the founding of the Committee of Fourteen through the beginning of World War I, the reform impulse to close down red-light districts spread across the country.[6] By the 1910s reformers had successfully pressured politicians and police to shut down segregated vice. The Committee of Fourteen and the Committee of Fifteen chose to interpret their early success as evidence that prostitution was

★

virtually eliminated. According to the Committee of Fourteen's figures, "whereas in 1914, there were almost 500 arrests for Keeping a Disorderly House; in 1924, there were less than 25."[7] Streetwalking was also curtailed. In Chicago the committee estimated that immoral resorts had been reduced by 40 percent and streetwalking by 80 percent. New York City Women's Court reported that the number of streetwalking cases were "negligible." A 1918 reformer proclaimed that New York City was the "cleanest city in the world." Chicago reformers concluded that prostitution had been "wiped out."[8]

If in 1917 you strolled through any number of white ethnic neighborhoods in Chicago or New York, the commission's glorious pronouncements might seem accurate. In some instances entire neighborhoods had been "reformed," left without a single dance hall, brothel, or streetwalker. One Chicago man recalled: "A few years ago I could point out 100 joints right in this neighborhood [a predominately white area]. Now I don't know of one." The "go-betweens of vice"—taxi drivers, doormen, and porters who earned money on the side for connecting prospective customers with prostitutes—testified to the movement's success. A New York taxi driver reported that he and other go-betweens had "practically discontinued aiding and abetting prospective customers," because "the resorts are closed or have been forced to move before we get a chance to send a customer." For the average resident living in certain white neighborhoods in Chicago and New York, it was quite possible to believe that prostitution had been eliminated.[9]

If, however, you resided in any number of other neighborhoods, the sexual geography had changed in more subtle and complex ways. Rather than eradicated, prostitution had scattered in different directions and relocated in new neighborhoods. A Committee of Fourteen official predicted one consequence of the dispersal with this rhetorical question: "If prostitution was to be driven from the 'dwellings of the poor,' where was it to go but to the dwellings of those better off than the poor?"[10] The commissions acknowledged that some prostitution had the unfortunate consequence of escaping repression and reemerging in middle-class neighborhoods.[11] According to one Committee of Fifteen report, "In both northern and southern cities, prostitution was spreading outside of the segregated districts." Investigators reported that "girls of respectable families in this city were being approached on the streets in an attempt to lead them astray." Some prostitutes, who formerly were found in the rear room of saloons, began to solicit customers in "certain classes of restaurants." After 1913 in Chicago some prostitution moved into the outlying areas and suburbs, including the roadhouses. Suburban prostitution was virtually all white.[12]

Some prostitutes did take up residence in the areas of the "better off," but, in answer to the official's question about the destination of vice: prostitution migrated deeper into African-American neighborhoods. The movement was more pronounced in Chicago than in

THE PROGRESSION OF VICE IN NEW YORK FROM THE LATE-NINETEENTH CENTURY TO THE MODERN ERA

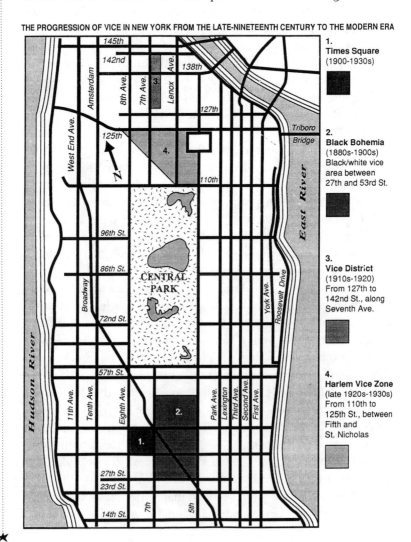

1.
Times Square
(1900-1930s)

2.
Black Bohemia
(1880s-1900s)
Black/white vice
area between
27th and 53rd St.

3.
Vice District
(1910s-1920)
From 127th to
142nd St., along
Seventh Ave.

4.
Harlem Vice Zone
(late 1920s-1930s)
From 110th to
125th St., between
Fifth and
St. Nicholas

New York.[13] In 1932 the social historian Willoughby Waterman observed the transformation of New York's urban geography. In just six years prostitution had migrated from those areas that the Progressive social scientist George Kneeland had identified in 1913, when "the region of greatest concentration continued to be on West Side Avenue between 34th Street and 56th Street." As early as 1919, however, in Harlem, a "very pronounced vice area was already establishing itself between 132nd and 143rd, especially along Seventh Avenue."[14] In addition, the closing of the older establishments

THE PROGRESSION OF VICE IN CHICAGO FROM THE LATE-NINETEENTH CENTURY TO THE MODERN ERA

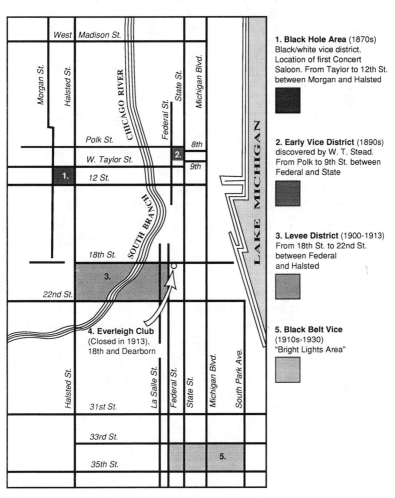

1. Black Hole Area (1870s)
Black/white vice district.
Location of first Concert
Saloon. From Taylor to 12th St.
between Morgan and Halsted

2. Early Vice District (1890s)
discovered by W. T. Stead.
From Polk to 9th St. between
Federal and State

3. Levee District (1900-1913)
From 18th St. to 22nd St.
between Federal
and Halsted

5. Black Belt Vice
(1910s-1930)
"Bright Lights Area"

25

resulted in the increase of tenement-house prostitution, again in predominately African-American neighborhoods. Waterman had identified a pattern of diffusion, temporary scattering, and the gradual resettlement. He applied the model to New York, arguing that it was "conspicuously true as regards Harlem." By the end of the 1920s Times Square continued to be a major vice district, increasingly popular among tourists, but in a sense the most "vicious" of vice activity was to be found above Central Park. According to Waterman's data, arrests in Harlem accounted for "thirty percent of the total convictions for the whole of Manhattan and the Bronx." By the late 1920s, hundreds of Committee of Fourteen entries and investigation reports indicated that prostitution thrived in the area from 126th to 152nd Street between Fifth and St. Nicholas Avenues. Harlem was becoming the city's clandestine sex district.[15]

By the 1920s prostitution in Chicago also relocated to African-American neighborhoods. In the 1870s the heart of vice was between Lake and Halsted and Washington and Sangamon. Within this district was the so-called Black Hole, "a group of Negro Saloons, cribs, and bawdy houses at Washington and Halsted Streets." In 1873 the first concert saloon, the major leisure institution preceding the dance hall, was established in the Black Hole.[16] In the 1890s the English journalist W. T. Stead had identified the area between Federal and State Streets as a center of vice; in 1895 Jane Addams Hull House had discovered vice as far south as 18th Street. By the beginning of the twentieth century the most famous vice district was the Levee, a twenty-square block comprised of "500 saloons, 6 variety theatres, 1,000 concert halls, 15 gambling halls, 56 pool rooms, and 500 bordellos housing 3,000 female workers." The most famous symbol of Chicago prostitution was the Everleigh sisters, two madams who owned a lavish Levee brothel catering to the wealthy. "The sisters had a million dollars in cash, some two hundred thousand dollars' worth of jewelry, uncollectible ious from customers totaling twenty-five thousand dollars." Notably, the Everleigh sisters attained celebrity status, and their brothel became something of a tourist attraction. Prostitution was illegal but unofficially tolerated by the reformers, police, and city governments.[17]

With the ascendance of Progressivism in Chicago, the Levee came under attack. By 1913 the Committee of Fifteen directed investigations into neighborhoods along 21st Street and Cermac, and police targeted many areas of vice, especially the Levee. In his melodramatic narrative, the popular historian Herbert Asbury described a typical raid: "Five minutes after the first patrol wagon rumbled into the South Side Levee, the district was in wild disorder." According to Asbury, "Into the street poured a crowd of half-dressed women, some with treasured belongings tied in tablecloths." For some time, then, the Levee was in fact "cleaned up," with the Everleigh sisters forced out of business. But prostitution was never wholly destroyed, and in some cases the older establishments reopened. By the 1920s the Everleigh sisters' palace on South Dearborn had become a second-rate brothel. Rather than highly paid white hostesses, the establishment was staffed primarily by African-American women. More significant, in Chicago the sociologist Walter Reckless concluded that between 1920 and 1930 the greatest concentration of vice had relocated to areas with the highest percentages of African-Americans.[18] By 1930 the Levee was closed and prostitution thrived in the Bright Lights district, located around 35th Street and State. In New York and Chicago the patterns were clear and undeniable: "Segregated vice" was giving way to racial segregation.[19]

In the early 1910s the internal migration of vice into growing black neighborhoods was covert, quiet—its purpose to elude police. The changing sexual terrain of Chicago and New York was not obvious but was hardly invisible. Chicago's Committee of Fifteen had evidence that 38 vice establishments could be found on the white ethnic West Side, whereas on the relatively affluent North Side, only 10. On the black South Side, however, the committee discovered 119 vice establishments. In New York the Committee of Fourteen conducted an investigation into black prostitution, but then ignored their findings.[20] They calculated that there had "been an increase, as compared with 1913–1914, of cases from tenements on the East Side and in Harlem, while decreases were noticed in the central part of the city, which included the old tenderloin." The committee publicly downplayed the concentration of prostitution in Harlem, emphasizing instead that the predominately African-American tenderloin had been "practically cleaned up, there not having been a case in the past year." Neither the police nor other social reform organizations responded to the committee's 1914 findings; the committee remained virtually silent on the issue for another thirteen years, when the problem of black vice became too serious to ignore.[21] Just years after the closing of the red-light districts, and the internal migration of prostitution from predominately white to African-American areas, another related development shaped the process through which black/white vice districts developed into interzones: Prohibition. Passed as the Volstead Act in 1919, enforced as Prohibition in 1920, the legislation forbade the production and consumption of alcohol. Like the repression of prostitution, however, the prohibition of alcohol ultimately resulted in the development of an underground economy—of distilleries, criminal distributors, and makeshift clubs in which to serve the drink. These clubs, the famed speakeasies, have become a central symbol of 1920s urban America. Most of these institutions were temporary, usually well hidden, but were not necessarily located in poor or undesirable neighborhoods. Some in fact could be found in prestigious brownstones or in the salons of famous urban bohemians. The most notorious speakeasies, infamous as institutions of criminality and sexual deviance, emerged in the black/white vice districts in Chicago and New York, in the center of the interzones. However, these institutions were not entirely unique to the era of Prohibition; in fact, the famed speakeasy of the 1920s had its origins in what were known as Black and Tans, nineteenth-century clubs catering to an interracial clientele.[22]

Contrary to what many would expect, between 1790 and 1900 in New York, and from the mid-nineteenth century in Chicago, institutions tolerating the expression of interracial intimacy were not wholly segregated from same-race institutions. African-American and mixed clubs were few, and, as Timothy Gilfoyle has shown, they were considered disreputable. In the early nineteenth century, one witness characterized a room over a local concert saloon as a place where "black and white promiscuously mingle, and nightly celebrate disgusting orgies." Another observer characterized black/white sexual relations as "naked deformity."[23] The interracial clubs were more likely to include public sexual behavior than were all-white establishments, but they were not geographically separated from the white establishments, nor were they as stigmatized as they would become in the twentieth century. According to Gilfoyle, the "racial divisions characteristic of much of nineteenth-century America vanished in this mixture of promiscuity, poverty, and loneliness."[24] In other words, Gilfoyle's findings may be interpreted to suggest that it was the presence of commercialized sex, and not racial mixing per se, that in the nineteenth century defined the borders of New York's sexual geography.

By the opening of the twentieth century, more and more young people traveled to the vice districts, attending dance clubs and local dives. As youth became increasingly attracted to popular dance establishments, they also participated in black/white institutions. Vice Commission and Juvenile Protective Agency reports provide important information on the changing racial composition of leisure institutions before the rise of the 1920s speakeasy. At first, the commission seemed to respond more strongly to class than racial issues. In 1913 one reformer reported that within a particular dance hall there existed "a social mixture such as was never before dreamed of in this county," but he was not referring to racial mingling but rather to the mixing of people from different class backgrounds. The cross-class interaction persisted nonetheless, and young working men and women enjoyed dance so much that they transformed it into one of the most popular leisure pursuits of its time. By the 1910s the older saloon, with a dance hall incidentally attached, was transformed into the glittering dance palaces, becoming the central leisure institution of a new generation of industrial workers. In the postwar era, the middle class patronized restaurants with dance floors and cabarets. According to David Nasaw, the young men and women who attended dance halls, working class and white-collar middle class, were part of a "public of pleasure seekers that cut across all social divisions"[25] — that is, almost all divisions. African-Americans, although often the musicians and choreographers, were not admitted to most dance halls.

Within their neighborhoods African-American men and women created their own unique, more modest leisure institutions, ranging from nightclubs to apartments doubling as saloons. In tenements or storefronts, small clubs opened; jazz bands played in private homes. African-Americans threw rent parties, in which families invited friends and acquaintances to their homes and for a small price provided cheap entertainment. The proceeds usually went toward paying the next month's rent.

In response to the new culture of public pleasure seeking, leisure institutions once located in the most dangerous urban areas, patronized by what Luc Sante has termed the low life, gradually evolved into highly respectable cabarets and dance halls.[26] Some Bowery concert saloons remained open, but they were relics of the past, and along with them, among the ruins of urban reorganization, were the clubs that tolerated black/white mixing. Frequently referred to as Black and Tans, these interracial clubs did not gain acceptance, or move into the geographical mainstream, but stayed in the slums. In fact they defined the slums.

Beginning in the late nineteenth century, discussion of the so-called Black and Tan surfaced in reform reports, sociological studies, and newspapers. The term Black and Tan apparently originated in the South, "from the palmy days when the negro was a factor in southern politics." The expression was coined to denote interracial cooperation, when black and white men combined in an election to defeat a white supremacist party, known as the "Lilly Whites."[27] The victorious coalition was known as the Black and Tans. Black/white relationships were also referred to by the term. One writer described an "underworld romance" as a "tangled thread of a strange 'black and tan' love."[28] Most cities with a sizable black population probably had at least a few Black and Tans, but some urban areas were reputed for their black/white vice districts. Chicago, New York, Detroit, and Cleveland reportedly included numerous racially mixed clubs. By contrast, racial mixing was less prevalent in Washington, D.C., prob-ably because the older model of Jim Crow black/white relations con-tinued to define patterns of leisure.[29] Of all the northern cities, Chicago was probably the most notorious for racial mixing. In his recollections a Harlem pianist recalled that there was more "mixing of the races in Chicago than there was in New York."[30] One *Pittsburgh Courier* front-page headline, referring to Europe's exotic reputation, even proclaimed: "Chicago Is Worse City Than Paris." According to J. A. Rogers, the black writer and leading expert on racial mixture, Chicago "had thousands of mixed married couples, chiefly of the laboring class."[31] In speculating why "Chicago was known for race mixing," one paper observed that there were "No Blue Laws in Chicago" (prohibiting the sale of alcohol on Sundays), which supposedly resulted in a more immoral atmosphere.[32] Black/white socializing was considered immoral because of the pre-vailing system of racial separation. Of all the forms of public, inter-racial contact, black/white dance elicited the sharpest, most impassioned responses from authorities. Thus the dance halls that welcomed black and white patrons but prohibited interracial dancing were often viewed as more respectable than the typical Black and Tan. In Chicago the Committee of Fifteen reported on a Black and Tan they had helped to shut down. When the club reopened under new management, the committee again sent an investigator. The new club was deemed respectable—in large part because "there was not mixing of the races in couples on the dance floor."[33] Racially mixed clubs that included black/white dancing were sometimes tolerated if they conformed to the racial double standard. As one black newspaper summarized the standard: "It has been the policy of clubs to frown upon negro men dancing with white girls, but at the same time allowing white men full association with colored girls."[34] When black/white dancing between black men and white women did occur, it was widely condemned. A prominent Chicago judge termed interracial socializing jungle dances, outraged that "orgies of the jungle could have been permitted in a public cafe in Chicago month after month."[35] In vice reports, investigators saved their harshest moralizing for the Black and Tans. Commissions refrained from publishing all the details submitted by investigators because, as the Committee of Fifteen stated, "no printable account could come within a mile of telling the depravity to which performers and patrons sank."[36] In part, these reactions stemmed from a visceral sexual racism; in part the negative views represented anxiety over the potential for racial conflict. In short, as one white commentator put it, tolerating the Black and Tan was like "Playing with Dynamite."[37]

From the perspective of black commentators as well, the Black and Tan was viewed as intrinsically immoral. A black writer described a Black and Tan as the site of "obscene, lewd, and indecent dancing and performances,"[38] yet the author never provided a detailed description of the patrons. They may simply have been performing the same dances popular everywhere, but because they were interracial they were condemned. Like some white newspapers, the *Age* concluded that black/white "dance halls . . . breed immorality and vice."[39] Black/white dancing was seen as immoral in large part because it suggested sexual relations.[40] Respectable African-Americans disdained black/white socializing and "disapproved of dance halls, cabarets, ragtime, jazz and leisure time."[41]

Whether expressed in a vice commission report or a newspaper headline, many groups held the belief that the Black and Tan was socially and sexually immoral. Although both whites and African-Americans rejected the Black and Tan, the black middle class expressed a specific concern with the dance halls that reflected the precariousness of their social position during the era of migration. Like white newspapers, black newspapers such as the *New York Age* believed that "dance halls wherein races mix are certainly the worst nuisances," and asserted that "colored and white persons cannot mingle happily." The racially mixed clubs "brought bad elements of the white and colored people together under inflammatory conditions and eventually that was certain to bring about a race collision, which might easily have the most terrible consequences."[42] Another black newspaper characterized the local Black and Tan as "a continuing menace of the most serious character, especially to our reputable colored residents who might be the chief sufferers from an outbreak of race passion."[43] The black middle class feared that interracial socializing would disrupt the already fragile system of paternalistic relations between the white and African-American middle class.

Given the history of southern whites justifying the lynching of black men by alleging the rape of white women, these fears seem historically grounded and perfectly reasonable. In the North, interracial socializing could trigger white violence. A Chicago newspaper reported that "patrons of the Golden Lily Cage—[the] latest South Side nightclub to go colored—[were] scared Wednesday when a bomb exploded in the kitchen." Police authorities suspected that "whites who frequented the club, owned by the Chinese, were seeking revenge for permitting Negroes to patronize it." Another source of conflict may have been the replacement "of the white orchestra with a negro orchestra."[44] The Black and Tans were sometimes targeted by local authorities. As one paper reported, the "Rose Tea Room, said to be a notorious 'black and tan joint' [was] raided by federal agents and Unit #1 police." The raid was described as spectacular, with many of the patrons trying to "make their escape by getting out of windows and running along the house tops in Olive Street."[45] Eventually, local black residents also wished to shut down the Black and Tans. In Chicago members of a local black church, Quin Chapel, passed resolutions "lamenting the lawless conditions" in their neighborhoods, including black/white dance halls. In 1922 the

★

Chicago Committee of Fifteen reported, "The respectable colored people are expressing hearty approval of the work of the Committee." In the effort to close a particularly infamous club, according to the committee, "a negro secured signatures to a protesting petition representing many thousands of colored people."[46] While Progressives grudgingly accepted public dance, most middle-class moralists—reformers, church leaders, local residents—tried to shut down the establishments that operated for black/white couples.

By the end of World War I, then, a traveler touring Chicago or New York would observe a distinctive pattern of leisure, quite different from the map that characterized the terrain of Victorian cities, when saloons were reserved for prostitutes and their customers, the working class remained more closely attached to family or ethnic community, and the middle classes eschewed leisure pursuits in public institutions. If, as historians have argued, Prohibition represented a kind of response to changing moral values—and, I would suggest, to new forms of urban leisure—then the effect of repression was the opposite of its intention. By the 1920s the saloon-style dance hall was dead—and dancing, without alcohol, seemed to many less exciting and pleasurable. For at least a moment it seemed that Prohibition had in fact destroyed urban leisure. Soon, however, new institutions replaced the concert saloon hall. In their place emerged the modern speakeasy, more lewd and inebriated than ever before. This irony of repression also had a racial dimension: the most infamous speakeasies featured black/white socializing. Relocating the saloons brought about another transformation in leisure institutions: the traditional saloon became the modern speakeasy. The Committee of Fourteen summarized the development: "With the adoption of the Eighteenth Amendment, the conditions [of vice] improved; but instead there now exist all-night 'speak-easy' clubs." Repression had not merely produced relocation but was intricately involved in the very transformation of the saloon itself.[47]

As outlawed institutions, the modern speakeasies were extremely cautious. "In some, the unknown prospective customers were sufficiently questioned as to their identity; in others a sponsor was necessary; and in still others, documentary proof, such as a letter, business cards." Speakeasies could open, close, and reopen with unbelievable speed, virtually overnight. The committee described this institutional pattern as a "rapid and mushroom-like growth."[48] Unlike brothels and hotels of assignation, the speakeasy could be constructed any-where, whether in an abandoned storefront, a tenement apartment, or a basement, in almost any neighborhood. One New York investi-gation revealed the process through which a speakeasy might be opened: "A half dozen young men rent a flat and call it a dance club. Girls are admitted free to supply the entertainment."[49] Many speakeasies were highly secretive and excluded unfamiliar cus-tomers, probably because police departments increasingly relied on undercover investigations and entrapment. Also, customers valued the covert nature of speakeasies, in large part because they too wished to remain anonymous. As one frequent patron of the clubs put it: when visiting hotels the customer was in danger of "someone seeing you," while in the speakeasy "you can come in the front way . . . and no one would see you."[50]

Locating a given establishment was difficult in itself. The more plush clubs were in brownstones, but the majority were hidden in alleys and basements, known only to regular customers.[51] The speakeasy was more racially diverse than virtually any previous leisure institution, expanding to include racial, ethnic, and even sex-ual minorities. Because the clubs were so elusive, it was difficult for the Committees of Fourteen and Fifteen to study the speakeasy problem. It remains even more difficult, therefore, to locate evi-dence detailing the institutional shift from neighborhood saloon to speakeasy. In general, the pre-Prohibition saloons were racially seg-regated. Many black clubs, as well, refused to admit white patrons. For example, while investigating the Chadwick Novelty Café, one investigator stated that when he "knocked at the door, a colored man on the inside motioned me to go away. I told him to send the boss out." The manager replied that "the captain [of police] told him not to let any white men in."[52] Even within saloons that wel-comed both white and black patrons, there frequently was segrega-tion. At the Lincoln Hotel and Café, an investigator observed a singer, pianist, five black men, and three white men. The investiga-tor was white. He approached a black woman, whom he suspected of being a prostitute, and asked if she would join him for a drink. According to the investigator, the woman accepted the drink, "but did not sit at my table. She said they don't allow blacks to sit at one table with the whites."[53]

★

Unlike saloons, speakeasies were renowned for fostering black/ white socializing but, unlike the majority Black and Tans, a class of speakeasies frequently included homosexuals. Chicago speakeasies were famous for attracting "criminal associates" and other supposed members of the urban lowlife. Although located in African-American neighborhoods, and often staffed by black residents, the majority were owned by white proprietors.[54] The business that drove the speakeasies was the sale of alcohol. Prostitution was a close second. The rise of the speakeasy certainly disappointed the Prohibitionists, but the reemergence of prostitution within the clubs must have shocked the antiprostitution movement. In 1927 the Committee of Fourteen initiated 14,399 investigations into leisure institutions in New York, and 1,330 of those were directed at speakeasies. Although speakeasies represented only 9 percent of the total number of institutions investigated, they accounted for 78 percent of all legal violations of prostitution that the committee uncovered. The speakeasy had become the "greatest source for the making of new prostitutes."[55] In the end Progressive repression resulted in an internal migration of vice: brothels and prostitutes moved into the South Side of Chicago and Harlem. National Prohibition accelerated the movement, also eventually reconnecting prostitution with alcohol. The irony was that Progressive repression of "miscegenation" had resulted, ultimately, in the creation of a new urban margin in which black/white sexual relations thrived.

In the first phase of reform, Progressive reformers accomplished a stunning success: red-light districts were closed across the country. Throughout the 1910s, however, prostitutes migrated to other, less carefully regulated parts of the city, frequently to African-American neighborhoods. During Prohibition the black/white districts in a sense matured, becoming vital centers of the illicit sale of alcohol and sex. In the 1920s reformers did not, and then could not, ameliorate the social distress created by the growth of the interzones.

★

3

INTERZONES 2

Reform and Representation

Slowly and ineffectively, vice commissions discovered and then responded to the black/white vice districts and, in the process, were themselves influenced through their observations and experiences in social uplift. More than merely learning from their mistakes, vice commissions were in effect reconstituted through their reform work. The interchange between reformer, commercialized sex, and ideologies of difference reveals a kind of circular development, or historical cycle, that recurs throughout my story. In the case of late-Progressive reform, the changing culture of the interzone circled back into the liberal mainstream, transforming late-Progressive-reform discourse. New conceptions of reform and of prostitution itself emerged. Ultimately, however, more is at stake in my analysis than the explication of social historical processes. The lag between the creation of the zones and the response of the vice commission represents a historical tragedy, and antiprostitution reform efforts to relieve stigmatized people living in the interzones failed. Progressive vice reform ended just as the working conditions of prostitution rapidly deteriorated.

Throughout the era of migration, reformers had collected enough evidence to verify what random investigations had suggested since the 1910s. Black women were disproportionately represented among the ranks of prostitutes. In June 1924 the New York City Women's Court found that the number of prostitution cases was 10 percent more than in May and 35 percent above the monthly average in 1923. However, within this pattern of growth in commercialized sexuality, they identified that "the proportion of cases of negroes increased from the highest proportion of 35 percent in June 1923 to 46 percent in 1924."[1] They established that "the negro population constitutes a tenth of the whole in Manhattan, upon which basis the number of arrests of negro women is over 4 times the proportion."[2] In Chicago the evidence revealed a similar disproportion. In 1920 black women represented roughly 2 percent of Chicago's population but were between 16 and 20 percent of convicted prostitutes; by 1930 black women represented 3.5 percent of the population, but they accounted for 69 percent of the total number of convicted prostitutes.[3] In 1928 the Chicago Morals Court indicated an astonishing statistical reversal: "In former years the percentage of prostitutes were 85 percent white, 15 percent colored, but now 20 percent white and 80 percent colored."[4]

The statistics were flawed to a certain degree because of racially biased regulation, but even so the available data suggest a marked racial disproportion. The organizations reporting these statistics acknowledged certain biases because of the policing of vice. The data were calculated from reports submitted by morals courts, and were therefore biased because of the particular methods used to arrest prostitutes. Waterman stated that in 1924, 46 percent of the women arrested for prostitution were African-American but noted that arrests were accomplished through so-called jump raids.[5] Police observed a prostitute, reported the incidence of vice, and then sent squads to converge on the neighborhood. As the Women's Court indicated, "Many of the cases brought to the Court were the product of jump raids—random investigations conducted by police without a warrant." As with many aspects of police enforcement, jump raids were flawed because they selectively enforced the existing statutes. They were used against the more visible prostitutes and did "not involve the high priced prostitute who is difficult to apprehend."[6] African-American women made up the ranks of streetwalkers, debatably the most difficult and dangerous form of prostitution; they solicited from tenement house windows, doorways, and stoops.[7]

Thus virtually all the available data are biased because black women were more likely than white women to be arrested, but the same evidence suggests that black women were more likely than white women to become prostitutes. The statistical data can also be read or interpreted as cultural representations. Sociological tables, arrest rates, and diagrams provide a wealth of what social scientists refer to as "qualitative" data, even if they do so unintentionally. As Joan Scott has argued, the positivist use of numerical information — as unproblematic reflections of social reality — denies the "inherently political" nature of statistical data.[8] In applying her theory, Scott shows how the gathering of statistics of women workers served to define a gendered conception of labor. For the most part, the exact circumstances under which the data on prostitution were collected remain unknown, but a cultural analysis of the numbers begins to suggest the increasing significance of race in the modern urban commercialization of sex. In the framework utilized by the Committee of Fourteen, elite sex workers were not necessarily defined as "prostitutes." They were classified as "hostesses." Vice commission reports acknowledged that hostesses danced with men for money and dated outside the dance halls, and that sometimes "hostesses" supplemented their incomes with prostitution. Yet in reporting on their data, the committees distinguished between the hostess and the rank-and-file prostitute. So, too, did the morals courts: one committee report indicated that after a police raid and arrests, dance hall hostesses were brought before magistrates but were not then convicted, supposedly because of "insufficient evidence." The distinction between hostess and prostitute was institutional, reflecting the greater respectability afforded to the dance halls compared to the brothels, but color was also a source for drawing social distinctions. Excluded from the brothels, black women were viewed as "natural" streetwalkers, deserving of harsh punishment.[9] The geographical shift from "segregated vice" to racial segregation, then, coincided with the development and operation of racially stratified markets of sexuality (a subject to be discussed in chapter 6).

The remapping of prostitution, and this cultural reorganization, effected social change in at least two directions: it shaped the lives of sex workers and then reconstituted the perceptions of the social scientists who studied prostitution. A discussion of the changing discourse on the causes of prostitution makes the point. In the mid-nineteenth century the leading scholars of prostitution, William Acton and William Sanger, each furthered what might be termed a moralist analysis of the causes of prostitution. They tended to blame lustful men who demanded prostitution, and they characterized women as the unsuspecting victims of evil seducers. Acton did articulate a nascent theory of innate moral corruption, observing that some women "evince[d] a natural disposition" toward the profession. By the turn of the century, social reformers were more likely to emphasize economic deprivation as the root of the social evil. Jane Addams, for instance, pointed out that an "immoral woman" could earn between seven and fifteen times the average salary of a department store clerk. Social welfare workers increasingly emphasized family backgrounds. Indeed, historians surveying the life histories of prostitutes have found high rates of divorce, desertion, or parental death. One New York study indicated that 25 percent of prostitutes came from "broken homes." A leading female Progressive reformer, Maude Miner, found that many of these women were homeless from a young age.[10]

By the 1920s social scientific opinion on the causes of prostitution had moved closer to an economic theory. However, some reformers questioned the economic theory, rejecting the argument that there was "a direct relation between unemployment of women and their participation in prostitution."[11] In its place, over the decade, putatively noneconomic theories emerged. Popular European theories of innate criminality did not gain a large following among American reformers, and yet by the 1920s, the biological category of feeblemindedness increasingly served as an explanation for some types of female social deviance. Thus one social scientist argued that 35 percent of prostitutes were "mentally retarded." A morals court in Chicago found that 50 percent of prostitutes were "feebleminded." Still, serious studies of prostitution continued to further a loosely environmental, economic interpretation that also accounted for changing patterns of regulation. Waterman's study of vice in New York concisely summarizes a prevailing theory. He argued that prostitution was caused by the combination of "the driving urge of poverty" and "the let-down in police activity."[12]

★

What remains significant about these theories of prostitution is not so much the shift from moral to economic to biological theorizing, and back again, but rather the relative absence of race as an explanation. In fact, the economic interpretation seemed to dominate social scientific discourse throughout the era, with sporadic bursts of biologism. There were a few exceptions. In her pathbreaking work, *The Colored People of Chicago*, Louise DeKoven Bowen pointed up the connections between race and vice. She noted that black families often were forced to take in lodgers, which led to immorality. Significantly, Bowen observed that "the boys and girls of colored families are often obliged to live near the vice districts."[13] Perhaps the most familiar analysis of African-American women and prostitution was articulated by racialist social scientists and reformers, who linked the incidence of black prostitution to the supposed immorality of black people. Chicago sociologist Walter Reckless emphasized the "open Negro community life"—the "badlands" and "blackbottoms"—among the factors accounting for the disproportionate number of black women among prostitutes. For the most part, the more influential theories followed Waterman, who developed a version of the last-of-the-migrants thesis. He argued that because black women were among the "latest group to enter, they must start at the bottom." He also invoked the lodger theory—that when African-Americans were forced to take in nonfamily members as boarders, the family suffered "attacks on privacy, morality, and their integrity." The black sociologist E. Franklin Frazier also argued for the centrality of the damaged black family, although he located the roots of "pathology" in slavery.[14]

The problem with the last-of-the-migrants thesis, and the pathology thesis, was that they either failed to compare ethnic group participation in vice or drew conclusions based on flawed historical interpretations. A synthesis of the nineteenth-century studies of vice, combined with my original research, provides a kind of corrective to the scientific study of prostitution—and to the current historical interpretations of white ethnic prostitution. Although rarely a theme in celebratory histories of immigration or remembered in neighborhood ethnic festivals, many immigrant women had entered prostitution, at least temporarily, because of the difficulties families faced in locating employment. Prostitution did not require formal training nor did a prostitute have to be fluent in English. In his study of vice in Chicago, Walter Reckless stated that "the Ghetto [Jewish neighborhood] and the Italian colonies are usually devoid of prostitution."[15] Ruth Rosen argued that "those ethnic groups that tended to emphasize family solidarity and female chastity—Jews, Irish, Italians—were underrepresented in the foreign-born prostitute population." A closer look suggests, however, that these and other ethnic groups suffered severe social strains and that, as a result, white ethnic women did participate in prostitution. Between 1845 and 1854, when approximately three million Irish and German immigrants entered the United States, Irish women were disproportionately represented among all arrested prostitutes in East Coast cities.[16] In New York, for instance, William Sanger calculated that 61.9 percent of the prostitutes he interviewed were of foreign birth. In part, Irish entrance reflected uneven sex ratios; Irish women outnumbered men by roughly a third. In Chicago, reformers blamed German women for the increase in the numbers of prostitutes. But family dislocation, compounded by restricted opportunity, was the primary cause of the entrance of young women, and in some cases girls, into commercialized vice. Moreover, like black women in the 1920s, Irish women in the 1850s were also more vulnerable to arrest than native-born women.[17] Ruth Rosen cites a 1911 study demonstrating that foreign-born women were underrepresented among all prostitutes, but recent historical analyses suggest the opposite. Katherine Lineham detected an important pattern of ethnic succession in Chicago, among both madams and pimps. According to her data, the number of foreign-born women managing brothels represented half of all madams. In turn, by 1900, the older Irish "pimps" had been supplanted by Southern and Eastern European immigrant men. Although she does not provide an analysis by ethnic group, Lineham persuasively concludes that in the late nineteenth century, Southern and Eastern European immigrant women were replacing older immigrant groups in the ranks of prostitutes.[18]

Foreign-born women entered prostitution because of family instabilities resulting from migration. And like black women, they too were disproportionately represented among the arrested and convicted. White ethnic women's experience diverges from the experience of black prostitutes in the 1920s in one important respect: white ethnic participation in commercialized vice was often temporary. In part, it was temporary because white ethnic heads of household eventually found employment or because white ethnic women could enter trades that were closed to black women, but the influence of social reform, specifically the resources directed at uplift and what I term gender restoration, also played a significant role. The data on black women's length of participation are not available, but the absence in itself actually strengthens the argument. For these statistics were gathered by social reformers and nascent social scientists, intent on ameliorating the problems of fallen women and attempting to rescue them. That reformers failed to collect more data on black prostitution can be interpreted to demonstrate their lack of concern with black women. This factor accounted for the difficulties that black prostitutes faced in New York and Chicago. Combine restricted opportunities with dwindling reform resources, and the situation facing black women becomes clear.

Through a comparative analysis of ethnic group participation and reform, it is possible to understand the worsening situation of African-American sex workers in particular. Beginning in the 1830s some reform groups attempted to assist prostitutes. In Chicago the "Home for the Friendless" served fallen women by providing food and shelter, and by fortifying their moral capacity. In Boston reformers led a kind of white slavery campaign against prostitution, attempting to save German immigrant women from the perils of prostitution. In New York female moralists also tried to "rescue" fallen women, including the foreign-born. Again in the 1850s, at the height of German and Irish immigration, a small-scale white slavery scare erupted, and immigrants formed organizations to rescue "their own." As I have shown, moreover, white slavery not only supplied an explanation for prostitution and justified its abolition, but in the process also supplied the cultural apparatus necessary to restore white women to respectability. By proclaiming that women were trapped into prostitution and were not willful sinners or permanently degraded deviants, these nascent movements could help to exonerate a woman and help her achieve respectability in home and community. The so-called new immigrants fostered reform efforts, and in the process the immigrant family also benefited. The phenomenon remains understudied, but recent research indicates that in New York, for example, Jewish community leaders formed organizations to rescue Jewish women from prostitution.[19] There existed a motif of population movement, female entrance into prostitution, and restoration through reform. Not since the late 1910s, either among community groups or social welfare agencies, has there developed as extensive or widespread concern over the plight of urban sex workers.

By the era of the third wave of ethnic migration to the urban North — the influx of African-American women — the older model of ethnic reform had declined. The failure of reform ranged from the more powerful, mainstream organizations to the peripheral groups working within urban black communities. Mainstream vice commissions were valuable insofar as they provided information to authorities, especially the police, regarding the location of establishments and the names of their owners, but the commissions were late in collecting and disseminating information about vice in Harlem and the South Side. Moreover, the success of the vice commissions before World War I had almost assured the "invisibility" of the problem of black prostitution. By the 1920s, even as whites went slumming to black areas, the growth of prostitution was not anything like a major urban political issue.

Indeed, as the zeal for reform faded, by the 1930s the leading vice commissions were in a state of decline. Always in search of more funds, the Committees of Fourteen and Fifteen had enormous difficulty raising enough money to survive, in part because of the Great Depression. By the 1930s the Bureau of Social Hygiene abandoned the rhetoric of antiprostitution and protection of female virtue, because these causes were no longer popular, and therefore failed to stir public interest or generate revenue.[20] In a sense, reformers had contributed to their own demise. By removing vice from public view and pushing it into black neighborhoods, reformers removed prostitution from a public agenda concerned with "white" social problems.

At the same time, local workers and neighborhood social reform organizations did not for the most part direct their efforts on the problem of black female prostitutes. In general, by the 1920s, white women's organizations were less likely to engage in "rescue" work, partially because their Protestant moralism had been discredited as sentimental, unprofessional, and old-fashioned. Thus the Chicago Erring Women's Refuge and Reform Organization, a local grassroots effort to assist (predominately white) prostitutes, closed in 1913, after the end of the white slavery campaigns.[21] Some white women probably left reform altogether, and a new generation of middle-class women trained as social workers entered federal and state agencies, which did not necessarily have a specific policy regarding prostitution. Even for the women who remained in grassroots social reform, prostitution receded as a public social problem. Between 1910 and 1920 many of the shelters originally constructed for prostitutes became houses for unmarried mothers. Moreover, as Regina Kunzel has argued, with "the closing of the red-light districts, rescue workers joined in the general rejection of the prostitute and turned to another fallen woman—the unmarried mother—who better conformed to their notions of the role." Thus the Salvation Army shifted from rescuing prostitutes to assisting unwed mothers. Under certain circumstances, such as in publicized cases of women who promised to leave prostitution, some agencies did at least temporarily open their doors to sex workers. In Chicago the Salvation Army and the Juvenile Protective Agency (JPA) each announced that they would assist *former* prostitutes, women who had renounced sex work. Moreover, the distinction between unwed mothers and prostitutes can be overdetermined, since many prostitutes became pregnant. Nevertheless, it does not seem unreasonable to accept Kunzel's argument that, after the "abolition of white slavery," many white reformers turned to what was perceived as the next social problem on the *white* reform agenda, namely, single motherhood.[22]

Just as white reformers withdrew from the war on prostitution, African-American social reform organizations were hobbled by lack of resources. Even so, throughout the period between roughly 1900 and 1930 black reformers did initiate efforts on behalf of black women. In Philadelphia at least eight homes were serving black women who had "fallen," probably including prostitutes.[23] In 1904, in Chicago, Richard R. Wright, Jr., opened the Trinity Mission, which received contributions from wealthy philanthropists; Wright's settlement worked directly with black prostitutes. Because of unstable leadership and loss of community, the Trinity Mission closed in 1914. In New York Victoria Earle Mathews headed the White Rose Mission, which helped black women adjust to the city by assisting them in finding employment. Mathews's mission served to prevent impoverished and homeless women from falling into commercialized vice. However, by 1910 the numbers of black women in need of assistance had overwhelmed the White Rose Mission, and it closed its doors. A year later it reopened as an industrial organization, designed to prepare women for the labor force.[24] On the whole, mission-style organizations in black neighborhoods were few, and their numbers were dwindling. The black middle class followed the dominant trend in urban social reform — the settlement house movement — but the black settlements were more likely to be connected to neighborhood churches, increasing their conservative outlook. The staffs of the Frederick Douglass House or the South Side Community House preached purity, thrift, and morality, and offered legal aid, kindergarten, nurseries, lecture classes, art, and probation work. The temperance societies, sponsored by women such as Mrs. Booker T. Washington, were another major organization of black middle-class reform.[25] These racially segregated clubs sought to serve a nascent African-American working class but did not necessarily reach out to the most impoverished or marginalized. Some black leaders were critical of the settlement houses, arguing that they were "not of the slightest benefit" to the masses.[26] At the same time that the missions closed and the settlements emerged, the major black social welfare organization — the National Urban League (NUL) — generally ignored the issue of vice. By the 1910s the consolidation of several industrial organizations into the NUL signaled a turn toward improving social conditions for men and away from dealing directly with employment problems of black women. The NUL did participate in the social hygiene movement, which included a major campaign against venereal disease, but even this kind of sexual reform was aimed at an emergent black middle class.[27] Black women leaders, including Ida B. Wells-Barnett, criticized the Urban League for its policy regarding women. In response, some black women's organizations, notably the Phillis Wheatley homes, established employment bureaus and probably helped some women avoid prostitution.[28] But the issue of the fallen woman gradually descended down the African-American social reform agenda.

Local black leaders did voice concern about the vice problem in their neighborhoods, but the most vociferous outcry came not from black women but from black men. Neighborhood ministers denounced gambling, drinking, and prostitution. The Reverend Adam Clayton Powell advocated cleaning up the speakeasies and tearing down the brothels. According to historian Julius Nimmons, however, the denunciation of vice from the pulpit did not result in action, only in moralism. For their part, the most powerful black women's organizations did not effectively respond to commercial sex. Famous social workers like Jane Edna Hunter probably worked with black unmarried mothers, but that was as far as the still redeemable could have fallen. Although they provided classes and other support services, the "colored" YWCAs ignored the problem of black fallen women. Rather than assisting single women, reformers like Nannie Helen Burroughs and Mary Church Terrell railed against "black flappers" for their immoral style and leisure habits, suggesting the extent to which sexual conservatism pervaded the African-American middle class.[29] In part, the failure to address prostitution stemmed from a kind of middle-class moralism that in the nineteenth century had also defined white social reform agendas. As Christina Simmons has argued, African-American sexual reformers continued to rely on this Victorianism well after white reformers had moved on to a more modern social welfare policy. Black women reformers were hampered by a legacy of sexual stereotyping that continually undermined their moral authority, and can be seen as the reason for the persistence of sexual conservatism within African-American social reform. In a sense, black women were a generation behind white female reformers, caught in the difficult predicament of maintaining their moral authority while trying to assist the putatively immoral. The predicament was all the more difficult because of the tendency of racial overgeneralization—mistaking respectable black women for immoral women—which could, in a flash, erase carefully cultivated distinctions of social class.[30]

In the end neither race nor class alone can explain the complex historical process through which urban vice was transformed. To an extent never before recognized, early Progressive reform was a deeply racial movement, supplying the ideological program for assimilating white women into the role of female respectability. In this era, however, because of the relatively low numbers of black women involved in prostitution, white reformers' silence on race was not as noticeable as it would become. Vice commissions, police departments, and social reform organizations were aware of the trends of increasing disproportions between black representation in the population and their participation in prostitution, but no one effectively responded. In a very real sense, then, a reform policy based on sexual racism—the elision of black women—was responsible for the creation of unpoliced black/white vice districts and the emergence of an underclass of black female prostitutes.

It would be wrong, however, for us to turn away from the limitations of African-American social policy. Even a general survey of black reform organizations reveals a pronounced hesitancy to deal with such highly charged issues as prostitution, particularly because, as we shall see, black prostitution frequently represented black/white sexual relations. A few neighborhood centers thrived for a short time, but the general trend in black social reform was to emulate the white settlement movement. The problem was that rather than targeting a stigmatized underclass, the settlements frequently served as cultural institutions designed to instill middle-class values in upwardly mobile workers. Moreover, the black settlements never really gained the kind of authority or possessed the kind of resources that were available to the major black political reform organizations, especially the National Urban League. In turn, the NUL did not deal with the employment problems faced by black women, much less by black prostitutes. As Hazel Carby has argued, the black middle class was invested in controlling female working-class sexuality, but, I would argue, not necessarily in uplifting the sexually stigmatized. Reforming prostitution was an unacceptable risk. Even if one corrects for the history of sexual racism, and the sexual stereotyping that constrained African-American female reformers, the failure to address the issue of prostitution seems undeniable.

The major black policy on prostitution, although not explicitly stated, was in effect to sacrifice those already "fallen" and focus instead on strengthening the African-American community by finding employment for black men and housing for black families. In itself this was not necessarily a flawed social policy. Unfortunately, however, the creation of vice districts actually signaled a more pervasive historical trend: white reformers' abandonment of African-Americans settling in the urban North. In other words, it may well be more than historical happenstance that the last major antiprostitution movement in the United States focused on white women and thrived before the influx of African-Americans into the cities. It may also be no mere coincidence that once white prostitution was more or less "controlled," philanthropists and white social service organizations took up issues such as single motherhood and child welfare.

Finally, it was also not by chance that as the general issue of "vice" — a redeemable fault of diminished virtue — gave way to concepts like pathology, the social problems of the urban margins increasingly became the province of the state. By the 1930s the New Deal and its particular kind of liberalism endeavored to serve the injured middle class and sometimes gestured toward a jeopardized working class but generally ignored the "undeserving" men and women living in the vice districts. The state did not "rescue" the "fallen" but rather institutionalized the "pathological" and punished the "criminal." Prostitution reform declined in the United States with a failure that devastated people living in the interzones.

Throughout the nineteenth century the opportunity for interracial mixing expanded. In the vice borderlands, intimacy between blacks and whites had become part of a more generalized marginal culture. The modern sex districts — and specifically the interzones — were distinct from the older, Victorian underworlds of dives and snares. Interzones were highly developed, distinctive social geographies, the result of a modern reform apparatus and direct social repression. Indeed, what remains so striking about the interzones, then, was the extent to which, as we shall see, they represented a world in which racial and sexual conventions were not merely transgressed but were inverted, mocked, or completely ignored. Even more striking is the growth of the rebellious vice districts in an era of increasing moral conservatism. In other words, interzones represented more than sites of social oppression or dreary margins of despair. They were in themselves complex social worlds, perhaps sites of cultural resistance, but certainly worthy of historical analysis.

PART II

Crossing the Color Line

in the 1920s

4

LEISURE AND SEXUAL RACISM
In-between Men in the Dance Halls

Beginning in the 1920s, sociologists became more committed to studying the texture of urban life, to understanding the ways in which the modern city shaped the psyches and personalities of isolated social strangers and processes of social adjustment. Studies of sex delinquency, prostitution, slums, and dance halls appeared throughout the 1920s. In the introduction to Paul Cressey's classic study of leisure in the city, his mentor, Ernest Burgess, observed that the popular dance halls "represent the full commercialization of sexuality, which can be seen in the name Taxi Dancer: Like the taxi-driver with his cab, she is for public hire and is paid in proportion to the time spent and the services rendered."[1] Concepts such as modernization, anomie, and pathology were part and parcel of an emergent sociological tradition. The new discipline concerned itself with individuals, often immigrants, as they adjusted to the impersonal forces of the metropolis. Those who did not, or could not, adjust were deemed pathological or, in the lexicon of the Chicago School sociologists, labeled social deviants. Participation in the taxi-dance halls represented maladjustment because the institution included interracial relations between Filipino men and white women. As this study demonstrates, however, the taxi-dance hall was not the center of vice—nor were dance hall sex relations between Asian men and white women considered the most polluted. In arguing as much, sociologists mistakenly gave the wrong impression. Throughout the era, black/white sex was understood to be so obscene as to be outside the pale of permissible academic discourse. Sociologists dared not study the issue, much less publish works on the topic. However, the absence of evidence speaks volumes. Black/white speakeasies were at the center of urban vice, not the taxi-dance halls, and black/white sex was the definitive sign of social deviance. That is not to diminish the significance of the taxi-dance halls or the considerable sexual racism Filipinos struggled against. In fact, a reading of the interzone map suggests that the antimiscegenation taboo located in the center of vice districts dispersed outward to shape life on the moral borders dividing mainstream Chicago and New York from their underworlds.

These urban/sexual borders were discursive, institutional, and ultimately social-historical. Taxi-dance halls were peopled with "in-between men," patrons distinguished by their color difference, such as dark-skinned Italians, Chinese, and Filipinos. Accepted neither as wholly white nor excluded (like Jack Johnson) as black, these men of color faced significant challenges for acceptance into the nation. White ethnic and Asian men struggled on various realms for access to resources—in urban politics, education, and employment. In the taxi-dance halls, they competed for status and for social acceptance.[2]

The taxi-dance hall, the quintessential border institution, served to distinguish the family-centered ethnic neighborhoods from the public, commercialized leisure districts, the authentic American from the suspicious "stranger," and respectability from immorality. The making of the border is a story of segregation; the story of in-between men in the dance halls, I argue, is one of institutionalized sexual racism.[3]

These histories can be illuminated through a discussion of public dance. As I demonstrated, during the nineteenth century in New York and Chicago, establishments termed "concert saloons" provided dancing, but they principally served as inexpensive clubs where single, common male laborers could solicit prostitutes.[4]

★

Victorians might attend a private ball but never a public saloon. By the opening of the twentieth century, with public leisure growing in general, dancing became increasingly popular. By the 1920s more than fifteen distinctive types of dance halls could be found in Chicago or New York. Traditional dance halls, located in ethnic neighborhoods and rented for holidays or weddings, were popular, but the fastest-growing institutions were the glittering, elaborate public dance palaces. As Kathy Peiss has shown, when more single women entered the paid labor force, consumer demand for public leisure greatly increased, whether in restaurants, amusement parks, or nickelodeons. Independent wage-earning women were particularly passionate about dancing. The turn toward public leisure in general, and dancing in particular, expanded beyond the new working class, effecting an important change in middle-class leisure habits; and, by the 1910s, respectable restaurants offered dancing, and plush dance cabarets opened in white entertainment zones. In New York, reformers estimated that the dance halls were "patronized by 35,000 to 50,000 boys and men per week." In Chicago authorities estimated that at least forty-three thousand couples went dancing each night.[5] In a profound rejection of the Victorian obsession with restraint, American urbanites—men and women, working class and middle class—were moving to the music.[6]

The revolution in leisure indicated by the popularity of dancing should not be interpreted as inevitable. Respectable Americans were in a sense sold on dance. In the nineteenth century, before the full emergence of the dance halls, most mainstream city dwellers were at least vaguely aware of the concert saloon as a club where prostitutes sometimes danced with customers. The phenomenon of the concert saloon crossover—from the Black Hole to its emergence into the mainstream—was not a natural progression but rather was facilitated by a complex combination of industrialization and careful marketing. Workers with more leisure time created a demand for public amusements. Before World War I the boundaries between margin and mainstream—the concentric circles of the interzones— remained fluid, barely formed. Dance hall proprietors had to resist the continual pull toward the immoral center of vice by subtly interspersing the culture of antimiscegenation—that is, by consistently contrasting their institutions with the Black and Tans. Mainstream dance halls were often extravagant, stylish, and plush, the opposite of the standard Black and Tan. Indeed, popular dance halls forbade interracial socializing.

Lurking in the shadows of the dance palaces and cabarets was the figure of Jack Johnson. Like his expulsion from the nation, Johnson was symbolically excluded from the dance scene. Yet, like Johnson, African-American men represented a pervasive presence, precisely through their absence.[7] Because racial purity indicated respectability, white urbanites were able to attend public dance halls without sacrificing their moral authority. By the early 1920s even conservative reform organizations had come to accept public dancing. As the Committee of Fourteen asserted, it had "no quarrel with the properly regulated dance hall."[8]

If African-Americans were absent, white workers were present, dancing in clubs not far removed from the middle-class cabarets. But white *ethnic* workers, and other men on the margins of mainstream respectability, patronized the so-called taxi-dance halls. In this case the vice commissions were critical of dance institutions. The taxi-dance halls, also known as the Closed Dance Hall, had emerged virtually overnight and then multiplied rapidly.[9] Committee of Fifteen vice investigators reported that "in 1923 there were but two taxi-dance halls in Chicago sufficiently well-established to be money-making concerns; in three years the number of closed dance halls had increased to 300."[10] The vice commissions deemed the taxi-dance hall unrespectable because, to quote the Committee of Fourteen, they were "laboratories of vice and crime."[11] In my map, the taxi-dance halls were the border institutions because of their reputation as working-class institutions and because they tolerated interracial socializing:[12] "In Chicago at least a fourth of the patrons of taxi-dance halls are Oriental who are elsewhere ostracized because of color. Of these Orientals nine-tenths are Filipinos, and the Chinese contribute virtually the remainder."[13] So stigmatized was interracial dance that even in the peripheral taxi-dance halls, men of color had to fight for admission. As Cressey observed, the "Mexican, Filipino, Chinese, and Japanese men were not so freely admitted." In general, "the attendance of very dark-skinned patrons" was carefully regulated.[14]

If in the interzones black/white vice developed in relative isolation, and if in the mainstream respectable whites could dance assured of their status as white, it was on the volatile borders in between where the most intense social conflict erupted. As we shall see, these conflicts took on complex class and ethnic dimensions. Historians of leisure have demonstrated that white ethnic workingmen did in fact articulate a kind of class consciousness in the saloons, where they asserted their virtue by reinforcing reciprocal relations through occasional treating, or buying drinks for one another. More often, however, in the dance halls workingmen aspired to assimilate to the culture of the respectable middle class.[15]

Proprietors of the taxi-dance halls sought to satisfy working-class desire for respectability by creating clubs with the facade of cabarets, dance palaces, or even dance academies. The facade, or taxi-dance hall "fronts," also supplied a kind of camouflage, helping to elude vice investigators and police raids. Taxi-dance halls frequently were located on the borders of the interzones, relatively close to the rooming-house districts where patrons resided but a calculated distance from the inner zones of black/white vice. Again, concerns of class appeal combined with entrepreneurial considerations. In a conversation between the leading sociologist Paul Cressey and a dance hall owner, Cressey stated that a particular Chicago neighborhood, located near Wilson Avenue, seemed "a pretty good place to start a hall." The proprietor disagreed. Posing as a dance hall patron, Cressey continued the discussion: "Well, then, you've got to get out beyond Racine because of the hoboes." The owner agreed: "Yes, you've got to go out further than that." In this system of respectability, immigrants living in rooming houses were the targeted patrons, whereas a class of men beneath the immigrant singles—the hobo— were viewed as undesirable and therefore were consciously excluded. Workingmen were welcomed as desirable patrons; but, in reality, even in what appear to be purely "class" concerns, racial codes were just beneath the surface. Thus, in another conversation concerning the most profitable location for a Chicago dance hall, the proprietor reminded Cressey that "the only thing you've got to look out for is the Chinks. The West-side guys [white ethnics] out there won't come. Once a girl goes with these Chinks they're too low down for any decent American guy to want to dance with."[16] Asian participation tarnished the reputation of the dance halls and, from the perspective of some white men, diminished the sexual appeal of the white dance hostess.

Operating a successful dance hall required the careful negotiation of a worker culture in which conceptions of class respectability were virtually inseparable from notions of white superiority. Thus, in describing his dance academy, one owner bragged: "Our patrons are high-class people. They won't go to the same places where these chinks or whatever they are go." Another proprietor asserted: "No really white guy is willing to go in and dance with these Chinks or Japs or whatnot. He's got to have a little nigger in him to be willing to do that."[17] Even if one were to attempt a kind of sociological diagram of the above sentences, it would be virtually impossible to separate conceptions of class respectability from assertions of white supremacy. These working-class people wanted to emulate the comportment of the putatively respectable. They wished to be "high-class people." In some instances, however, the standard of success was to be measured by how "really white" a given patron could become (or remain)—by making certain that in fact one did not "have a little nigger in him." Many proprietors, through discussing their marketing strategies, revealed much about the ways in which systems of domination—cultural codes of race and class—operate simultaneously and inseparably in American culture.[18]

Despite the taxi-dance hall's facade as a respectable, all-white institution, ethnic diversity in the taxi-dance halls was inevitable, in part because of the diversification of the urban population caused by the so-called new immigration. The population movement beginning in the 1890s consisted primarily of southern and Eastern Europeans, but after the U.S. victory in the Spanish-American War, the flow of immigration expanded to include Filipinos. In the 1920s Filipino immigration increased dramatically: from ten thousand in 1920 to approximately eighty thousand in 1930.[19] The majority of Filipinos settled in Hawaii, California, Illinois, and New York. Filipino immigration was distinguished by its uneven sex ratio; 93 percent of Filipino immigrants were men.[20]

Because of the disproportionate sex ratios, Filipinos lived in what were often referred to as bachelor communities. Without opportunities for personal intimacy or sexual contact, Filipino men seemed destined to solitude, bachelorhood, or, as sociologists indicated, to a life of sexual vice: the Filipino's search for physical intimacy "finds its way to vice; leisure time produces personal disorganization."[21] Sympathetic liberal academics asserted that commercial vice was inherently pathological, but in the context of studying Filipinos and other men of color, that assertion also presumed the pathology of interracial association. To the extent that Filipinos built clubhouses, attended church, or socialized with Filipino women, sociologists classified them as "socially adjusted." To the extent that Filipinos participated in public leisure institutions and, more specific, dated white women, sociologists classified them as "socially unadjusted."[22] As one scholar summarized the supposedly obvious distinction: "That much promiscuity and disorganization results from this intermingling of the races . . . must be apparent."[23]

Rather than transparently reflecting the everyday reality of Filipino life, sociological discourse constituted the Filipino as "disorganized" and the taxi-dance hall as an archetypal institution of modern anomie. Life in a bachelor community significantly narrowed the Filipinos' chances for successful adjustment and increased the probability of their entrance into interracial vice. In the language of a leading researcher of the taxi-dance halls: "Being a patron of a taxi-dance and night club seems to be the last stage of disorganized life." For the Filipino or Chinese patron, this "last stage" was symbolized by a kind of social descent into interracial relations.[24] Once descended, others were likely to follow. The discursive creation of "the transgressive Filipino" shaped the experience of each successive group of Asian men who entered the dance hall scene. In one interview, or discursive interchange, a University of Chicago graduate student interacts with a Chinese laundry worker who regularly attended the dance halls. In fact, the Chinese man admitted that he went "to the dance hall almost every weekend."[25] Through the subject's mode of confession or the sociologist's mode of transcription—and probably through both—the Chinese man's life story became one of gradual descent into the zone of interracial vice. At first the Chinese man avoided the dance halls that friends and co-workers attended. Then he decided to join the scene: "My sexual impulse was overwhelmingly aroused." He moved from visiting a Chinese prostitute in the Old Chinatown areas to frequenting burlesque shows. Eventually, according to the man, some "people took me to see white girls—you know, in some of those hotels in the loop. Then, when I had money, I went to places alone. Later I went to dance halls and night clubs, becoming an old hand!"[26] From immigration to a bachelor community to commercialized leisure within the Chinese community and eventually to commercialized sexual relations with white women, in telling and retelling of the story, the concept of interracial association as intrinsically immoral and the structuring mode of "descent" defined oral narratives. These personal histories circulated in the culture, shaping immigrant experience. The resulting journal articles influenced increasing numbers of scholars and others who might read them.

ON THE DANCE FLOOR

An analysis of the sociological study of popular leisure yields information about the cultural hierarchies organizing leisure, the ideology of urban pluralism and its exclusions, and the discursive creation of subjects caught between national acceptance and rejection. Such an analysis suggests diverse relations, between morality and immorality, class and race, scholar and subject. By narrating another set of relations—among in-between men as they struggled for cultural inclusion and experienced sexual racism—we can achieve a deeper understanding of social life on the borders. In all leisure institutions blackness was a presence/absence, but in the taxi-dance halls the influence of black/white sexual relations was more direct, pervasive, and profound. As an immigrant of color living in a "bachelor community," the Filipino man was caught in an exceptional predicament, but his relationship to the taxi-dance halls and to white women was ultimately defined by a common culture that prohibited "miscegenation."[27]

Once settled and at least partially assimilated, Filipinos experienced a series of problems that went beyond uneven sex ratios. Many felt a growing sense of alienation from their native culture. As one man lamented, "I'll always have to remain a bachelor. I'm a product of a crossing of Filipinos and American ways, and there's no Filipino girl who's had the same kind of experiences and same kind of attitudes I have."[28] Filipino immigrants believed they had become "Americanized" but, like African-Americans, their status as accepted citizens was precarious, always open to challenge. Filipinos faced intolerance and prejudice. As one Filipino testified, "If it weren't for race prejudice I'd marry an American girl." However, the Filipino man had learned, through racialized experience, that his was a group set apart; he learned to conceive of himself as a member of a race. According to one Filipino man, "There will always be difficulties because of the differences in race." And according to another: "Whenever I took Elizabeth out we were always being stared at. I knew they all thought she couldn't go out with a Chinaman, as they usually think I am. But sometimes she'd come to understand what people meant by that stare and then she'd be unhappy." To avoid such public disapproval, a Filipino man noted, "Whenever I took Marjorie anywhere . . . I always take a cab rather than travel in a street car."[29] The social response to the spectacle of Filipino/white intimacy closely resembled the social response to black/white couples.

In a sense, then, the taxi-dance halls represented refuges from public disapproval, but they were nonetheless sites of sexual racism — again, shaped by the circulating "miscegenation" taboo. More precisely, black/white sexual culture — and the "miscegenation" analogy — made its way into the lives of the taxi-dance hall patrons through numerous modes of interchange, including the Black and Tans themselves. Cressey noted that among Filipino/white couples "to go cabareting [was] a mark of prestige," discovering that the "'black and tan' cabarets of the colored belt are favored." In part, these couples traveled to the Black and Tans because they were "hospitable to racially mixed couples." As Cressey pointed out, "A few of the more notorious 'black and tan' cabarets . . . have constituted the night resort held in high esteem in the world of the taxi-dance hall."[30] The very language that patrons and white hostesses used to describe their experiences derived from the cultural system regulating black/white sexual relations. For example, the urban spaces in which the black/white clubs were located came to be known in the white and Filipino halls as "Africa." White women who frequented the Black and Tans were commonly understood to be "playing Africa." Racial language was also used to describe participants in the taxi-dance halls. White immigrant men customarily referred to Filipino men as "niggers." A white hostess who dated, or even danced with, a Filipino was called a "nigger lover." The reverse — accepting dates from only white men — was understood to be "staying white."[31]

The generalized racial taboo of "miscegenation" directly shaped intercultural relations on the dance floor, but so too did gender relations. Still deeper into the interzones, where black/white prostitution thrived, ideologies of womanhood became central, as we shall see in the following chapters, and yet the gender of men, more specifically masculinity, shaped relations in the taxi-dance halls. If one defines masculinity as something like the cultural accoutrements determining manhood and ultimately supporting gender dominance, then the issue becomes one of understanding how masculinity interacted with race, of how an ideology of dominance becomes complicated by systems of racial subordination. To begin to understand this intricacy, it is important to note, first, the status of the white dance hostess. From the start, one must acknowledge that all women of the vice district were directly subordinate to men. Women became dance hostesses for a variety of reasons that reflected deep social inequality.[32] As customers, men wielded significant power over the white women employed as hostesses. The Jack Johnson episode demonstrated that men of color also suffered a specific kind of subordination. The Black and Tan triggered such anxiety among white people because it both represented and symbolized the prevailing racial order turned upside-down: black men were on top. It was more than a matter of race, however. Within the world of the Black and Tan or the taxi-dance hall, because of contested inversions, even the gender hierarchy—that women were subordinate to men—remained unstable. For at various moments, and in different ways, the presence of the woman's *whiteness* undermined the inversion. A black or Filipino man might take the lead in a dance with his white partner, but when the music stopped and the dance was over, the white hostess exploited the high premium on her favors gained from the interracial taboo, charging Filipino men more than white patrons.[33] In the history of black/white sexual relations, and in the taxi-dance halls as well, a recurrent and complex tension is ever present: racial privilege pulling against gender privilege, with the eroticism of sexual transgression exacerbating the already volatile situation.

The reality was that because of the power of sexual racism, gender relations were thrown off balance. Thus in the dance halls, the so-called Oriental patrons were termed "fish." The term presumed, first, that white hostesses disliked Filipino men, and, second, referred to the vulnerability of Filipino men "because they do not have women of their own race, and are prohibited by social mores from dating American girls." In one view, then, hostesses supposedly exploited the social predicament of the Filipino patron. Attempting to defend her reputation when asked about her dances with Filipinos, one hostess proclaimed no affection or attraction: "Oh, these Niggers (Filipinos) and 'Chinks' (Chinese) are just 'fish' to the girls." A conversation between an undercover investigator and one hostess exemplifies how the white hostess exploited Filipino patrons: "We mustn't go far away. My fish might get jealous!" The investigator asked, "What is that?" "Oh, that Chinaman over there," she replied. The investigator attempted to extract more information: "Why do you call him your 'fish'?" Smugly, the hostess replied: "He gives me about twenty dollars every time I ask, and he only spends two evenings a week up here."[34]

From the perspective of white investigators, the phenomenon of the duped "Oriental" was common among the dance halls. One investigator reported: there were "three dancing instructoresses [white]. I danced with two of them, but they wouldn't 'talk open.' . . . In fact later on when Chinese, Japs, Filipinos and other of that kind started to come, they left all white men that were there already and danced with them." Eventually more dance hostesses, as well as more Asian men, arrived on the scene. The investigator observed that the "Chinese and Oriental dance with these girls imitating sexual intercourse by rubbing their bodies." Again, however, the investigator's explanation for the sexual behavior turned on the supposed inequity. The investigators believed that the Filipino patron "spoiled" the dance hostesses. As one man put it, "The Orientals were buying these girls cigarettes, candy, and sodas."[35] One investigator overheard a conversation in which a "Chinamen was asking one of the instructresses [*sic*] to go out with him all night." Although the usual price for a white hostess was approximately fifteen dollars, in this instance "[the hostess] said that it will cost him one hundred dollars." The patron agreed to the price.[36]

Because of demographics and sexual racism, the only alternative available to Filipino men eager for intimacy were the dance halls, where they were vulnerable to exploitation. Once in this predicament, some Filipino men probably also internalized the dominant sexual values privileging white womanhood. Within and outside the vice districts, particularly in the modern era, white women were idealized as the epitome of erotic sexual beauty. As one Filipino patron acknowledged: "I'll always get more kick out of having sex relations with American girls because they are more skillful coquettes in love. When the boys get a chance to have sex experience with American girls they don't want to go back home. They like their 'white meat' too well."[37]

White women exploited the Filipino's demographic predicament and, in effect, traded on their own whiteness. "Oftentimes, many Filipinos have been cheated by taxi dancers. In many cases, these women have lived with the Filipinos. Sometimes, they even get married to the Filipinos to rob them of all their money and then they disappeared to live with other men." Another report told of "a pathetic example" in which "a dance hall girl talked a Filipino into buying her some clothes in one of the downtown credit clothing stores. The amount of the purchase was $150. The Filipino signed the contract. A week or so later, the girl was reported to have disappeared, leaving no clues behind."[38] White women relied on racial privilege to get as much money out of the men as they could, but the documents also reveal that investigators and sociologists were seemingly obsessed with the notion of "fish." These white men were directly challenged by their observations of Filipino men with white women.

Indeed, contrary to what the "fish" discourse indicated, not all white hostesses exploited the Filipinos, nor did all white women view their relations with Filipinos as a matter of business. Of course, "some girls refuse to accept dates from Flips [Filipinos]; they want to stay white." Other hostesses drew a distinction between dancing with and dating Filipino men. "The Flips are all right for anybody that wants them. But they're not white, that's all. Of course, I'll dance with them at the hall. But I won't go out with them. I'm white, and I intend to stay white."[39] However, some hostesses shifted from one position to another, gradually becoming more intimate with Filipino patrons. According to one woman, when first offered a job as a dance hostess in a club frequented by Filipinos, she recalled that it seemed potentially lucrative and "that sounded good to me." Then, the proprietor stated that her duties included dancing with Filipino patrons. "I didn't know what they were, but went on downstairs," she remembered. After discussing several matters with her co-workers, the young women "asked a girl who these Filipinos were." "She laughed and said I'd just been dancing with one. I looked at the man closer and found that they were different and they were all alike. I got so I didn't mind their color." In fact, many white hostesses claimed that they actually preferred Filipino to white men.[40] It was the incidence of these favorable responses toward the Filipinos that probably disturbed some white investigators and scholars. Given the possibilities of such prejudice, we must exercise caution in reading the documents. The notion of the "fish" as the duped "Oriental" exploited by the calculating hostess was a kind of story—really the only story—that white investigators could use to explain their observations of affection and even attraction between white women and Asian men.

The least discussed and least studied aspect of the taxi-dance halls concerns not the relations between Filipino men and white women but those between white men and men of color. The dance hall was a site of intense conflict between white ethnic men and Filipinos and Chinese. The immediate conflicts took the form of episodes of interracial male aggression for the attentions of white hostesses, but from a different perspective, the confrontations can be interpreted as intricate cultural rituals performed to secure the rights and benefits of national citizenship.[41] In the era of the new immigration, Nordic, native stock Americans turned against "darker" Europeans. The rise of xenophobia reflected a widespread resistance to the social inclusion of certain white immigrants; eventually immigration was drastically reduced in order to stop the entrance of southern and Eastern Europeans. Of the immigrants who settled, as Robert Orsi has demonstrated, Italian Americans were cast in the national role of "social in-betweens," among the most stigmatized.[42] For the native-born sons of Italian immigrants, ethnic chauvinism and prejudice reached beyond federal immigration policy, off the job, into the taxi-dance halls.

Simultaneously, as the gates of citizenship closed and Nordic nationalism ascended, a paradigmatic shift in the construction of masculinity reshaped definitions of male sexuality. In the Victorian era the prevailing ideology emphasized the necessity that white, middle-class men save their sexual energy and avoid overindulgence; by the 1920s it was widely believed that white men had overcompensated in their sexual restraint, causing, among other problems, male sexual impotence. In the Victorian era, the central negative ideal supporting sexual restraint was a discourse of black male hyperpotency; by the 1920s that discourse of stigmatized black hyperpotency persisted, but it was complicated by several important cultural shifts.[43] For one thing, some men began to view black masculinity as a source of sexual inspiration. More important for our purposes, conflicts between white and black men over access to white women—symbolized by the persecution of Jack Johnson—

also shaped conflicts between Filipino and white men. Part of the sense of lost manhood that so many white men experienced was perhaps intensified by their everyday observations of white ethnic and Filipino men dating—and sexually appealing to—white, native stock women. Racial masculinity was now also a source of jealousy. In an interview, for instance, one white, native, middle-class patron condemned the taxi-dance hall as disreputable because "you have these young girls being exposed to Chinese and Japs, and Filipinos, and to those even worse among the white race." Perhaps this repulsion in fact derived from a kind of sexual jealousy. White men were losing out to the Other.

Meanwhile, intense conflict also erupted between the regular patrons of the taxi-dance halls.[44] Formal political inclusion into the national polity was founded on white manhood. For men whose citizenship was challenged—the historical symbol was, of course, black men—exclusion was partially experienced as diminished manhood. Filipino men were denied citizenship outright; white ethnic men had to "assimilate" to become full cultural citizens. It was not surprising that these "in-between men" compensated by asserting their sexual prowess and appeal to the dance hostesses. When a native stock white women—Lady Liberty, if you will—danced with and dated an immigrant man, she symbolically embraced him into the nation.[45]

From the perspective of some patrons, then, the taxi-dance hall represented more than a leisure institution and the hostess more than a temporary partner. Their participation represented an attempt at upward social mobility and inclusion. According to Cressey's interview with an ambitious Italian immigrant, "currently a bricklayer who planned to become an electrical engineer," the dance halls were important "because they provided an opportunity for him to meet available women and potential wives." As the sociologist William Foote Whyte demonstrated, Italian youth preferred native stock, especially blonde women over Italian women.[46] The few historical studies of ethnic assimilation suggest that upwardly mobile men dated, and married, non-Italian women. Thus, among Italian police officers, of the thirty-five who married, twenty-one chose non-Italian women, and of two who divorced, both remarried native-born women. In the words of an Italian dance hall patron, "Sure I'm gonna marry an American. I don't wanta marry an Italian, do I."[47]

In studying these men Cressey seemed to believe that the patrons realized their aspirations of national inclusion. Like many American theorists, he took the mere presence of diversity—whether in the nation or the dance hall—as an indication of cultural equality. The problem with this interpretation is that Cressey's own evidence indicated otherwise.

In reality, rather than affording cultural equality, the dance halls were sites of conflict and exclusion—institutions of sexual racism. To understand the relations between white patrons and men of color, we must interrogate the complex hierarchies that organized relations of masculinity within the dance hall. First, as indicated, there were tensions between first- and second-generation white ethnic men, and sometimes conflicts erupted. Although investigators subsumed several different ethnic groups—Chinese, Japanese, Filipino—under the category of "Oriental," dance hall insiders drew important distinctions between these three groups. Among the so-called Orientals, the Filipino probably was the least stigmatized. Cressey's research indicated that "the acceptability of the Filipino, in preference to other Oriental groups, is explained by such factors as his Occidental culture, represented in the Spanish influence in the Philippine Islands."[48] Filipinos were seen as more like white men than were either Japanese or Chinese men.

In fact, the Filipino stood on the line between white and black, closer to white than any other men of color. The Filipino thus posed a significant threat to white ethnic patrons, who wished to assert a racial prerogative to dance with white hostesses. In the contests between Filipinos and white ethnic men "race" made the difference, and the difference was often violent. In one case, recorded by Cressey, "three men were stabbed and seriously wounded . . . in a riot which started in a pay-as-you-go dance hall on North Clark Street, when a Filipino group from the West and South Side tried to monopolize the dancing school." In this scenario the young white ethnics viewed the numbers of Filipino men as a challenge to their racial hegemony on the dance floor. In fact, according to reports, the "Pinoy [Filipinos] have been molested for many months by these gangs of white fellows." Repeatedly, these sexual conflicts reveal a central dimension of masculinity: violence. As one subject described it, "They get after the Pinoys [Filipinos] because they can get dates with some of the girls and the gangsters [Italians] can't. So they began attacking Filipinos when there were only one or two together. They would jump on a couple of Pinoys and tear their clothes and take their money."[49]

These clashes were similar to the everyday conflicts that erupted between black and white men. Not long after the race riot in Chicago the press referred to one Filipino/white incident as a riot. According to a dance hall insider, "The big fight on North Clark Street came as a reprisal. . . . Just last week two boys were caught and beaten up so that the doctor had to take stitches." The Italian men resented that white women dated Filipino men; they not only attacked the Filipinos but also disturbed the hostesses: "Just the night before a quiet little Filipino was asked by his roommates's girl to take her home because she didn't want to go with the Italian boys who were after her." Their purpose, to be sure, was to stop Filipino/white intimacy, but, again, the parallels with resistance to black/white relations can be detected. As the Italian assailant described it, "Us guys was standing outside on those dance halls on Madison waiting for the 'niggers' to come out."[50] The ideology of miscegenation—forged in the era of Johnson—came to define public masculine relations between Filipinos and whites.

In one final sense, the reference to Filipino men as "niggers" suggests the centrality of blackness in the construction of racial masculinity. What I refer to as the Filipino's predicament put him at a distinct disadvantage in the sexual competition for the favors of white women, as revealed in the interviews and narratives. The racial politics of that competition—the operation of sexual racism—frequently manifested itself in white attacks on Filipino men, but the injuries of white supremacy were not only physical. The costs of racism were psychological as well. Sociologists studying the Filipinos were probably correct in their assessment of the Filipino psyche as demoralized, even if one might assign a different meaning to the term. Rather than a sign of social deviance or maladjustment to American culture, demoralization might well be considered an understandable response to an unreasonable situation. The social operation of racism had a particular consequence or effect on masculinity. As Robert Staples has argued, black manhood conflicted with the norms of masculinity because the codes "imply power, control, and authority," which were "denied to black men since slavery."[51] In response to this contradiction, black men assumed an air of "coolness." Black male self-presentation served a specific social-psychological purpose. Scholars of masculinity argue, for instance, that "the purpose of styling, then, is to paint a self-portrait in colorful, vivid strokes that makes the black male somebody."[52]

Filipino men, in response to the dilemmas of their predicament, also assumed a kind of coolness and expended great effort at self-presentation. Social scientists called it a "hyperaddiction to personal sophistication," attributing the "evil" of style-consciousness to the dance halls. In assessing Filipino social maladjustment, they observed that the Filipino dance hall patron was "a natty fellow, almost always immaculately groomed, well garbed, with a flair for style of dress." He was bold and ostentatious: "If he has a car it is frequently a sport model."[53] In turn, this supposed hyperaddiction to style was symptomatic of anomie and modern alienation. Finally, from the perspective of sociologists, the Filipino male's participation in the interracial world of leisure was a sign of personal demoralization. Documenting his concern with hygiene, a scholar described the routine of dressing: "The hair is combed with patent leather slickness; the face dabbed with soothing cold cream, finished afterwards with liberal touches of baby powder." By lavishing such attention on himself and the vice scene, the Filipino revealed himself to be disorganized and a victim of anomie. "The finished product is a human mannequin."[54]

To the extent that the sociological discourse presents a fair representation of the Filipino dance hall patron, it suggests how race and nationalism were connected. Outside the dance halls Filipino citizenship was legally denied, and sexual racism in the dance halls was but another facet of this national exclusion. Yet Filipinos continued to fight for their right to belong. In these contests over whiteness and nationalism, Filipinos honed certain skills and drew from their cultural repertoire. As Dick Hebidge and others have shown, leisure in general and style in particular represented realms of resistance in which the participants rework commodities to challenge the relations of capitalism.[55] In the taxi-dance halls the racial order—interlocking with the gender arrangements and class interests—was also contested and challenged.

To observers, the various incidents of sexual racism in the taxi-dance halls reflected the inevitability of conflict between social groups, the result of "natural" or "essential" differences. According to one scholar, "As long as Slavic and Italian youths and hot-headed Filipinos were allowed to mingle together on the same dance floor, frequent disturbances were inevitable."[56] As I have tried to demonstrate in this chapter, however, the conflicts between Filipino men and Italian men were anything but "inevitable." Filipino men entered the dance hall because of a difficult social predicament, and, once inside, they confronted discrimination. Some white women exploited them, as sociologists and investigators reported, but perhaps their most dangerous obstacles were other men. Many white ethnic men who attended the dance halls pursued native white women but not necessarily because of restricted access to women of their own social group. Rather, they sought assimilation through interethnic socializing, sexual relations, and, in some instances, marriage. But when Filipinos danced with white women, the cultural capital that could be gained from the white dance hall hostess—her appeal as an icon of virginal whiteness—was, from the perspective of white men, greatly diminished. Anything but inevitable, the conflicts on the dance floor reflected, in a microcosm, the broader conflicts between socially "marginal" men over racial privilege and prerogative.

Off the dance floor, in the cities, the history of public dance institutions revealed another dimension of the history of black/white sexual relations. Like some historians of American leisure, Cressey believed that the Chicago dance hall scene reflected the unique character of American pluralism—that "the patrons make up a polyglot aggregate from many corners of the world."[57] The history of the Filipino experience belies the uncomplicated pluralism that Cressey invoked. The taxi-dance halls were not institutions of unity or inclusion; they were sites of sexual racism and sometimes violent racial struggle.

But perhaps the most telling feature of Cressey's American pluralism thesis centers not on the presence of conflict but rather on an absence. As dancing became more and more popular, and as dance halls rapidly multiplied, it is important to note that the vast majority of the establishments excluded black men from entering. In that sense, perhaps the dance halls did reflect the nature of American pluralism. For as I have tried to suggest, the transformation of leisure institutions—the movement of the dance hall from the nineteenth-century margin into the early-twentieth-century mainstream—was made ideologically possible by the marginalization of the Black and Tans. The Black and Tans were immoral—and, to outsiders, even frightening—in part because they represented a world in which the rules and conventions of the mainstream were literally inverted. In the Black and Tan, black men were in the lead—blackness was on "top." The place of women in the black/white vice districts will be described and analyzed in chapter 6, where I reconstruct the history of black/white prostitution and explore the ways in which sexual margins influence the center. For now, however, we will examine further the ways in which the "antimiscegenation" taboo, and black/white sexual culture, influenced members of another social group who, because of prejudice, also found themselves relegated to the margin to seek intimacy. As we move further into the interzones, our historical inquiry shifts from dance halls to speakeasies, and from Filipino patrons to homosexual men and women.

★

5

INTERRACIAL INTERSECTIONS

Homosexuality and Black/White Relations

In the 1931 homosexual novel *Strange Brother*, the white author Blair Niles explores the world of Greenwich Village bohemians and urban speakeasies. In many ways Niles is critical of these sophisticated urbanites who, in search of pleasure and excitement, go "slumming" to the teeming underworld of black Harlem. Indeed, the novel's central character, June Westbrook, represents the stereotypical slummer, who admires but also exploits the black entertainers and patrons of the Harlem speakeasy scene. Another white character in *Strange Brother*, Mark Thornton, receives a more sympathetic treatment. Like June, Mark travels to Harlem to patronize the speakeasy scene. But Mark is a homosexual, and for him Harlem represents more than a slumming spot. He views the speakeasy scene as a refuge from intolerance and as an enclave of community.[1]

A brief analysis of the social history of *Strange Brother* suggests a kind of affinity between homosexuals, black/white sex districts, and African-American culture more generally. In the early 1930s the sociologist Ernest Burgess and his students at the University of Chicago conducted a survey of the city's rental libraries and drugstores, in order to document the circulation of novels with homosexual themes. Their reports indicated that in general retailers "can't keep up with public demand for risqué and sex books." Young homosexual readers, grappling with a conflicted sexual desire in its earliest stages of formation, sought to make sense of their feelings by reading texts that dared to mention the "unspeakable vice." In an interview between a graduate student and a homosexual, the subject recalled that he had read "'Weel of Lonlieness' [*sic*] as well as 'Strange Brother.'" The young man valued these books because he "would` like to live their lives."[2] Indeed, retailers reported that *Strange Brother* was among the most widely read books that they carried. It is significant that in several rental libraries, proprietors placed *Strange Brother* and other homosexual novels in the so-called colored section. Thus while Mark, a white homosexual, found affirmation and tolerance by traveling to black Harlem, urban retailers displayed novels with homosexual themes in black sections.[3] These proprietors distinguished *Strange Brother* from mainstream novels not by stigmatizing it as homosexual (they did not even have a "homosexual section") but rather by locating it within another, readily available system of social and spatial hierarchy—race. In other words, searching for a way to classify *Strange Brother*, the proprietors racialized the homosexual text.

This rare piece of evidence—of an explicitly homosexual text and its racialized marketing—actually suggests a pervasive pattern of *intersection* within the interzones. Throughout the 1920s, in Chicago and New York, some black and white homosexual men and women shared a sexual subculture forged within the Black and Tans, speakeasies, and public sex institutions. Homosexual involvement in the interzones can be divided into at least two phases—the first occurring at the turn of the century, within the culture of gender inversion, and the second phase marking the emergence of the modern homosexual. As historians have argued, sexologists and doctors first identified same-sex desire with what was known as gender inversion. The sources can be read to suggest the ways in which black/white heterosexual relations, particularly as institutionalized in the Black and Tan, helped to construct this theory. Later, in the 1920s, medical experts and particularly psychologists argued that instead of gender inversion, homosexuality could better be understood as a mental disorder that was not necessarily contingent on

★
74

gender reversal. Masculine men could also be homosexual. In both phases of homosexual formation, I argue, certain elements of African-American culture ought to figure more prominently.

In an essay assigned for a seminar on "social deviance," one University of Chicago graduate student argued that the homosexual, like other casualties of modern anomie—the Filipino dance hall patron and the Negro delinquent—suffered from social ostracism.[4] The student's comparison was more accurate than he realized; some homosexual men were shaped by black/white vice districts and institutions. As early as the 1890s historians have located male inverts in several northern cities. According to the sexologist Havelock Ellis, "The world of sexual inverts is, indeed, a large one in any American city." Moreover, "every city has its numerous meeting places: certain churches where inverts congregate; certain cafes well known for the inverted character of their patrons." Inverts met in clubs that, according to one observer, "were really dance-halls attached to saloons, which were presided over by [invert] waiters and musicians."[5] In Chicago reformers reported on "men who impersonate females [and] are among the vaudeville entertainers in the saloons. Unless these men are known, it is difficult to detect their sex." A similar report stated that the clubs included "men who dress in women's clothing and women who dress in men's clothing."[6] The central distinguishing feature of invert institutions, at least to outside observers, was the creative reversal of gender roles. Men behaved like women and women like men.

Reports of black inverts almost always include discussions of white inverts. According to one report, for example, invert meeting places included "certain cafes patronized by both Negroes and whites, and were [considered to be] the seat of male solicitation."[7] In 1893 a physician reported that "there is, in the city of Washington, D.C., an annual convocation of Negro men called the drag dance, which is an orgy of lascivious debauchery." Always subject to swift and punitive police actions, these and "similar organizations [were] lately suppressed by the police of New York City."[8] Those few institutions and dancers that eluded authorities were viewed, it should be noted, through a particular analytical lens—through a conceptual model of interracial relations. Thus one authority on sexual disorders, after witnessing an interracial inversion dance, believed that the participants were "Homosexual complexion perverts"—men who suffered from a kind of "social reverse complexion" syndrome. He theorized that color or racial difference substituted for the gender difference in the sexual relationship. Moreover, in discussing the prevalence of the disorder, the observer compared homosexual with heterosexual relations, noting that "even white women sometimes prefer colored men to white men and vice versa." In 1913 the prison reformer Margaret Otis observed intense relations between black and white female inmates, and in her nascent theory of "situational lesbianism," she argued that the difference in color substituted for gender difference. Otis refers to the white women involved with black women as "nigger lovers," suggesting the extent to which reformers understood black/white *homosexual* relations through reference to the ideology of miscegenation, just as in the case of Filipino relations within the dance halls. Likewise, one observer of a social gathering and ball including black and white homosexual men termed the event a *miscegenation dance*.[9] These references to race reveal the extent to which medical experts relied on the more pervasive theory of racial difference, as well as the ideology of "miscegenation," to conceptualize sexual attraction and relations between people of the same gender.[10]

What I am describing as racialization was more than a matter of reformers relying on race to understand inversion. Ideologies of racial difference also shaped the subculture from within, through subjective experience.[11] A young black male homosexual, in an interview with a University of Chicago sociologist, recounted his earliest experiences socializing with other male inverts. Leo reported that at age sixteen he had read about same-sex desire and learned that men who desired men were effeminate, a lesson that made a deep impression on him. At eighteen Leo was introduced to the sexual underworld of inverts "through a friend from Milwaukee," who invited Leo to a party: "I saw boys dance together, calling each other husband and wife, and several of them were arguing about men." Indeed, Leo's choice of terms that denoted homosexuality—words like *sissy* and *nelly*—each ultimately described a kind of gender reversal.[12] One can read this evidence from both black and white participants in the invert clubs to reveal a shared language, a common set of social practices, and similar constructions of sexuality. At the same time the (admittedly slim) evidence of black/white male homosexuality before 1900 almost always indicates that black men

★

adopted the female role.[13] The opposite was true of black female inverts.[14] If placed in their urban context—of white supremacist backlash against interracial socializing—it does not seem unreasonable to suggest that inverts drew on the stigmatized, socially dangerous culture of miscegenation to invent their sexual practices and construct their sexual subjectivities. To that extent the invert's performance of polarized gender roles—the exaggeration of the difference between the extremely feminine female roles and the masculine male roles—was paralleled by the constructed opposition between blackness and whiteness. "Miscegenation" dances were, first and foremost, racial events, with a history stretching back to the politics of slavery and Reconstruction. Yet miscegenation was invented in the North, in the midst of riots located in something like an urban vice district. It should not be surprising, therefore, that people forced into the margins or interzones easily assimilated certain concepts and idioms derived from the culture of miscegenation. As inverts hosted black/white dances and attended interracial invert cafes, the fundamental opposition between "races" historically central to "miscegenation" rituals probably enhanced the pleasurable opposition between gender roles.

By the beginning of the 1910s another formation of same-sex desire, distinguishable from inversion, dispersed through the sexual zones of Chicago and New York. This development can be viewed more clearly in the medical literature. As George Chauncey has argued, beginning in the 1890s, scientists and physicians reconceptualized the theory of same-sex desire, from one based on a model of gender inversion to a theory more recognizable as modern homosexuality. This shift has been the subject of much scholarly study, so it remains unnecessary to rehearse the arguments, but in general the development reflected the emergence of sexuality as a discrete source of social identity. In the theory of inversion, the man who desired other men adopted the gender identity of a woman, which was the only way to account for same-sex desire. By the 1910s, however, physicians were more likely to formulate theories of individual deviance, and attributed enormous power to sexuality as a force in human personalities, drawing from and popularizing Freudian theories of polymorphous perversity. From the perspective of physicians, then, it had become increasingly possible to conceive of a man who desired men and who behaved like a man. At the same time, within the subculture, the older cultural tradition of gender inversion did not disappear but rather persisted alongside the new more distinctively *sexual* identities.[15]

Medical discourse probably reflected, rather than created, the new sexual identities. How, then, do we explain the proliferation of homosexual subjectivities? A partial answer can be found in the fledgling black/white homosexual subcultures located in Harlem and Chicago.[16] If the absence of discussion among the actual reformers is any indication, homosexual institutions in Chicago were well hidden. Indeed, in their report on vice, the Chicago commission was surprised to discover the existence of homosexual establishments. As Dr. William Healy, an authority on juvenile delinquency, stated: "Most of us had thought of Chicago as being a place particularly inhabited by virile people, rather of the Western variety. There wasn't a soul on that commission who thought for a minute there was any extent of it in Chicago."[17] In the 1920s Harvey Zorbaugh's classic urban study of Chicago indicated that the bohemian section of Chicago, Towertown, included homosexual men and women. Also known as the "Village," this enclave was inhabited primarily by white homosexuals. One man was described as a "beautiful boy," who worked as a blouse maker. Noting the events of a Sunday tea party, Zorbaugh observed that "there was a good deal of taking one another's arms, sitting on the arms of one another's chairs, and of throwing arms about one another's shoulders. Soon the men were fondling each other, as were the women." These were white "fairies" and "lesbians." Indeed, as an example of racial prejudice, Zorbaugh noted that a man named "Alonzo," who claimed to be a Spaniard, was shunned by "Village" homosexuals because he was reputed to be an "octoroon." The more renowned homosexual restaurants were also predominately white. Zorbaugh did overhear a conversation between two men in a tearoom change suddenly when "a group of 'homos' from the South Side also came in." They were probably white, but their proximity to the Black Belt remains significant.[18] Public sex institutions—bathhouses "frequented by queers" or public toilets "notorious" for same-sex activity—were located on the predominately white North Side. But that does not, of course, indicate these institutions were all-white, since African-American men had occasion to travel to the North Side and to use the toilets. In addition to the bohemians, there were also the

★

so-called hoboes who formed homosexual attachments, often involving age difference; their ranks could have been interracial, but the manuscripts dealing with homosexual hoboes does not indicate racial background.[19]

If it seems likely that black men participated in white homosexual areas, the evidence also suggests the presence of homosexuality in African-American areas. In his interview entitled "My Story of Fags, Freaks, and Women Impersonators," a young black man, Walt Lewis, recalled in explicit detail his experiences with both men and women. One incident of public sex with a woman occurred in Washington Park, near Cottage Grove, deep in the heart of the Black Belt. Washington Park was also well known as an area where white and black homosexual men found sexual partners.[20] In general, the evidence about black lesbians in Chicago clubs remains scarce. One source indicates that some separation characterized relations between homosexual men and lesbians. In a Chicago report, the investigator pointed out that "there are very few lesbians and those that do come do not seem to mingle with the others."[21] Clark Street was also the location of black transvestite prostitutes. According to the German sexologist, Magnus Hirschfeld, "In Chicago I was introduced to a Negro girl on Clark Street who turned out to be a male prostitute." In general, the black/white clubs and dance halls that catered to, or at least tolerated, homosexuality also included prostitution.[22]

In New York, homosexuals congregated in several areas, including Times Square and Greenwich Village, but some men also participated in the black/white vice districts in Harlem. It was not uncommon for Harlem residents to cross these and other urban borders. The black gay writer Richard Bruce Nugent recalled his numerous visits to the Village; the black showgirl Mabel Hampton remembered that the Village was the "place where other lesbians hung out."[23]

In 1927, the Committee of Fourteen opened a special investigation into Harlem. Most of their findings concerned prostitution, as we shall see, but they also mentioned the existence of black/white homosexual institutions. In their published report on the investigation, the committee made only a veiled reference to the establishments, referring to "dives" that catered to "specialized types of degeneracy and perversion." The investigators, however, filed far more explicit descriptions. Some reports simply mentioned the presence of homosexuals. Thus an investigator noted that in "the largest speakeasy house of prostitution and assignation discovered in the entire Harlem investigation," there were the usual trappings—"a large speakeasy room and four rooms for prostitution," with "liquor being served from a five gallon jug." "Couples committed acts of sexual intercourse, unashamed, in view of others." Indeed, on "one visit the investigator saw three couples in the act at the same time." These, then, were the typical colored speakeasies. Near the end of the report, the investigator, almost as an afterthought, noted that in addition to black and white prostitutes and customers, there were "some fairies."[24]

Committee of Fourteen vice investigators acknowledged homosexual attendance of speakeasies, which accounted in part for their negative view of the "Colored Speakeasy." The "Colored" clubs were located primarily in Harlem and probably a few in Brooklyn. The black vice district in general, and the black/white homosexual clubs in particular, were located in the area from 126th Street to 152nd Street between Fifth and St. Nicholas Avenues. Investigators reported the incidence of lesbian sexual practices in a basement speakeasy located on 138th Street; another basement speakeasy, catering to "faggots" and prostitutes, was down on West 131st Street.[25] Some of these clubs were black/white clubs, which more openly catered to a racially mixed clientele, although the investigator also classified some as colored clubs, even though white homosexuals also patronized these establishments. One Committee of Fourteen file contained reports of approximately four hundred investigations, of which perhaps eighty were classified "White and Colored." An additional sixty were considered "Colored." The remainder were exclusively white clubs (in which I found no evidence of homosexuality). A survey of the file reveals that the highest percentage of reports of same-sex behavior occurred in "Colored" clubs.[26] As an example of a report, one investigation report noted that "in thirteen night clubs and speakeasies, there were fourteen homo-sexuals of both sexes observed."[27]

From the perspective of the investigators, all black/white mixing was immoral, but homosexual behavior elicited the strongest responses. The clubs including homosexuality were the only establishments routinely to be labeled the "worst." In one investigation of a homosexual speakeasy, on the margins of the report, a New York investigator noted in pencil: "Very Bad." Another report opened with the familiar statement: "This place is very disreputable." Like the clubs that included black homosexual men, the lesbian clubs were also viewed as immoral. In one report, for instance, the investigator wrote that he was introduced to a "Pussy Party," located in a basement where "various forms of sex perversion [were] committed." Near the top of the entry, his hastily penciled note reads: "Very Bad."[28]

A handful of clubs were designed exclusively for homosexual men, but the majority of "Colored" speakeasies also catered to lesbians. Hence there was the random all-male club, in which women were not permitted to enter,[29] but most New York speakeasies included women and men. Even at a so-called women's party, in which lesbians performed various sexual acts on each other, some men were present. Even outside the speakeasies, black lesbians socialized with men, at rent parties and buffet flats. Mabel Hampton, a black lesbian who worked as a showgirl, remembered a series of parties given by A'Leila Walker; she attended one party with a white friend and witnessed homosexual men and women conversing, dancing, and sometimes engaging in sexual activity. The major exception to the rule that lesbians mixed with homosexuals seems to have been the "sex circuses," in which lesbians often engaged in sexual relations.[30] In general, there were fewer separate lesbian institutions than separate male homosexual institutions, probably because women had less access to the resources necessary both to own and to attend nightclubs.

The 1890s invert clubs did include men and women, but the majority of the invert drag dances and leisure institutions were predominately male. By contrast, in the 1920s the underground sexual establishments in Harlem almost always included both men and women. In my view, this cogendered context partially caused the gradual movement away from the predominance of gender inversion and toward new models of homosexuality. This development, I would argue, stems in part from the culture of the speakeasy. The key characteristic of the typical underground speakeasy was the diversity of patrons. As one observer noted: "Every night we find the place crowded with both races, the black and the white, both types of lovers, the homo and heterosexual."[31] Moreover, the new underground speakeasies included Chinese and Filipino men (who, according to the evidence, were heterosexual). This multitude of differences—racial, gender, sexual, ethnic—helped to create a speakeasy culture of fluidity that sharply contrasted with the ritualized rigidity of gender or racial dichotomy characteristic of the old-style Black and Tan or invert drag dance. The earlier invert rituals persisted into the 1920s—Langston Hughes called them the "Spectacles in Color"—but in this instance gender reversal and cross-dressing had become less a direct expression of a thriving subculture and more a performance for white tourists in search of the exciting and the exotic.[32]

Indeed, from the perspective of the investigators, cross-dressing itself no longer served as the privileged signifier of homosexuality. In writing about the presence of fairies or lesbians in a given establishment, investigators did not often report men wearing women's clothes, nor consequently did they themselves rely on the presence of gender reversal to classify homosexuals. If there was cross-dressing, and there probably was, in sharp contrast to the witnesses of turn-of-the-century invert rituals, 1920s vice investigators did not find the practice especially notable.

Nor did sociologists, who were now more likely to employ a popularized version of Freud to describe same-sex phenomena. The tradition of inversion persisted—at least to the extent that some social scientists believed that the homosexual personality was "effeminate"—but now gender inversion was but one among several theories of same-sex desire. In a discussion of homosexuals and speakeasies, a University of Chicago graduate student pointed to a club "located in the Negro district of the south side where a cabaret of the black and tan variety operates mainly for their [homosexuals'] benefit." In his view, in such clubs "the social taboos of a conventional society have been raised and the repressed individual can find full expression for those smoldering desires burning within."[33] Throughout his essay, the student draws on concepts like "polymorphous perversity," "instinctive craving," and "neurotic state" to make sense of his observations of black and white homosexual men dancing at a Black and Tan. The student's relatively novel conception of Freudianism—the opposition between society and individual desire, the language of "repression" and "expression"—mark this description of homosexuality as decidedly more modern than the racialized

★

language employed by the authorities who studied inversion. But the significance of race did not decline with the dispersal of Freudianism. For the point of the graduate student's Freudian description was to suggest that a black context—a "black and tan" cabaret in a "Negro district"—was critical to overcoming and releasing the internalized inhibitions of civilization. On the one hand, because they were the most marginalized of dance clubs, the Black and Tans or speakeasies tolerated stigmatized behavior, providing a context in which homosexual men and women could experience their sense of desire. Yet the above description ultimately reveals the extent to which Freudianism in America relied on a particular racialistic conception of the id. Some black men may have absorbed the Freudian model and organized their subjectivity through popular currents of the theory. In his correspondence, the gay black social worker Glen Carrington sometimes invoked Freudianism, particularly the drive theory of homosexual desire.[34] Nevertheless, psychological concepts like internal drives and sex instinct were associated with the primitive, which, in the modern era, had become closely linked to the construction of black sexuality.

The contacts between African-Americans and homosexuals in speakeasies constituted direct cultural exchange through the creation of sexualized social practices. The reports can be read to suggest that in the diverse, fluid context of the speakeasy the single unifying theme was explicit sexuality. In one speakeasy, for instance, the investigator reported that "two men were dancing with each other kissing and sucking tongues." In another club, an investigator observed, the "women were dancing with each other, imitating the motions of sexual intercourse and the men were dancing with each other, all indecently." Another report on an all-black speakeasy indicated that "the women were dancing with one another and going through the motions of copulation, and the men were dancing with one another."[35] Patrons probably danced the "Black Bottom" or the "Turkey Trot"—dances imported from the South that circulated in a variety of northern urban venues—but the underground homosexual speakeasy versions were intensely sexualized. These reports support the thesis that African-American cultural practices, especially dance, shaped homosexuality not in some abstract, indistinct way, but directly through the communal molding of dance forms that were often indistinguishable from sexual intercourse.[36] It does not require a huge leap of faith to believe that this public, interactive construction of sexualized dance extended its influence off the dance floor, choreographing the supposedly "private" performance of sexual intercourse.[37]

The music of the speakeasy, a large subject worthy of further study, shaped the sexualized dancing. As the historian Eric Garber has argued, black blues singers, including Gladys Bentley, Alberta Hunter, George Hanna, and Ma Rainey, became increasingly popular in the 1920s. These singers performed songs with sexually explicit lyrics, which included the speakeasy language of homosexuality, featuring terms like *sissy* and *bulldagger*. Some of the lyrics hinted at the fluidity of sexual desire: "If you can't bring me a woman, bring me a sissy man." Lyrics dealing with women suggested the superiority of lesbian sexual practices, entreating men, for example, to perform oral sex. Lillian Faderman interprets several of the blues songs as nascent radical lesbian texts, which proclaim the superiority of lesbianism and the obsolescence of men and heterosexuality. In a sense homosexual themes were common among certain blues lyrics, but it would be wrong to deduce from their frankness that the blues reflected a broad acceptance of homosexuality in African-American neighborhoods. Faderman relies on evidence of Harlem lesbians who received marriage licenses and lived as a married couple, but the countervailing evidence of antivice rhetoric among black reformers and religious leaders suggests that such examples of tolerance were exceptional. Moreover, as indicated, the majority of Harlem clubs that tolerated homosexuality were deeply marginalized, frequently located in tenement apartments. Apparently the more visible and accessible a Harlem club became, the more heterosexual its patrons. The homosexual speakeasies were hypervigilant for good reason: they feared exposure and expulsion. And yet the clubs *were* located in Harlem and not in white neighborhoods. That Harlem had become a site of homosexual leisure perhaps represented the relative powerlessness of black Harlemites to rid their neighborhoods of institutions they viewed as harmful. The greater number of clubs in Harlem might also suggest a tolerance for the marginalized among people with a long history of exclusion.[38]

In either case, with titles like "Boy in the Boat," the songs left little to the imagination. Speakeasy dances provided a ready urban stage on which homosexuals constructed the performance and shaped the experience of sexuality. So central was the institutional culture of the speakeasy to the "practices" of homosexuality that it shaped white homosexual life outside the clubs. For example, in the 1930s, Earl Bruce, a University of Chicago graduate student, studied the patterns of behavior among white homosexual men at a private party. The men attempted to re-create the speakeasy scene, according to Bruce. "When we arrived at the apartment, one of the homosexuals sent out for a gallon of beer and a few pints of whiskey." The ages of the members ranged from twenty-six to thirty-seven. "The owner of the apartment, a homosexual about 25 years of age, runs a small dancing school downtown. Many of his pupils are homosexual." At the party a "Mr. J. [the host] played a number of pornographic records sung by some negro entertainers; a homosexual theme ran through the lyrics." These homosexual men could be found "swaying to the music of a colored jazz orchestra," providing the "unconventional sight" of "two young men in street clothes dancing together, cheek to cheek."[39] During interviews, white homosexual men revealed not only that they liked to dance but that they "like music, singers, especially negro singers."[40] Mabel Hampton also noted the historic significance of private parties, particularly because the gatherings were not only lesbian but also black/white. Of course, in the background of the typical gathering one could hear jazz — a word that not only denoted black music but, in the parlance of some African-Americans, prostitutes, and homosexuals, also meant sexual intercourse.[41]

The vernacular of jazz among members of the urban sexual margins suggests the historical potential for the circulation and exchange of cultural forms. Because of the racial segregation of vice, African-Americans represented the primary group influencing the fundamental culture of the interzone. Because of social repression, some stigmatized white groups temporarily inhabited the districts. Sharing space in the speakeasies resulted in shared music and dance, common idioms and social rituals. At the same time some African-American men indicated that their earliest homosexual experiences were with white men already initiated into the homosexual subculture,[42] suggesting the historic centrality of the white culture of gender inversion. As several scholars have argued, Freudian theories of homosexuality detached gender from sexuality and declared sexuality a discrete and powerful dimension of the psy-che.[43] In the urban construction of sexuality Freudianism may have supplied the modern theory of homosexuality, but African-American dance and music shaped the practice.[44]

A great many homosexual contacts occurred outside the dance halls and speakeasies. Although rarely discussed by historians, male solicitation was an important aspect of the commercialization of sex-uality. The current literature on male prostitution centers on the early-twentieth-century Northeast and focuses on what was com-monly known as "trade," usually heterosexual men who sold their sex-uality to "queer" or "inverted" men.[45] As Jeffrey Weeks has argued for nineteenth-century London and George Chauncey for 1920s Times Square in New York, a new model of male prostitution emerged in urban centers. In New York class relations were important to the orga-nization of male solicitation, but the presence of "fairies" reveals the continuing centrality of gender in male prostitution.[46]

A comparison between white and black forms of male prostitu-tion helps to illustrate the significance of race. Throughout its his-tory white prostitution, almost without exception, has been segre-gated by gender. White male prostitution was prevalent in Chicago and New York, but men were more likely than women to be street-walkers. In part this reflects the prevailing sexual hierarchy. Heterosexual relations were privileged over homosexual relations: male prostitution institutions were deeply repressed and therefore few and far between. Nonetheless, some "Colored" speakeasy houses of prostitution offered their male customers both male and female prostitutes. For example, in one case the investigator made an inquiry to the resident madam, Virginia "Cotton" Canfield, about the type of club she managed. According to his report, "I asked the madam what kind of a party she called this and she said 'A freak-ish party, everybody in here is supposed to be a bulldagger or a c——.' I said, 'Well I am neither, I like mine in a normal way. Aren't there any regular girls around this place?'" It is difficult to know pre-cisely which type of club the investigator describes. It may have been a sexually mixed brothel or even a predominately homosexual speakeasy house of prostitution. In either case, Virginia Canfield was neither intimidated nor impressed by the investigator, and replied to his query with a terse, "I don't know." He asked her, "Are you one of these so-called things here or are you a normal, regular girl?"

Obviously she could have solicited the undercover investigator, but instead she replied to his inquiry into her sexual status that "everybody here is either a bull dagger or a faggot and I am here." This was a predominately black club, and the investigator too was black. As the investigator wandered through the "party," he was "solicited for an act of perversion by one of the men present."[47]

Although rare, the evidence does indicate the existence of black male prostitution alongside female prostitution. For example, one white investigator working in Brooklyn reported that at "about 4:15 P.M. while passing this address I observed a colored man and two colored women standing on a stoop. As I passed they all spoke at once, saying 'Come on in,' beckoning with their heads." But rather than a solicitation from one of the women, the investigator received a proposition from "the colored man, Sam," who said, "How would you like to take a boy?" Sam was about 5 feet, 7 inches, 155 pounds, with dark brown eyes and hair, and a "yellow complexion." To Sam's invitation, the investigator replied, "I don't care about boys." But Sam persisted, promising, "I'll give you a good time." It is significant that the investigator did not pursue the matter with the man, perhaps because solicitation from a man did not, from the perspective of white investigators, constitute "prostitution" and therefore did not interest them. In any case, the investigator replied that he would prefer a woman. Sam responded by asserting, "It don't make any difference, but there they are." The investigator then approached two women, inquired about their prices, and learned that an act of prostitution cost two dollars. Finally, as the investigator prepared to leave, Sam solicited him again: "Why don't you take a boy?" The investigator inquired about the price, which he learned was the same as for an act of prostitution with a woman, two dollars.[48] One can make too much of this dialogue, to be sure, but we should listen carefully to Sam's claim that the gender of the prostitute was not particularly significant. To Sam's mind, the important difference was between a white customer and a black prostitute. The point is not to privilege one category of difference over another—to underplay the significance of the hierarchy organizing relations between sex worker and customer—but the evidence can be read to suggest the power of racial ideology in black/white male prostitution. Unlike the gender segregation of white prostitution, black men and women solicited side by side. Unlike the white prostitutes, black male prostitutes solicited customers who were above them in the racial hierarchy. Color difference coded and socially reinforced the class hierarchy positioning the customer or "john" over the prostitute. Following regulations of the committees, investigators assiduously documented racial difference; on each report they classified the objects of their investigations by color, ranging from "dark" to "yellow." Investigators sometimes inferred the ethnicity but did not document the color of "white" hostesses. Within and outside the subculture of prostitution, race remained a central form shaping the commercialization of sex.[49]

From the perspective of a gender analysis, the ideology of male prostitution diverged significantly from the ideology shaping female prostitution. According to the norms of heterosexuality, the purpose of sexual relations between men and women was either to procreate or to provide satisfaction between married adults.[50] Those norms also supported the view that sexuality ought to be located in the home, away from the public, commercial realm. Thus female prostitution represented a kind of negative ideal, an example of illegitimate sexuality; it was a public sexual transaction structured by the exchange of money. All homosexual relations were, by definition, illegitimate. Sexual contacts between people of the same gender were outside marriage; they were public and, if not located within vice zones, were then indirectly formed by a public culture of commercialized leisure. In the majority of investigative reports, what may well have been acts of homosexual prostitution were viewed merely as homosexual behavior, whereas investigators of female prostitution attempted to discern whether a given act constituted public dating or paid dancing or an "authentic" act of prostitution.[51]

Thus the distinctions threaten to disintegrate when one attempts to classify homosexual behavior in public sex institutions, such as bathhouses and toilets. The evidence of black/white contacts within these institutions remains rare, but it seems reasonable to suggest that, given the prevalence of racial segregation in housing and employment, bathrooms provided the most opportunities for black/white sexual contacts. Some of these contacts were for pleasure only, some for financial gain, some for both. In one investigative report, filed under the category "miscellaneous" about a "colored pervert," the scene was the rest room of the Harlem subway station at 125th Street and Lenox Avenue. After entering the lavatory the investigator noticed "two sets of legs in the toilet enclosure." He observed "a white man in an intoxicated condition sitting on the stool and a large bundle alongside of him and a colored man on his knees committing an act of perversion." Presumably the African-American man, described as "fairly well dressed" with a "high yellow complexion," was performing oral sex. Some time later the African-American man returned to the platform, but then he followed another man back into the bathroom. The investigator followed and reported the "colored pervert standing by the urinal watching the white man who was standing next to him." This man was either uninterested in a sexual encounter or uninitiated into the homosexual codes and soon left the urinal. Returning to the platform, he asked the investigator, "What the hell's the matter with him?" The investigator replied, "He is a fairy." I want to create several different interpretations from this document. One can view the so-called colored pervert as a homosexual man who pursued multiple partners in the bathrooms. Or it may well be that the man was a prostitute who, when the investigator was not looking, received money from the white man in the toilet stall. It is significant as well that the subject of the report was the colored pervert, who performed the oral sex, and not the white man receiving it. The man assuming the female position was viewed as the pervert; that he was a black man engaging in sex with a white man reinforced the investigator's perception of the perversion. And the investigator's voyeurism is worth noting, since his perceptions were shaped by his position as a hidden powerful authority.[52]

To bring the example of black/white homosexual contact out of the interzones, further toward the mainstream, I want to introduce another example of a "colored pervert," but in this case the African-American writer Wallace Thurman, one of the most gifted members of the Harlem Renaissance. Thurman grew up in Salt Lake City, Utah, attended the University of Southern California, and moved to Harlem in 1925. Soon after arriving Thurman found himself virtually alone, with few resources, and unemployed. According to his and other accounts, he had extreme difficulty in locating a job. Writing about himself in the third person, Thurman recounted his initial hardship to William Rapp, a close friend: "He [Thurman] had a little stake which has soon gone. He found no job. He had no room rent and was hungry." Thurman secured a job as an elevator man but then lost the position. That day "he returned homeward." According to Thurman's recollection, "At 135th St. he got off the subway, and feeling nature's call went into the toilet. There was a man loitering in there. The man spoke." At this point in the letter, at precisely the moment when the homosexual act surfaces, Thurman switches from the third to the first person. Thurman wrote: "He did more than speak, making me know what his game was. I laughed. He offered me two dollars. I accepted." At some point during the sexual exchange, according to Thurman, policemen burst out of a porter's mop closet and arrested the two men. Thurman found himself in night court. He was fined twenty-five dollars. At this point, in recounting the story, Thurman draws a distinction between himself and the man who propositioned him, a "Fifth Avenue hairdresser" who had previously been arrested for approaching men in bathrooms.[53]

The central purpose of his correspondence to Rapp was to deny allegations of homosexuality. Thurman may have been disingenuous when he claimed to have entered the bathroom only at "nature's calling." He might have entered the homosexual meeting place in search of either money or pleasure or both. Moreover, it seems that Thurman understood the codes of the bathroom, suggesting that this experience in the rest room was not his first. Since the man who approached Thurman had been arrested for solicitation, he would have tried to avoid undercover policemen. Maybe he was reckless. Or perhaps he minimized the risk of entrapment by soliciting men only through the use of "insider" codes. If this was so, then it would seem that Thurman was enough of an insider to interpret the codes and respond with the appropriate signals. To be sure, Thurman proclaimed, "There was certainly no evidence therein that I was homosexual," although he did so in the context of public divorce proceedings. In either case it seems clear that what Thurman represented to Rapp as an isolated event, caused by the exigencies of financial need, had a more complex history.[54]

Seven years after his arrest for the homosexual incident, Wallace Thurman published a roman à clef of the Harlem Renaissance, entitled *Infants of the Spring*.[55] The novel, more than any other of the several works about Harlem in the 1920s, centered on black/white sexual relations. Indeed, the central black character, Raymond, becomes enamored with the central white character, Stephen (a

Swedish man visiting Harlem for the first time). Raymond believes that their relationship can transcend race: "There was something delightfully naive, and childlike, about their frankly acknowledged affection for one another. Like children, they seemed to be totally unconscious of their racial difference."[56] *Infants of the Spring* represented the first known example of an African-American writer portraying black/white homosexual relations.

By the end of the 1920s Thurman's characteristic cynicism toward bohemians had devolved into harsh criticism of the Harlem Renaissance. In his writing he focused on the excesses of the young black literati, its decadence, and what he judged to be its mediocrity. At the center of his commentary were black/white sexual relations, for he believed that the growing obsession with interracial sex represented yet another attempt by young upstarts to transgress Victorian conventions in the name of modernist rebellion. Popular experimentation with homosexuality among self-styled sophisticates was little more than a case in point. Wallace Thurman knew better. His intermittent participation in the subculture of homosexuality imparted a sense of the continuing marginality not only of same-sex desire but, more forbidding, of black/white homosexual relations. Interracial same-sex relations emerged in urban areas only haltingly and against great odds. In both New York and Chicago certain spaces in black neighborhoods offered these men and women a rare opportunity to form a community. Homosexuals frequented rest rooms where, given the prevalence of racial segregation, it was uniquely possible for white and black men to share an intimate social experience. Repression from without had forged cultural bonds between people living on the margins.

Despite the freedom offered by speakeasies, Thurman and his brethren of gay black men did not live in some urban utopia. Two other social realities must be addressed. The white homosexuals in Towertown who scorned another homosexual man because of his reputed black ancestry, or the prevalence of middle-class homosexual restaurants in Chicago that were all-white, suggest the existence of racism among white homosexuals. At the same time, Wallace Thurman's fear of exposure or W.E.B. DuBois's decision to fire Augustus Granville Dill, managing editor of the *Crisis*, after his arrest for soliciting in a rest room, suggest the existence of homophobia among African-Americans.[57] African-American gays and lesbians, living on the borders between margins, experienced both sides of the social history of black/white homosexuality. They suffered numerous exclusions based on prejudice but continued to survive at the cultural and institutional intersections of race and sexuality.

Mark Thornton, the fictional man who found affirmation in Harlem, would have cherished, and identified with, Thurman's novels. In fact the two might have met at a club or exchanged sexual favors in a restroom. Whether through dancing to jazz in a speakeasy or discoursing through a Harlem novel, African-American culture and artists did in fact help to shape the emergence of homosexuality. The interzones formed the basis for a significant transformation in American culture. As we travel further into the circles of the underworld, the culture of the interzone becomes both more complex in its transgressive dimension and powerful in its transformative effects. The subject is black/white prostitution.

★

6

NEW FALLEN WOMEN
Black/White Prostitution

If the persecution of Jack Johnson served to create a uniquely northern system regulating black male sexuality, the story of Johnson's
wife, Lucille Cameron, and of his accuser, Belle Schreiber, config-
ured the other side of the emergent race/gender system. The sensa-
tional story of the women who became sexually involved with
Johnson produced a series of stereotypes that, after dispersing and fil-
tering across the cities, structured the everyday lives of women in the
vice districts. Both Cameron and Schreiber were prostitutes. The
newspaper discourse helped to circulate the conception that all
white women involved with black men were prostitutes. It is also
important to remember the fate of Cameron in the era of white slavery. When she refused to cooperate with federal authorities, she was
imprisoned, the ultimate punishment for perhaps the most sexually
immoral transgression.[1] Another historical coincidence is central to
the story of interracial prostitution: Schreiber, Johnson's accuser,
had worked at the infamous Chicago Everleigh Club. As I pointed
out, with the closing of the Levee, the Everleigh Club had deteriorated, and by the 1920s its new tenants were predominately African-

American women. In fact, by the end of World War I the ranks of prostitution had become increasingly, and in some areas predominately, African-American. More than historical coincidence, that Schreiber's former workplace had become predominately black represented one of the most significant trends in the history of prostitution.

The most basic demographic data suggest the depth and extent of the racial revolution in prostitution.[2] As indicated, the available historical evidence reflects a bias in the policing of prostitution: black women were more visible and therefore more vulnerable to arrest. Yet the numbers combined to produce a striking statistical portrait. Black women were easy prey to police, who possibly were under pressure to inflate the number of arrests.[3] Black prostitutes were more likely to be convicted and, after conviction, more likely to receive maximum sentences. After serving their sentences, black prostitutes were less successful on probation than were white women and more likely than white women to return to prostitution. Indeed, their rates of recidivism were higher.[4]

Even if corrected for the biased policing, the statistical evidence demonstrates that black women were more likely to enter the underworld of "sex work" than were white women. Although social scientists conceived of several theories to explain black women's participation in prostitution, their theories centered on social scientific models emphasizing either internal pathology ("inheritances from slavery" and family breakdown) or external causes (customer demand and economic deprivation). The prevailing interpretation of the causes of prostitution held that women turned to prostitution because of poverty. Social scientists of the era, and historians of prostitution, have usually relied on a combination of internal and external theories to explain prostitution. As I suggested earlier, the problem with such theorizing is that scholars have not fully addressed the issue of African-American prostitution, so the analytical category of race has been absent; nor have they located prostitution in general within the historical scholarship on women's labor.

An analysis that combines race and female labor must begin with the fact that, historically, the work patterns of black women did not parallel the work patterns of most white women. African-American women's work has not been defined or structured by the ideology of public and private spheres,[5] the concept that woman's role is in the private sphere, performing duties of wife and mother. In the case of black women, beginning with their enslavement, the public/private dichotomy did not define patterns of labor, and black women routinely worked alongside men, outside the domicile. Despite efforts to reorganize gender arrangements, after emancipation black women continued to labor outside the home. Because the public/private dichotomy did not apply to black women, they were more susceptible to sexual harassment, lacking the protection afforded by the ideological distinction between bodily labor (that which can be extracted for a price) and their body and sexuality (that which is private and not for sale). In the North, black women suffered sexual harassment, even when they secured the kinds of jobs furthest removed from the sexual realm. DeBoven Koven pointed out, "There is no doubt that the few colored girls who find positions as stenographers or bookkeepers are much more open to insult than white girls in similar positions."[6] To an extent, the ideological vulnerability of black women originated in the South, during the era of slavery, but the particular historical problem of the disproportionate representation of black women in prostitution must also be situated in the social context of modern urban capitalism. In the North, African-American women worked within racially stratified markets.[7] A white progressive reformer, for instance, found that African-American "high school girls of refined appearance, after looking for weeks, will find nothing open to them in department stores, office buildings, or manufacturing establishments, save a few positions as maids in the women's waiting rooms." The evidence indicates that black women were more likely to be servants and laundresses, whereas white women were more likely to be seamstresses. Moreover, as migration continued, the percentage of black women in domestic service continued to rise.[8]

If black women were relegated to domestic service, it is important to note that even within that system they were forced into the least desirable positions.[9] In Illinois, for example, protective labor laws forbade employment agencies from sending white children to work in parlor houses or brothels; yet, following the pattern of Progressive color blindness, the statutes remained silent concerning African-American women. As the Progressive reformer Mrs. Celia Parker Wooley stated: "The law upon Illinois statute books prohibits white girls from acting in any capacity as servant in houses of prostitution.

While colored girls and women at any age beyond sixteen are permitted with the greatest freedom to work as servants."[10] Demographic disproportions also shaped African-American women's employment options: in Chicago, for instance, there was a surplus of black women, so some women had difficulty finding an African-American partner and therefore had to seek employment outside the home. In New York, where black men actually outnumbered black women, black women were nevertheless disproportionately in the ranks of prostitution, but the numbers are not as dramatic.[11]

Racism in the market—black women's relegation to domestic service, their vulnerability to sexual harassment, and segregated service in brothels—combined to increase the probability that African-American women would enter prostitution. At the same time, racism operated within the markets of commercialized sex, forcing women of color to negotiate yet another set of racial stigmas and hierarchies. For the most part, black women worked in interracial prostitution, which represented a distinctive form of sex work. In the West, of all prostitutes who worked for white men, "African-American women and Mexican women occupied the lowest rung on the ladder of social acceptance."[12] In some cases the stigma against interracial prostitution operated within the generally subordinated group. Thus, as Lucie Cheng Hirata has argued with regard to Chinese prostitutes, "The best prostitutes went into higher-class brothels reserved only for the Chinese, while the rest were sold to inferior dens of prostitution, which served a racially mixed clientele."[13]

In Chicago and New York the type and prestige of the institution, whether brothel, hotel, or tenement, determined the financial prospects of a prostitute. As we have seen, dance halls served as conduits for prostitution but were not readily acknowledged as such. The institutional fronts afforded them a kind of respectability that in turn inflated the prices a given "hostess" could charge. During the era of Prohibition, investigators identified at least three classes of sexual institutions. The first was the standard speakeasy. Rather than being employed by the proprietors, prostitutes congregated at the establishment to make the necessary contacts. The next level or type was a speakeasy "where prostitutes [were] employed under the guise of hostesses and where drinks are served." Like the nineteenth-century saloon, this speakeasy featured women as waitresses, but the establishments were in fact popular because it was possible to find a waitress who might exchange sex for money. The final type of club was viewed, by reformers and the general public alike, as the most notorious. According to the committees, "the most flagrant type has been designated for convenience, the Speak-easy House of Prostitution." A report offers the standard description: "There is a main room where customers gather and where they are introduced to prostitutes who are either residents or sitters, and where drinks are served." Bedrooms in the back provided the space for sexual exchanges. For our purposes, it should be pointed out that the "White and Colored" establishments were almost always the notorious "Speak-easy Houses of Prostitution."[14]

Historians of prostitution agree that the type of sexual institution determines to a great extent the amount of financial remuneration a given prostitute could expect. Thus elite white dance hostesses earned between fifteen and twenty dollars for a sexual exchange. In one New York club, for example, two so-called hostesses attracted the attention of the undercover investigator. The prostitute Ruth Ross offered to "commit an act of prostitution for the sum of $15.00."[15] Dance hall rituals—conversation, protocol, customs— were complicated, and constructed into a facade, to impart the impression that the hostesses were not actually prostitutes. In one reported scenario, a "chaperon came over to our table and asked if we would like to have an instructress." Soon the men were introduced to Miss Ross. Then the investigator sought to confirm that the hostesses acted as prostitutes. Miss Ross replied: "Do you think we are here out for good health?" They charged "twenty dollars each for the evening."[16] The dance hall hostess was not shy or demure; her comportment suggested sexual availability. In a report from the Orpheum Dance Hall, an investigator observed the standard erotic play, in which "she rubbed her sexual parts against my body." The undercover man inquired if she "stepped out for a wild time." She replied that "she did not step out for charity." The dance hall hostess crossed the blurry boundaries of treating, that is, exchanging various sexual favors for dates, entertainment, and gifts. Yet hostesses, as their name suggests, still retained some of the gendered artifice of Victorian respectability. In effect, the typical customer of the dance halls could assure himself that the hostess was not, by his estimation, a "whore"; he might even believe she was a relative innocent whose agreement to accept his proposition was unique.[17]

The central difference, then, between a streetwalker and a hostess derived from a constellation of rituals constructed within the commercialized sex institution. Miss Rose and other elite prostitutes benefited from their employment in "respectable" dance halls and restaurants where they could meet a relatively elite clientele. In the course of an evening a hostess and her "date" might go uptown to Harlem or across town to the South Side of Chicago, but their status as sex workers was in part secured by their position within all-white establishments. Even so it should be noted that—as much as the glittering dance floor lights or the sensual music—the ideology of whiteness supplied the erotics of culture on which sex workers traded.[18]

A few black women were able to attain the kind of sexual status as white women. These cases were rare. The *Baltimore Afro-American* reported a case of a white man who kept a black mistress. In this story, appearing with the headline "Brown Skin Got His Goat," the paper reported that a "wealthy New Yorker [was] declared to be keeping a West Indian beauty in a Rich Apartment." He was described as hopelessly infatuated by her "brown skin." According to the sources, including an interview with the man's wife, the "husband found the woman in Jamaica, and now supports her in an apartment—an apartment the shades of which are always drawn."[19]

Whatever the exceptions, the general trend was that white dance hostesses earned more than white streetwalkers. But all white women working in same-race prostitution earned more than African-American women. As in the general market, institutional ideology remained significant: where a woman worked greatly determined her financial remuneration. If you correct for institutional location, however, the significance of race is highlighted. As with the white taxi dancer who danced with Filipino men, the white streetwalker who solicited black men earned significantly less than streetwalkers who "stayed white." Women who worked in black/white prostitution, whether white or black, typically charged between two and six dollars. Among the most destitute streetwalkers, the cost for a brief sexual contact could dip as low as one dollar. In studies conducted in New York, social scientists calculated that the average prostitute, probably white, accepted propositions from approximately fifteen men each day, earning up to eighty dollars. For black streetwalkers, the majority of reported prices hovered around two dollars; even if they conducted twenty sexual exchanges, their daily net probably was half that of the average white streetwalker.[20]

Some speakeasies were for whites, some for blacks, but the majority were probably black/white clubs, the institutional descendants of Black and Tans. A portion of these probably specialized in offering black/white sexual contacts, and others simply operated with an open-door policy. As one proprietor put it, "We take anybody that has the money."[21] Many speakeasies catered to a particular black/white dyad, whether black men seeking white prostitutes or white men seeking black. Spann's, for instance, was widely known as a club of "white inmates for colored men."[22] Mrs. Branch, the madam and initial contact who informed the investigator of the club's existence, brought the investigator into a "dining room in the rear of the apartment where Marion Edward [a white prostitute] and a colored man were sitting talking." Another club was described as a speakeasy house of prostitution in a "tenement, with white inmates, operated for colored men only."[23]

The undercover investigators tended to perceive the milieu of white houses of prostitution that catered to black men as more immoral than same-race sex institutions. Indeed, these reports, perhaps more than other reports on different aspects of prostitution, suggested the bias of white investigators. A survey of several reports on white brothels catering to black men reveal a recurrent concern with black/white dancing. Of one establishment, the Greenleaf Melody Club, an investigator reported that "the dance was very sexual and indecent." Another report observed that the white prostitutes "provoked" the black customers by their "shimmying." In another black/white brothel, an investigator described a white prostitute as "degenerate." According to the investigator's rendition of their conversation, the white woman "was a hostess in a Broadway nightclub" but she also "consorted with black men" in Harlem. She frankly stated that she preferred "the colored man's technique." The investigator summarized his estimation of the club in a word: "obscene."[24] In a Chicago club an investigator noted that "black men were seen dancing with white girls and vice versa." He then indicated that the "actions of these people were absolutely disgusting." Such condemnation was not often applied to same-race dance halls but rather to black/white situations, particularly in the case of white prostitutes and black customers.[25] Another report included a lengthy discussion of "aggressive" black prostitutes, significant in itself, but then focused on the fact that "there were nine white women, eight of whom were there in the company of black men."[26] From the point of view of white male investigators, when black men consorted with white women, the interactions were almost always deemed hypersexual, sometimes obscene, even to the extent that black/white prostitution was perceived as a different kind of commercialized sex altogether.

These sharp moral reactions against black/white prostitution were not "reflexes" but, rather, white male perceptions as filtered through urban racial/sexual ideologies. In part the ideology derived from the southern racial system in which black men were denied sexual access to white women. But the historical reality was that the Great Migration represented a significant, and enduring, challenge to the interracial taboo and ideologies of sexual segregation. Although after the Civil War black men did not in fact have access to white women, in the North the growth of commercialized sexuality provided increased availability of white women. Although rarely referred to in migration studies, this difference must have made a significant impact on the experience of black men settling in Chicago and New York. What had been deeply taboo in the South was readily available in the North. Yet the promise of freedom, whether in employment or sexuality, was ultimately quite deceptive. The consensus that brought down Jack Johnson in 1913 had not significantly changed in the 1920s and, in order to survive, African-American men learned the sexual boundaries of the North. Crossing the color line could be treacherous. Of all the problems in locating evidence on black/white sexuality, by far the most difficult is the case of African-American men involved with white women. Historical sources of illicit sexuality almost always surface in regulatory institutions—the police, the courts, the prisons. African-American men who desired to cross the sexual color line were seemingly skilled at eluding authorities. When they were not, many were arrested and imprisoned; others were probably murdered. In a rare piece of evidence, a trial transcript of a case in which a black man was arrested for associating with a white woman, the power of "antimiscegenation" ideology is revealed. According to the black man, he often spent time in a club where "white girls meet up with colored fellows." Referring to specific women involved in a supposed crime, the judge inquired whether he knew "what nationality she was?" The black man replied, "When I met her she was passing as a colored girl. She was supposed to be colored when she was at 34th and State." Then, to reassure the judge, and to protect himself, the man declared: "If I knew she was white when I met her I never would have had anything to do with her." Nevertheless the man was found guilty of pandering. The judge imposed the maximum penalty of one thousand dollars, court costs, and one year in jail.[27] Despite the power of the taboo and the strictness of its enforcement, the fact remained that for black men migrating to the North, the availability of white prostitutes in predominately black urban areas must have represented a significant change from life under Jim Crow. What was held up in the South as both most desirable and most taboo—white womanhood—was in the North readily available to the African-American man able to spend five or six dollars.

If African-American sexuality was in fact reshaped by moving North—and by the increased availability of white women—the prevailing conception of the white women who consorted with black men also changed considerably. In the North, at least by the 1920s, it had become increasingly possible to view black/white relations as consensual, not as rape, and therefore less possible to view white women sexually involved with black men as helpless victims of black violence. In the modern urban North, then, white women involved in black/white prostitution were highly stigmatized. Because there were fewer white than black prostitutes available to black men, however, white sex workers could charge higher prices. Chicago and New York records indicate that white women were more likely to benefit from working in formal brothels, and speakeasies, than were black women, who frequently worked in tenement basements doubling as saloons. If you correct for institution, the significance of race increases: some white streetwalkers earned more than black prostitutes who worked in brothels.

And black women were more likely than white women to become streetwalkers. Although reformers argued that streetwalking was eradicated in the 1910s, investigators increasingly reported on the "flagrant solicitation" methods of black women streetwalking in black neighborhoods. Although investigators believed that streetwalking generally was the least desirable and lucrative form of prostitution, historians of sexuality remain divided. Ruth Rosen has argued that streetwalking was far less prestigious than brothel work and consisted of primarily older and less attractive women. But Louise White has argued that streetwalkers had more autonomy and often made more money because the "middle man" was elimi-nated.[28] An analysis of race and prostitution in the 1920s suggests that both positions have merit. According to an interview between a pros-titute, Blanche, and a sociology graduate student at the University of Chicago, Cynthia Cohen, some prostitutes preferred streetwalking to working in formal houses.[29] In Blanche's view, for instance: "It's nicer on the street, you can pick your man. It's awful to be in a house. Do you know how much those girls realize for laying down their body?" Answering her own question, she said: "Just about .85 though the charge is two dollars per man. The owners take out so much for towels, so much for protection, so much for examination." These ser-vices, although seemingly valuable at first glance, were in Blanche's estimation "all hooey; you get pulled in just the same." As she testi-fied, "[A brothel] I was working in the other night was raided, I got pulled in."[30]

Not only was the promise of protection often broken but women who worked "in" often had less autonomy than those who walked the streets: "Then, too, when you work in a house you have to take in any man that comes along and you have all kinds of dirty experi-ences." A streetwalker, in contrast, had the opportunity at least to make a judgment about each client and choose whether to engage in prostitution.[31] For Blanche, as for many white prostitutes, the free-dom to choose one's client was important, particularly for white women who wished to avoid contact with black men. When asked if she would consider having a black pimp or accepting a black cus-tomer, Blanche curtly replied, "Not me."[32]

Black streetwalkers earned less money than black women who worked in brothels or tenements. And the majority of black women probably were streetwalkers. In a report submitted to the Chicago Committee of Fifteen, "At night some were seen along the streets in the thickly-populated colored areas on the South Side, employ-ing semi-flagrant methods of soliciting."[33] This information re-futed the common wisdom of most vice reformers who had fought against streetwalking throughout the 1910s. They believed, as a Committee of Fourteen report revealed, that "street soliciting by prostitutes is so rare that it may be considered as being practically

★

negligible."[34] As was the case with white slavery reform, post–World War I reformers excluded black women from their analyses. In fact, the reports actually revealed extensive and open solicitation in black areas, on the streets, and from windows and doorways. On a routine patrol one white investigator reported: "Two colored women standing in the doorway called to me. I stopped and was offered sexual intercourse for only $1.00, and the other sexual intercourse or perversion [oral sex] at $1.50." Later he returned to the scene, "and five additional colored prostitutes were gathered in this doorway." These black prostitutes "openly accosted all white men who chanced to pass."[35] In another report on black streetwalking, the investigator voiced a peculiar optimism: at least black streetwalkers "were confining such advances to members of their own race."[36] Reformers once believed that streetwalking in Chicago and New York had been totally eradicated, a conclusion they could draw only by ignoring race. Now, with evidence of open and aggressive African-American street solicitation, reformers could at least reassure themselves by emphasizing that much of the activity was between black prostitutes and black customers. Black/white prostitution remained hidden. White men had access to illicit sex—and to black women—but it was not public and therefore not the source of public controversy.

Although streetwalking persisted among black women, it seemed that the nature of prostitution, as a sexual act, had changed in significant ways. Race and institution interacted to create what might be called "speakeasy prostitution." Speakeasy prostitution was at the other end of the spectrum from the ritualized prostitution conducted by "call girls" or hostesses within the dance halls, cabarets, and restaurants. The black streetwalker—exceedingly public, flagrant, flashy—was not presumed to be, nor presented as, quasi-respectable but rather as just the opposite: a whore, a fallen woman. Elite white dance hostesses and black women within the upper tier of nightclubs often spent the night with their clients and engaged in traditional intercourse, performing their sexual exchanges in ways that mimicked or emulated noncommercial sexual relations. These elite hostesses were something like a middle-class man's mistress; they concealed or denied the commercial aspects and dramatized the affective or romantic dimension of the exchange. The typical white brothel worker did not spend the night with her client, yet she, too, probably engaged in traditional coitus and made some sorts of romantic gestures.[37]

By contrast, streetwalking encounters in general and speakeasy sex in particular were entirely different sexual propositions. African-American female prostitutes performed the kinds of sexual services that were deemed most degenerate, most immoral, the least "domestic," and, for some, the most desirable. The point is that not only did urban geography and commercial institution divide the hostess from the streetwalker; so too did sexual behavior. Speakeasy sex included a number of distinctive acts of intercourse. In a survey of Chicago streetwalkers, investigators observed that only "5 offered the 'normal' coitus." More than a hundred apparently offered fellatio and declined traditional coitus. According to the report, "90 percent of the street solicitations coming to the attention of the staff in the month of May 1934 consisted of offers of gross perversion." The term *gross perversion* often referred to oral sex. Investigators also noted "the rapidity with which the entire transaction can be completed." Speakeasy sex was performed in corners of dark hallways, beneath a staircase, behind a trash bin in an alley. It was aggressive, quick, groping, highly impersonal sex, stripped of any pretense of Victorian romance. A speakeasy sexual act in a Harlem tenement represented the ultimate example of modern anomie, of bodily interpenetration and complete emotional estrangement.[38]

The interaction between a racially stratified labor market, geography, and institution directly determined the sexual system in which black and white prostitutes worked. I am arguing, however, that racial distinctions, mapped onto female bodies, created internal hierarchies, shaped working conditions, and ultimately choreographed the sexual exchange.

Finally, however, it is important to discuss another set of factors that shaped black/white prostitution. Analysis of this hierarchy allows us to isolate historically, and then carefully analyze, the precise role of color in the commercialization of sex. In other words, by analyzing the hierarchies of color that distinguished subgroups of black prostitutes, we can begin to understand the ways in which the racially perceived body—as separated from the law, institutions, and geographies—constituted the historical phenomenon of "race."

A survey of the New York files reveals that color differences corresponded to differences in prices for sex acts. Madams often quoted prices in accordance with color. As one report of an "ordi-nary speakeasy" revealed, the "madam had a large list of call girls at prices varying from $3.00–$7.00, depending on the girl and her color."[39] As one might expect, the lighter the skin, the higher the price. In a club named the Kewpie Doll, one investigator observed a scene in which there were "white prostitutes and four light col-ored negro prostitutes . . . varying in price from $4.00–$7.00."[40] Dark-skinned women usually earned the least. In one report focus-ing on a colored tenement, the investigator inquired whether the house had a "french girl." One of the women replied: "If you want that it will cost you an extra dollar." In this instance, the term french meant a light-skinned black woman; her price was four dollars. The remainder of the prostitutes, reportedly ranging in color from "medium" to "dark," each charged three dollars.[41] Likewise, an-other investigator reported a monetary hierarchy of color in a black brothel, which primarily served local black residents of Harlem, with "dark" women charging two dollars and "light" or "mulatto" women charging between three and five dollars. In a Brooklyn es-tablishment, investigators distinguished between "dark-chocolate" and "High yellow complexion." Certainly customers differed in their sexual tastes—some probably preferred dark-skinned women over light-skinned women—so these price differentials were not universal. There were exceptions: some dark-skinned women com-manded higher prices than light-skinned women.[42]

In a sense the color hierarchy is not surprising, given the history of a kind of aristocracy of color within black communities. In the South light-skinned black people benefited from their white ances-try, gaining status within both white and black communities. In the 1920s urban North, the status hierarchy affected African-American more than white communities, but clearly the color order persisted. As the advertising found in virtually any African-American newspa-per indicates, the black middle class had become obsessed with skin tone and supported a thriving market in skin lighteners and hair straighteners. Color consciousness was not new, but it persisted in part because of black/white prostitution. Black streetwalking repre-sented a highly visible, constantly reinforcing symbol of the color hierarchy: the lighter the skin, the more desirable the body, and ulti-mately the more valuable the woman.[43] Black prostitutes earned less money than white women for basically the same work, yet, despite their subaltern position in the hierarchy, they should not be viewed as victims. Although slim, the evidence suggests that black women who serviced white patrons nevertheless maintained some worker autonomy. To the extent that most other employment opportunities were greatly restricted, black women were "forced" into prostitution, but they were not victims, even taking account of the inequalities of social power between white customers and black prostitutes. Thus, in a club named the Old Kid Morris Dance Hall and Speakeasy, an investigator reported finding five colored women and nine colored men. According to the report, "While seated at the table with two girls and one fellow, drinking, one of the girls by the name of Harriet Clark invited me to dance with her, which I did." Harriet, according to the report, was "colored," though her precise racial position, at first ambiguous, was clarified by the investigator's statement that she was a "mulatto." During the dance, as reported by the customer, Harriet "rubbed her body against mine in an indecent manner." The investigator encouraged her, saying, "Oh baby, shake it." She replied, "I mean I can do it!"[44]

Engaging in a kind of sexual repartee, the investigator retorted, "Yes, you have such a little of it you ought to be able to do it." To which the young woman replied, "It may be little, but there is enough of it to snatch the come from you." Steering the conversation toward prostitution, the investigator replied, "Yes? I don't believe it." She dared to show him, and then he inquired about the expense. In this case, Harriet treated black and white customers differently. Harriet revealed that she charged "white men $5, but colored men only $3."[45] Although a small gesture, her difference in price reflected a kind of racial consciousness and even reveals a certain amount of historical agency. Another, perhaps clearer example of resistance and autonomy concerned a rarity—a black dance hostess. In this establishment, "a colored dance hall in which the majority of the people who patronize it [were] negroes," there was "indecent dancing" among the men and women. The white investigator reported that he "danced with a mulatto girl named Ella Greene." In an effort to lead the conversation toward prostitution, and ultimately to entrap the woman, the investigator "asked her if she stepped out for a wild time." But his efforts went unrewarded. The young woman curtly replied, "I don't do anything like that white boy."[46] Whether or not it was true, the tone of her reply suggests anything but degradation or docility.

Through these simple gestures—by charging white customers more than black or setting definite sexual limits on the sexual exchange—some black women exerted a kind of social agency not usually attributed to marginalized sex workers.

Although the story of black women in prostitution reveals that they exerted some influence over black/white encounters, fragments of evidence suggest that some white male customers viewed black/white prostitution differently from white prostitution. In a conversation between a taxi driver and an investigator, the driver stated that it had become difficult to locate a prostitute. His statement was racially coded, however, reflecting a perceived difficulty in locating white prostitutes compared to locating black prostitutes. As he informed the investigator, "If you don't object to a nigger, you can get fixed up there for a buck." The investigator indicated that he would "look the colored girl over." The driver countered that he had "a friend who runs a candy store, and he knows a very nice Jewish girl who charges $3.00." Here the racial epithet, the difference in price, and the clear ethnic distinction drawn between a black woman and a Jewish woman together shaped the perceived racial/sexual difference between prostitutes.[47] In another exchange, again between a taxi driver and undercover investigator, the problem of locating a prostitute surfaced. To a request for sexual services, the driver replied: "There are women around here who are putting out, but you've got to know where to go." In giving advice on how best to procure a prostitute, he advised, "You won't find a lot of big joints like you say there are in Milwaukee and Chicago. You could go up to Third Avenue, between 99th and 100th St. You'd find about 15 colored women in front of the houses there, but I know you don't want that kind of stuff."[48] Black prostitution was perceived as distinct from white prostitution, in part because of price and accessibility, but some white men perceived black prostitutes as more immoral and degraded than white prostitutes. Both the middle men and investigators described black prostitutes as "flagrant" and aggressive, repelling some potential white customers and perhaps attracting others.[49] For white men, as for black, the experience of interracial prostitution was apparently unlike same-race sexual encounters.

The transformation of the vice districts had transformed prostitution. The work lives of black women and white, black customers and white, had been dramatically altered. During the decade of migration, as black women entered the vice districts, mainstream white vice organizations did not effectively respond to the problem of race and prostitution. The failure of prostitution reform reflected a complex of social structural forces, failed policy, and blatant sexual racism. Forces from without had combined to alter fundamentally sexual relations on the urban margins. If, however, the focus has so far remained on the effects of demography and social policy on the urban margins, the final point to be made is that the resulting sexual change wrought within the black/white vice districts circled back and gradually reshaped gender conventions and sexuality of the respectable middle classes.

This intersection of vice and virtue was made visible in the rise of the New Woman. As historians of women have demonstrated, in the early twentieth century, the ideology of female domesticity and passionlessness was in decline. Working women experimented with new modes of sexual expression and adopted new styles of presenting themselves, creatively applying makeup, wearing shorter and flashier dresses, and sporting colorful accessories. To middle-class outsiders, such as the social reformer Lillian Wald, these women had a "pronounced lack of modesty in dress . . . their dancing, their talk, their freedom of manner, all rendered them conspicuous."[50] Working women's public rebelliousness was new, but its expression was not exactly original: much of the new style was in fact the result of careful appropriation from other public women, that is, prostitutes.[51] By the 1920s the dispersal begun by industrial worker emulation had reached white, middle-class women. As middle-class women entered the streets they routinely came into contact with working-class women, and their styles; the new dance halls offered other opportunities for contact and cultural appropriation. As one observer of the scene noted, they included a "social mixture such as was never before dreamed of in this country—a hodge podge of people in which respectable young married and unmarried women, and even debutantes, dance, not only under the same roof, but in the same room with women of the town."[52] Shopping during the day and out on the town at night, middle-class women directly challenged the gendered map of separate spheres. From all this emerged the New Woman, symbolized by the flapper.

The flapper symbolized what was widely known as "the revolution in morals." As one account characterized the shift, "Before the war a lady did not set foot in a saloon; after the war, she entered a speakeasy as thoughtlessly as she would go into a railroad station."[53] To some extent the style and manners of the middle-class New Woman could be attributed to the appropriation of styles from the early movie stars, such as Lillian Gish and Mary Pickford.[54] Bohemians living in Greenwich Village were also cultural pioneers of modern womanhood.[55] Most important, though, historians have established that the shifting styles and modes of presentation were evident before the so-called revolution in manners that supposedly transformed post–World War I America. One social commentator argued, for example, that "skirts had been creeping up for years before the war offered an excuse, if any were needed, to reduce the amount of cloth in women's clothing."[56] To corroborate that thesis, historians of working women have argued that the rise of the New Woman reflected but another cycle of cultural appropriation, this one of middle-class women inspired by the fashions that had been popular among independent wage-earning women as early as the turn of the century.[57]

Probably the most important signifier of the flapper was the "bob" haircut. Rather than the long, flowing hair of the Victorian woman (usually arranged on the top of her head), the modern woman's hair was cut short and blunt, approximating men's hairstyles more than women's. But if we return to the scene in Harlem or the South Side of Chicago and to the houses of prostitution, we see the same cut as the one donned by flappers. The proprietor of a black speakeasy, Virgie Canfield, wore a white silk blouse and black skirt; she had "black, bobbed, straightened hair." Helen Branch, another prostitute described in New York investigative reports, had "chestnut hair, bobbed." Ruth Ross, the elite white dance hostess, had a "short, clipped blonde bob." As early as 1913 a black prostitute in Philadelphia, Anna, wore a brown felt hat, beige polo coat, and "black bobbed hair."[58]

One can overemphasize style, and especially haircuts, but underlying the rise of the New Woman of the 1920s was the gradual blurring of stylistic distinctions between respectable and fallen women.[59] The development is complex and paradoxical; the gradual overlapping occurred not because of the emergence of a more benign, empathetic conception of the prostitute but rather as part of a pointed backlash. As I indicated in the opening chapter, in the era of white slavery, the dominant view was that innocent "women adrift" had been trapped into prostitution; the solution was to rescue and restore them to Victorian respectability. By the end of World War I reformers had become more cynical in their view of prostitutes, in part because of ideological changes in the mid-1910s. As Hobson has argued, "When World War I was declared, the prostitute was cast as the enemy on the home front."[60] The new view of the typical prostitute emphasized their voluntary entrance into vice rather than their "enslavement."[61] A Committee of Fourteen report illustrated the historical shift. Before the passage of the Mann Act, the "traffic in women was looked upon as synonymous with white slavery": it "involved direct compulsion." But "in the new traffic, compulsion is either indirect or non-existent—usually the latter."[62] The modern prostitute, far from being kidnapped, actually applied for the job. To be sure, as the committee indicated, these agencies were "shady" and the interviews were conducted privately, "behind closed doors." Some women who resisted these "interviews" by refusing to have sex with employment agents were raped. In addition, the committee noted other examples that shaped women's entrance into vice, including "certain influences of the lower class clubs and speakeasies, such as the breaking down in morale caused by the long hours of work, the constant drinking of bad liquor, the lack of adequate sleep, [and] economic pressure."[63] Despite these examples of coercion, vice commissions understood the modern "hostess" as a woman who chose prostitution.

Indeed, the rise of the New Woman was ideologically situated as the cross-current development of the backlash against the willful prostitute. Changing class ideologies between and among women, then, initiated the dramatic paradigmatic shift in female sexual ideology. Again, however, the significance of race should not be discounted, for the one mitigating factor protecting prostitutes in the era of backlash was their whiteness. If it is true that by the 1920s prostitutes were more highly stigmatized than the nineteenth-century fallen woman, it is also apparent that, paradoxically, their lives were less unique, at several points overlapping with the experiences of middle-class women.[64] The sociologist Walter Reckless, author of a major study entitled *Vice in Chicago*, centered his analysis on the changing character of prostitution during the 1920s. In his pioneering analysis of vice in Chicago, Reckless described the development

★

as a shift "From Outcast to No Caste." According to Reckless, in the 1910s "white slaves were in fact an outcast group with distinctive manner, dress, style." They were located "in the 'half-world'" and were "free to do what was tabu [*sic*] for the respectable woman."[65] What he termed *The Painted Lady* once had "an uncontested monopoly of rouge, the bleaching of hair, and strong perfumes, all of which have been means of sexual attraction."[66]

According to Reckless, with the rise of the New Woman of the 1920s, that monopoly was in effect broken. In his view, "women of ill-fame no longer form[ed] a distinct caste readily distinguished from other women by dress, manners, and place of residence." This reflected the dramatic shift in middle-class gender roles: "The activities of modern women—slumming, night life, exaggerations in dress, an unchaperoned life outside the home, entrance into business and sports—have erased the outward distinction between the painted sport and the paler protected lady." In his view, the rapid exchange of cultural forms in the modern metropolis was a potentially liberating, even democratizing, development. "The breakdown of the barriers of caste has made the escape easier from the life of commercialized vice. The inhumanity of the earlier form of exploitation of women consisted in the fact that once she had crossed the threshold of a house of prostitution there was no escape."[67]

All this is not to suggest a kind of gendered free-for-all. Normative gender conventions and negative ideals of the fallen woman did not disappear. Once arrested, a prostitute had less hope of redemption or genuine assistance than even a decade before. An analysis of unwed motherhood again makes the point. While reformers turned to other fallen women—white unwed mothers—the line between female delinquency and single motherhood blurred. Indeed, as Regina Kunzel has shown, unwed mothers increasingly became reformers' central focus, supplanting prostitutes. That is not to suggest that unwed mothers remained unstigmatized; in the 1920s to be a young single mother was to have fallen very far. Reformers could be brutal; some institutions were similar to prisons. As one unwed mother recalled of her "home": "I know now that any one of us could have gotten out of that place any time we wanted to. But I didn't know it then. We were all beaten."[68]

But however confining and potentially violent, these institutions were not prisons. Prostitutes were incarcerated. And by the 1920s the majority of prostitutes in prison were African-American women. Their visibility as imprisoned prostitutes constructed a critical racial/sexual discourse that, as much as neighborhood boundaries, shaped the modern urban sexual system. This discourse ranged from the random newspaper story to complex sociological analyses: together they converged in the concept of "female Negro sex delinquency." Sociologists turned their attention toward cultural patterns evidenced in black areas of major urban centers, exploring the nature of "pathology" and the causes of "personal disorganization." In academic projects with names like "Community Factors in Negro Delinquency," scholars argued that damaged community structures caused delinquency and unstable populations, as well as "pathological conditions generally."[69] Reform organizations also took up the distinctive problem of female Negro sex delinquency.[70] This theorizing about the causes of black prostitution is significant, but even more important was the underlying trend that the sudden interest in the topic reveals. The statistical, sociological, and reform discourses on prostitution combined to reconstruct the central stereotype of the prostitute, and of the fallen woman, as a young, "female Negro sex delinquent."

The prevailing ideology that connected black women with sexual transgression was not new to the modern urban North. As several historians of black female sexuality have argued, in the South during the era of slavery black women were viewed as hypersexual, in part to justify white slave owners' sexual violation. After emancipation and throughout the nineteenth century, this view of black women as sexually licentious and available persisted in the South.[71] With the Great Migration the ideology moved North and then was elaborated. Historians have held that in the discourse of unwed motherhood, class was the center of the debate; not until the 1940s would race become a dominant category through which to explain single mothers. My evidence suggests that in the transition from Victorian to modern conceptions of the prostitute as the most degraded of fallen women, class did not so much recede as become socially coded by race. Working women, even when in public and sexualized, could avoid the stigma of prostitute, because the older gender conventions of private/public no longer defined the urban terrain. Indeed, it may well be that the blurring of distinctions of respectability—between the white prostitutes, white working-class

★

women, and the middle-class flapper—was made ideologically possible by the reassignment of the sexual stigma of prostitution to
African-American women. When Reckless described the blurring of
distinctions of respectability as "the erasure of the outward distinction between Painted Lady and the *'paler'*" protected woman, he
was in fact witnessing an era during which the Victorian system of
identifying female impropriety through class codes of spatial location and style was shifting to a modern system in which all women
who were "*paler*" could enjoy the public status of respectability.[72] In
turn the New Fallen Woman represented the realignment of female
sexual impropriety with blackness.

So powerful was the sexual stigma of blackness that even association with it could sexually pollute a white woman. For example,
white prostitutes and dance hostesses who serviced black men, as
well as Filipino men, could lose their white clientele. Further, white
women who associated with men of color also lost status in the eyes
of their peers, as evinced by Paul Cressey's discussion of the intra-
caste epithet "nigger lover."[73] The story of one dance hostess, Helen,
illustrates how some white women chose to accept Filipino men as
customers. In an interview Helen stated that she was middle-class
but had trouble at home. First she sought employment at the New
Majestic dance hall; then "she went to the Black and Tans with
other Filipinos." Eventually Helen married a Filipino man, but he
was not wealthy enough to support her. When she returned to the
Filipino dance hall, she was rejected because of her reputation for
dating black men. Eventually she became a regular at the Black and
Tans and moved to the South Side.[74]

Within the dance halls, the "fallen" white women who consorted
with men of color eventually went through this mode of "retrogres-
sive cycles." The work history of a Polish woman, Florence Klepka,
illustrates this model of moral decline. Florence left home at nineteen and worked in burlesque shows. After becoming pregnant she
entered the dance hall scene, serving Italian and Greek men, but
then lost her business because of her reputation for promiscuity. By
1925 she had begun accepting dates from Filipino men but soon
became "common" to the Filipino group. She left dancing and
turned to prostitution, working in Filipino rooming houses. Another
Polish woman's work history followed the same trajectory, through a
"white cycle" and then a "Filipino cycle." But her decline was

steeper: she eventually moved to the South Side and "became known as an independent prostitute, carrying on her business chiefly with Negroes and Chinese." That was the farthest a white woman could fall. According to Cressey, when the woman attempted to return to the more lucrative Filipino dance halls, "there are always those who remember her and warn the others that she has already 'gone African.'" One common view of these white women who danced with black men was voiced by a white slummer in a dance hall with Filipino/white dancing: "I'd rather see my daughter dead than in a place like this."[75]

Even in a context removed from the realm of commercialized vice, in respectable neighborhoods, on the sidewalks, or in restaurants, the ideology created in the vice districts dispersed to stigmatize all white women seen with black men. In the North white women who attempted to wed black men were often arrested and sent to mental institutions. Only an insane woman, it was believed, would consent to marry a black man. Likewise, in divorce cases, the stigma associated with black/white sexual relations surfaced. Testifying against his wife, one husband claimed that she was too promiscuous. As conclusive evidence, he "continually referred to his wife as a 'damned nigger lover.'" His request for a divorce was quickly granted.[76] Although in the modern era white women who were once considered fallen could now achieve a kind of redemption or at least "pass" as respectable, those white women who openly dated (much less married) men of color were widely believed to be as guilty of sexual impropriety as black women, and in some cases more so. In a variety of contexts, without the slightest cause or piece of evidence, white women seen with black men were presumed to be prostitutes. One evening a black man, Harvey Jackson, was "beaten into insensibility" for no other reason than walking down the street with a white woman. Less than a classic lynching, designed to punish black men, his assault represented a modern example of the new views of the fallen woman. As the news article explained, the police believed that the woman with whom the man was walking was a prostitute. To verify this, they asked the woman, "You are white, aren't you?" The women replied that, to the contrary, she was colored. The police asserted, "Oh no, you're white, and this man is your pimp."[77] Through extensive interviewing of black/white couples in Chicago, a University of

Chicago graduate student concluded that intermarried couples were frequently stopped by police, "ostensibly to discover whether the woman is a prostitute or if the couple are engaged in some sort of illegal activity." As Robert E. T. Roberts indicated, the purpose of these interrogations was to harass the couples, but what is historically significant was the justification for the intrusion: that white women intimate with black men were assumed to be prostitutes.[78] By the 1920s, in the modern metropolis the racial code of the body and the transgression of the sexual color line were critical in constructing the boundaries of female immorality and defining ideologies of gender deviance.

The Great Migration and the relocation of vice had transformed the underworld of commercialized sexual relations. Black/white contacts increased in number, and interracial sex became more visible. Excluded from almost all "legitimate" forms of women's labor, black women were unofficially and, in some cases legally, channeled into sex work, whether as maids in brothels or as prostitutes. Black prostitutes worked in less prestigious institutions or walked the streets, and they earned less money than white women for the same work. At the same time the business of selling one's sexual self in accordance with an established racial/monetary scale revealed the stark reality of the devaluation of color. In the underworld racism was crystal clear: white was worth more than brown which was worth more than black.

The history of black/white prostitution is a story not only of racism but also of forbidden desire. For black men, the easy sexual availability of white women must have dramatically influenced the experience of migration, particularly in contrast with the violently defended taboo against black/white intimacy in the South. The North was decidedly not the promised land—for black women or men—but the opportunity to buy easily what had been so deeply taboo must have been a significant factor influencing black men's estimation of the differences between North and South. Further, the growth in black/white commercialized sexuality also shaped the experience of white men. Much of the evidence suggests that black prostitution was organized differently from white, and white men— investigators, middlemen, and customers—apparently viewed (and experienced) sex with a black prostitute as perceptibly different from an exchange with a white prostitute.

The rules and codes of black/white prostitution also influenced the lives of men and women who never directly participated in the underworld, specifically middle-class white women. As social commentators and scholars observed, the "revolution in morals" symbolized by the flapper signaled a historic shift in the definition of middle-class womanhood. From prostitute to worker to middle-class wife, all women could appear to be the New Woman. Almost all women. The New Fallen Women—Female Negro Sex Delinquents and Nigger Lovers—were negative symbols that helped launch the so-called sexual liberation of modern womanhood.

As we have seen in the first section of this study, because of sexual racism, the interzones developed in major cities. Life in the vice districts was varied, providing a haven for people stigmatized and relegated to the urban periphery, but the rituals of the interzones recapitulated the ideology of sexual racism that created them. Dance halls constructed exclusive policies and fomented racial competitions within the institutions. Repression from without caused homosexuals to search for community underground, but African-American homosexuals and lesbians struggled against crisscrossing racisms and homophobia, currents of prejudice that knew no urban borders. Finally, if the story of black/white prostitution follows a particular historical trajectory, it is that of sexual racism in its most brutal form. Arriving from the South impoverished and frequently alone, black women entered the city with hopes of making a better life and instead confronted two structures of racism. When they attempted to find a decent wage in legitimate employment, they were denied access, and when they then turned to prostitution, they struggled against yet more hierarchies of color.

The previous ethnographic analysis of black/white sexual relations ought to discourage interpretations of life in the interzones as unrelenting oppression, experienced by faceless figures bending to the pressures of racist sexual exploitation. These men and women were remarkable in their resilience and demonstrated agency. After all, they lived outside the conventions of respectability; their lives must have been exciting and adventurous, somehow freer. But we should remember that the interzones have never before been the subject of historical inquiry: the myths of the Roaring Twenties, the Jazz Age, of carefree pleasure and overwhelming abundance dominate professional historical writing and the popular imagination.

★

The glamorous flapper should probably be seen as a faint copy of the hard-boiled, hardworking prostitute, black or white, exchanging their sexuality for as little as a dollar—and then getting arrested by police because of it. Yet the culture of the interzones inspired street styles and dance and music. Black/white vice districts became the source of inspiration for writers and artists who were attempting to revolt against the constraints of Victorian culture. For a brief moment, interracial vice enjoyed unprecedented popularity and notoriety, selling novels and appearing in forward magazines and attracting rebellious audiences from across town. Then the interzones and black/white sexuality again became the source of national anxiety, as Americans across the country revolted against the revolt.

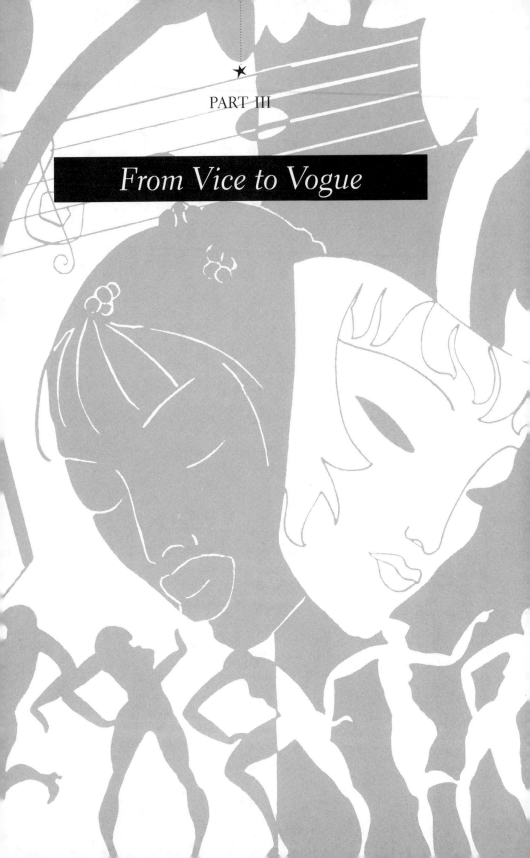

PART III

From Vice to Vogue

★

7

ON STAGE

The Social Response to All God's Chillun' Got Wings

In 1924, several months before the scheduled opening of Eugene O'Neill's drama *All God's Chillun' Got Wings*, the play was published in the *American Mercury*.[1] O'Neill's subject was racial intermarriage, and in his play he continually explored a central racial contradiction: that the color line in America was deeply drawn and unyielding, yet the social divisions of race were mutable. O'Neill sought to understand the experience of the men and women who crossed the color line, exploring their personal pain and social ostracism. Whatever the quality of the drama, or the particular politics of its representation of racial intermarriage, the astonishing social controversy surrounding *All God's Chillun' Got Wings* ultimately exposed not only the psychological conflicts experienced by the people who intermarried but also the profound anxiety of those who protested against them.

Soon after the play was published, rumor of the content of its plot and potential cast seemed to spread throughout the country. Almost overnight the press helped transform the short drama into a sensation. As the *New York Times* observed, "It is no risk at all to say that

'All God's Chillun' received more publicity before production than any play in the history of the American theater."[2] In places far removed from New York City and the small circle of drama enthusiasts, among people who had relatively little interest in the theater, O'Neill's drama stirred intense controversy.

This chapter describes the cultural history of one controversial drama, but its broader purpose is to suggest the source and direction of cultural change, the gradual movement of interracial sex out of vice districts and toward a new realm of avant-garde art. Most white middle-class urbanites were oblivious to the growing interracial subcultures in their midst. Yet evidence suggests that O'Neill's production participated in a stream of cultural change in the early 1920s that, by the end of the decade, would culminate in a spree of white slumming to black clubs and ultimately in an outpouring of texts exploring Harlem's sexual underworld. The early Progressive taboo against interracial sex was in the process of rearticulation. *All God's Chillun'* broke the silence surrounding *consensual* black/white sexuality in the North, and the social response elicited by this challenge revealed a more heterogeneous, variegated audience than many had believed existed. Moreover, for an artistic cultural elite, the images and discourses of interracial sex could be appropriated and employed in opposition to Victorian values. This urban vanguard acknowledged the boundary of immorality that restricted black/white sexual relations, and then they self-consciously transgressed it. To be sure, the social response to *All God's Chillun'* was not unusual or unexpected—it represented a kind of traditional sexual racism—but the support for the production was novel and ultimately historic.

Criticism of the play and historical analysis of the social response to the drama suggest the character of this turning point. O'Neill's production successfully moved the urban margin of Harlem, and the conceptions of interracial sex it fostered, to the center of attention of New York sophisticates. At the same time, the play explored the nature of black/white sexual relationships, pioneering new trends in the representation of black/white relations.

The drama's main themes are presented in the opening scene. Typical of many portrayals of racial difference during the 1920s, *All God's Chillun'* began by constructing a stereotype that associated natural release with blackness and internalized restraint with whiteness. O'Neill's stage direction called for the black actors to play "Negroes frankly participating in the spirit of Spring" but for the white actors to "laugh constrainedly, awkward in natural emotion." In O'Neill's view this "expressed the difference of race."[3]

Although in the opening scene O'Neill established a clear example of racial difference, he also suggested the potential permeability of racial boundaries, particularly among children, who seemed ignorant of the social consequences of racial difference. In an innocent exchange, Jim and Ella imagine trading skin colors. Thus Jim reveals that, following the the local barber's advice, he decided to drink chalk and water to become white; in turn Ella proclaims to Jim, "I like black. Let's you and me swap. I'd like to be black."[4] Yet their innocence is ultimately corrupted by the gradual encroachment of racialism, exemplified by the language they use to tease each other. Children refer to Jim as "Jim Crow," invoking the Southern system of segregation, and to Ella as "Painty Face," conjuring the image of the "Painted Lady," typically understood to be a prostitute. Soon thereafter, near the end of the scene, Jim and Ella hold hands and then skip away. As she departs, Ella turns back to see Jim and yells, "Here!" Then she kisses her hand, foreshadowing what was to become perhaps the most controversial kiss in American theater.[5]

The next scene both reasserts the dominant racial divisions and exacts retribution from Jim and Ella (who are now high school age) for crossing the divide. Two dialogues are central to the scene. The first concerns an exchange between Jim, his black friend Joe, and Shorty (a white youth). Although on his first attempt Jim fails the high school examination, he eventually graduates, unlike most of the other young men in his neighborhood. Jim's achievement provokes comment from Shorty: "Does you deny you's a nigger?"[6] In turn Jim's friend Joe asks the same question: "What's all dis denyin' you a nigger—an wid de white boys listenin to you say it?" That Jim succeeds in what is coded as a white pursuit elicits attacks on his racial integrity, not only from white characters, who wish to impose on him racial stereotypes of black intellectual inferiority, but also from black characters, who wish to impose constraints from within the group. Ultimately Jim is chastised; he concedes to Joe, "Yes, I'm a nigger."[7] In another, parallel dialogue, between Ella and Mickey (a white man Ella has dated), a similar pattern of challenge and retribution emerges. In this scene, Ella's affection for Jim, by challenging the sexual color line, represents her resistance to specific gender roles. Mickey confronts Ella about the transgression: "They say you been travelin' with Jim Crow." She replies that Jim has been a good friend to her. Shorty challenges her: "A Nigger!" Ella, invoking a childhood fantasy of the mutability of racial difference, replies: "The only white man in the world! Kind and white. You're all black—black to the heart." But Ella and Shorty are grown up now, and her childhood games cannot support Ella in her color blind fantasy. Finally Shorty responds with a simple but powerfully silencing epithet "Nigger Lover."[8]

One of O'Neill's key narrative strategies was to explore the possibility of racial harmony, symbolized by Jim and Ella's marriage, against the social backdrop of intense racial polarization and conflict. After Jim and Ella have married, traveled to Paris, and returned to Harlem, scene 4 focuses on the city's racial separation. In this instance the stage direction calls for the entire cast to portray the bustling area in which both black and white people live. As the curtain rises, many people—"men, women, children—pour from two tenements, whites from the tenement to the left, blacks from the tenement to the right. They hurry to form into two racial lines on each side of the gate, rigid and unyielding, staring across the stage at each other with bitter hostile eyes."[9] This direction pictures a world in which whites may occasionally live alongside blacks, but do not cross the racial line, a world outside the interzones.

In the following scene the dialogue between Jim's mother, Mrs. H., and his sister, Hattie, underscore the division. Hattie had objected to the wedding, but Jim's mother was seemingly more tolerant of the union. Questioning her mother, Hattie remains cynical about her brother's marriage, and wonders "if she [Ella] loves him." Mrs. H. replies that Ella must have loved Jim. Then, drawing attention to the prejudice the couple elicited by crossing the color line, she reminds Hattie: "Don't forget dat dis was hard for her—mighty, mighty hard—harder for de white dan de black!"[10]

Ultimately Mrs. H. represents the voice of wisdom, for her warning against interracial marriage proves prophetic. Gradually, from scene to scene, the relationship between Ella and Jim deteriorates. By the opening of the final scene, it has become clear that Ella is severely ill, but the precise source of her illness is obscured. Hattie

★

suggests that Ella is crazy and ought to be institutionalized; she recounts a conversation to Jim, the one in which Ella called Hattie a "nigger." Jim expresses disbelief. Hattie then speculates that Ella "may develop a violent mania, and is dangerous for you. Jim you'll go crazy, too—living this way."[11] In response, Jim tries to deny his wife's illness and to defend her from his sister's attacks. "Let her call me nigger! Let her call me the whitest of the white of the white. I'm all she's got in the world, ain't I? She's all I got. You with your fool talk of the black race and the white race! Where does the human race get a chance to come in?"[12]

In the end, however, Jim's plea for racial tolerance and for the triumph of love over bigotry does not prevail as the central theme. In the final scene, Ella is shown to have deteriorated, appearing confused and angry. She ultimately does call Jim a "nigger" but then forgets that she did so. The drama reaches a climax when Jim receives the results of his American Bar Association exam. Although Ella had claimed she wanted Jim to become a lawyer, in fact she had sabotaged his bar exam, by distracting him from his studies. On the day Jim receives the results, Ella descends into a mental state of fantasy. Fearful that Jim might actually become a lawyer,[13] she inquires about the exam, "You didn't pass did you?" Jim replies: "Good lord, child, how come you can ever imagine such a crazy idea? Pass? Me? It'd be miraculous, there'd be earthquakes and catastrophes."[14]

Of course the word pass serves a dual purpose here, for it not only means obtaining a passing score on an exam but also refers to the act of racial passing in which a black subject transgresses a racial boundary. The double meaning is not accidental, for throughout the drama Jim's intellectual success is equivalent to his denying his identity as a black man and attempting to become white. That, perhaps, is also the source of Ella's anxiety and mental decline—the fear that in the end race is far more mutable than she had believed. By failing the exam, Jim in effect becomes more black; in turn Ella seems to recover her sanity. Thus in her final speech, after learning of Jim's failure, Ella declares: "Well, it's all over now Jim. Everything'll be all right now. I'll be just your little girl, Jim—and you'll be my little boy." Only because the gesture has become meaningless does Ella suggest that they revert back to their childhood: "I'll put shoe blacking on my face and pretend I'm black and you can put chalk on your face and pretend you're white just as we used to do."[15]

Ultimately *All God's Chillun' Got Wings* closed by reasserting the central, contradictory themes of racial mutability and deep social division. In another sense, however, O'Neill's play had an extended run, for his story provoked intense social controversy, placing the topic of black/white sexual relations on a national stage. In this venue, the play served to demonstrate that its major themes—the mutability of racial division and black/white sexual relations—remain outside the pale of permissible discourse. Although O'Neill did appropriate certain themes from an interracial subculture, with that appropriation came the kind of prejudice routinely experienced by people engaged in black/white sexual relations. In the realm of representation, O'Neill himself faced the sexual racism he portrayed.

If one carefully examines the social response to the play, several trends can be identified. There were three distinct kinds of social responses: the reaction of hard-core racists, of mainstream cultural critics, and of modernists sympathetic to O'Neill's drama. This was the least popular response, expressed principally by the literary elite. An example can be found in a letter written to the National Association for the Advancement of Colored People (NAACP), which argued that "the furor of intolerance that is being raised against O'Neill's play is so absurd. White and colored people do occasionally get married, so why should not a serious dramatist use that phase of our national life as material for a big play."[16] At the other end of the spectrum was a seemingly less "reasonable" response—that of the hard-core racist. In a strange reference to Jack Johnson, a hard-core racist sent a letter to the NAACP, scrawled in black crayon; the author addressed the two-page note to "Nigger Johnson" and signed it "white man." He saw the production of the play as an effort to "help the black bastards to get what was in their rotten hearts for years." But in his view, the play was erroneous, at least compared to the movie *Birth of a Nation*, which showed "what a coon is." Moreover, to discredit even the potential for affection between a white woman for a black man, the author of the letter declared, "Mary Blair is a mullatto [sic]—not white." Like many in the press, this individual believed that the production would intensify racial conflict, rather than achieve black people's supposed goal of marrying white women: "But this play is going to spoil everything.

★

America is not for niggers—you shines belong in Africa. Bring on the Riot—that's what we want."[17]

What may be surprising about the overall social response, however, is the extent to which those in the mainstream fundamentally supported the viewpoint of hard-core racists, even if they articulated their opinions in a more respectable language and wished to avoid, rather than exacerbate, racial violence by stopping the production. From the start, that the play included a black man and a white woman was a source of controversy. The *New York Sentinel* provided the key headline: "Inter-Racial Play." The article briefly described the plot, summarizing *All God's Chillun'* as a play set "in the Negro District of Manhattan Island, with a white woman married to a Negro."[18] In another article the press declared that the cumulative effect of the initial press coverage amounted to "the greatest of sensations in the theatrical world, with every indication that the waves of comment and criticism will eventually reach all classes of the American public." The play did create a national controversy.[19]

Aside from giving the general outline of the plot, the media predicted that the play would cause nothing less than a race riot. In Cincinnati reporters suggested that "it needs no prophet to foretell the storm that will break when 'All God's Chillun' Got Wings' is put upon the stage."[20] In North Carolina the press conceded racial prejudice but argued that O'Neill's drama would only exacerbate the situation. According to the *Greensboro Daily News*, "Race prejudice exists and that may be regrettable; but even if one thinks it regrettable, there is no sense in ignoring its existence. Bubonic Plague is regrettable too, but the way to abolish it is not by creating conditions ideally designed to propagate it."[21] One southern paper named its article "Inviting Trouble," another paper "Inviting a Lynching."[22] Newspapers across the country predicted racial disaster: "Violation of that one principle of race integrity, which in America, at least, is regarded as vitally important to the welfare of the community, opens wide the door to all the evils of race hatred."[23] Finally protests emerged for closing the play. As Mrs. W. J. Arnold, a founder of the United Daughters of the Confederacy, argued: "The play should be banned by the authorities because it will be impossible for it do otherwise than to stir up ill feeling between the races."[24]

This was not the first time that racial controversy surrounded the staging of a drama. As one newspaper recalled, there had been a movement to stop the production of Thomas Dixon's *The Clansman*, but it had been supported primarily by black leaders. For the most part, white groups led the fight against *All God's Chillun' Got Wings*. In considering the contrast, one southern newspaper recalled, "There was much agitation against Thomas Dixon's 'Klansmen' when it first appeared, the negroes protesting against its showing in a number of northern cities." That protest continued with the adaptation of the play for the screen; when *Birth of a Nation* opened, the NAACP initiated an all-out but largely unsuccessful effort to ban the film. But according to one newspaper, there was simply no comparison between Dixon's and O'Neill's dramas: "That play was in its worst treatment of race questions mild in comparison with the mildest scene in O'Neill's play."[25]

Some northern black leaders agreed that the play would cause trouble. In an article focusing on the reaction of the Reverend Adam Clayton Powell, Jr., the headline read: "Race Strife Seen If 'God's Chillun' Is Staged." Powell viewed the ultimate outcome as "'Intensely Harmful' to His Race."[26] At times it seemed the media's prediction that the play could lead to violence was accurate. In the middle of rehearsals, for example, the cast received a bomb threat. Eventually guards were posted at the playhouse and at the leading lady's apartment.[27]

Although white groups were most vitriolic against the play, many black leaders and organizations also protested the production. Their objections centered on the negative stereotypes of black people that the drama supposedly fostered. According to one report, a black newspaper, the *Chicago Defender*, "recently made the point that the negro is not flattered that O'Neill has made Jim, an educated, high-minded negro, whose sister is a school teacher, take into his home a wife who comes from the streets."[28] Another reporter explained, "I doubt if any Negro with Jim's dogged determination to make a place for himself in the world would have chosen a moron for a wife. The infringement of law which the production of the play may involve is less potent than its infringement upon the standards of a race of people."[29] Later Reverend Powell echoed these sentiments. His comments were widely viewed as "the most bitter denunciation of the play." Preaching to his large congregation in Harlem, Powell argued, "It is harmful because it intimates that we are desirous of marrying white women. I am opposed to this play because I believe that it will only stir up ill feeling against our race. The kissing of a white woman by a big, strapping negro is bound to cause bad feelings. No thinking colored man desires to marry outside of his own race."[30] Paul Robeson, the actor who played Jim in the drama, was disturbed by the response of many black leaders and felt he was caught in a difficult predicament, in between two opposing factions. He experienced conflict as "being damned all over the place for playing . . . the part."[31] In fact very few black leaders actually supported the production. One exception was W.E.B. DuBois, who believed that the production of the play should be seen as an "experiment."[32]

After the play's initial prepublication controversy, focusing particularly on the casting of Robeson opposite a white woman, the discord continued, this time over the white woman's role. According to reports, the actress who was first asked to play the lead, Helen Mac-Kellar, eventually declined. Before ultimately declining the role, however, she had accepted "on the condition that a white actor and burnt cork play opposite her."[33] Then, "a rumor that Mary Blair had finally refused to play the part and a light mulatta had been substituted" for her was denied.[34] Finally it was announced that "after one leading actress and many near-stars had refused the part of the white wife," Mary Blair accepted the role.[35] In summarizing the problem of casting, the *North Carolina Herald* concluded that "naturally he [O'Neill] had great difficulty in getting a white woman to take the part" and that a lesser actress had finally accepted "that disgusting role."[36] Soon the controversy extended beyond press observations and the theater world into the realm of political social reform. Conservative church groups, the Society for the Prevention of Vice, and various other organizations protested the production. For example, a black group, the Ministerial Association of Salisbury and Wicomico County, Maryland, representing five thousand members, sent a letter to the NAACP stating that they "strenuously protest against the rendering of the Eugene O'Neill drama, in which Paul Robeson is a star, on the grounds that we deem it prejudicial to our racial group."[37] Then some women's groups followed suit. They viewed "the play as an insult to both the colored and white race." More specifically, according to news reports, "opposition of women's clubs [was] based principally on the fact that in the closing scene of the play Miss Blair is called upon to kiss the hand of Robeson, who is a full-blooded negro." Later another article doubled the number of supposed insults, reporting that "the woman is called [upon] twice during the play to kiss the negro's hand."[38]

Like the press, women's clubs and black political leaders converged on the interracial kiss. Eventually local city officials responded to the protest. The mayor of New York, John F. Hylan, "threatened an investigation." The turn of events was described by another paper: "Following a general outcry of protest which reached as far as Chicago, Mayor Hylan has asked for a police investigation." The *Herald* speculated that "there might be police intervention."[39] As one New York daily observed, "When Mayor Hylan investigates, something happens." And so it did: Eugene O'Neill announced that the play had been postponed a month but would nonetheless run for the full duration.[40]

New York City officials continued to feel the pressure of public protest and tried to stop the production. The opening scene required a cast of eight children, to play Jim, Ella, and their friends when they were very young, but in New York minors had to obtain a license to act on stage. According to the *New York Times*, however, "the eight children required for the play's prologue had been refused licenses by the Mayor's office." When the theater management questioned city officials as to why the licenses were denied, "no grounds were given." The management defended the opening scene, arguing that it merely showed "the friendship of the negro boy, Jim Harris, and a white girl, Ella Downey, and establishes the fact that the color line does not cross childhood."[41] In retrospect, given the furor that just the casting of a black man and white woman had provoked, the management's attempt to appease their critics by pointing to one of the drama's themes—that the color line was not absolutely impermeable—was hardly a good defense. Mayor Hylan continued to refuse the licenses, and Jimmy Light, the director, had to read the children's parts.

Eventually, O'Neill felt compelled to issue a formal statement defending his play. At a well-attended press conference he claimed that the controversy surrounding his play was "prejudice born of an entire ignorance of the subject," which he declared was "the last word in injustice and absurdity." Yet he expressed his commitment to production and promised both friends and foes that he would not "back down in the slightest."[42]

★

O'Neill tried to answer every charge directed against the play. He defended his choice of Robeson for the lead, not only on the basis of Robeson's talent but because, in O'Neill's words, "the question of race prejudice cannot enter here." Moreover, he rightly pointed out that this was not the first time that Robeson had been cast opposite a white woman, for Robeson had played against Margaret Wycherlin in a play called *Voodoo*. According to O'Neill, "In one scene, he was cast as the King and she the Queen. A King and Queen are, I believe, usually married."[43] But in a sense O'Neill was disingenuous, for the casting was only one of several elements that combined to spark such intense controversy. As he knew, in the end most of the criticism had converged on the interracial kiss. In responding to this criticism O'Neill requested that the press more closely analyze the text of the play, an appeal he would make over and over again, but he was probably correct in believing that many of his harshest critics never read the script. In any case, in an attempt to deflect some of the criticism centering on the interracial kiss, O'Neill replied, "If they would only take the trouble to look up this passage in the printed play, they would see how entirely innocent of all the inferred suggestion this action is."

From his perspective O'Neill saw the play as one with a social conscience designed to promote racial harmony, not to ignite social controversy or much less racial violence: "The play itself, as anyone who has read it with intelligence knows, is never a 'Race problem' play." O'Neill even suggested that "'God's Chillun' will help toward a more sympathetic understanding between the races, through the sense of mutual tragedy involved."[44] O'Neill's stated intentions were thwarted. The play did not encourage anything even closely resembling "a more sympathetic understanding" between black and white people. Nor did it result in a race riot, however. The play opened at the Provincetown Players Theater without much fanfare. Apparently police guards were posted outside the doors, as they had been during rehearsals. After the first performance a yellow book entitled the Ku Klux Klan was found in the theater. One newspaper predicted that the production would "permanently kill [O'Neill] as a playwright and attach an odium to his name from which it will never emerge."[45] Obviously, that was not the case. On the whole, as several papers reported, "Aside from the action by the Mayor's office, the premiere differed in no way from the seasons' other openings at the

Provincetown."[46] Indeed, according to Robeson's biographer, Martin Duberman, "Chillun' had a profitable run" and played to "standing-room-only crowds." In the end the play ran for a hundred performances.[47]

Yet the social response to the play revealed deep tensions in American culture. Unlike any theater production that preceded it, *All God's Chillun' Got Wings* stirred intense racial controversy, primarily among people who had little or no interest in the theater. Ironically their attempts to stop the production probably had the unintended effect of heightening public awareness of vice in general and of black/white sexual relations in particular. Moreover, in just a few more years, literary representations of black/white intimacy would become increasingly common; to an adventurous elite those fictions would provide a means through which to transgress middle-class conventions, breaking a taboo that O'Neill's play itself had helped to construct. More than the actual production, however, the scope and intensity of the social controversy surrounding O'Neill's drama established a kind of cultural division—between traditional conservatives, who believed that the discussion of interracial sex ought to remain outside the pale of permissible discourse, and a new avant-garde, who, by attending the play or reading the *American Mercury*, were able to position themselves as cultural pioneers. It was this group, defined initially as much by their conservative opponents as by their commitment to the representation of black/white sexuality, that would help complete the cultural transformation that O'Neill helped to create. Eventually, in an effort to stay on the cutting edge of modernism, more and more white urbanites would invade Jim and Ella's world of Harlem and black/white sexual relations. From the Provincetown to the Cotton Club, from high art to black burlesque, from exclusive salons to carefully managed saloons, through the modernists the black/white center was dispersing into the mainstream.

★

8

SLUMMING

Appropriating the Margins for Pleasure

If the fictional character Mark Thornton symbolized a modern cultural development—the extent to which white homosexual desire
had been formed within the interzones—his companion, June
Westbrook, also symbolized a related, if more familiar, historical
trend. By the late 1920s white bohemians evinced a growing fascination with African-American culture and institutions, especially with
Harlem. Rather than examples of sexual formation through cultural
interaction, however, the rise of bohemians represented a future
social trend—the dispersal of cultural forms across the urban landscape, through appropriation by social outsiders. At the end of the
1920s the process of cultural dispersion was accelerated by another
development: the influx of white mainstream urbanites who temporarily participated in the interzones, usually for pleasure, and then
returned to their homes and lives apart from the black/white vice districts. These leisurely crossings or social transgressions represented
yet more modes of cultural transmission and dispersal. In the broad-
est sense, white slumming represented an example of the accelerated circulation of social forms characteristic of American urban

modernism, a set of highly charged cultural loops. One uniquely American aspect of these circulations was that they tended to originate in black neighborhoods, signaling the extent to which it is possible to locate the origins of American modernism in African-American culture and social practices. As the decade closed, then, cultural interchange within the interzones produced cultural forms that dispersed first through the interracial pioneers, the homosexuals; then through bohemian involvement; and finally through mainstream leisure practices and texts.

As the possible modes of cultural interchange multiplied, and black/white sexual culture dispersed, the sex geography of the city did not change correspondingly. Racial segregation persisted. To take a taxi from Fifth Avenue to Broadway and then to Harlem was to journey across a geography seemingly as diverse as the terrain spanning London to Saudi Arabia to Nigeria. My analogy between urban slumming and world travel is not, in this instance, an exaggeration or, when viewed through race, merely coincidental. By the mid-1920s the increasingly popular impulse to travel—whether across national or urban borders—became a central social practice of the middle class. As studies of travel novels and innovations in traveling theory have shown, some travel writings and diaries of exploration actually represented the recorded experiences of imperialism. As the theorist Mary Louise Pratt has argued, the colonial travel narrative helped to effect the global transition to capitalism, in part through constituting the "native" as a "domestic" subject. In turn, I would argue, travel narratives have the effect of reconstituting their authors and, in yet another constitutive mode, their readership, completing the discursive cycle.[1]

These cycles of dispersion and redefinition, as in the modern history of reform, reflect a distinctly modern mode of cultural change. Among New York's cultural avant-garde, the impulse to travel was at least in part a quest for rejuvenation, an effort to escape from the banality of Victorianism by embracing the primitive, exotic, and taboo. In the modern era the imperialist project of travel competed with travel as a middle-class leisure pursuit, and travel writing was seen not necessarily as a form of literary fantasy or adventure but as a realistic narrative designed to impart practical advice on how to make a successful tour of a given city. In addition to the appearance of white modernist literature and dime-store travel guides, it is

★

important to understand the emergence of the so-called Harlem Renaissance. The subject of numerous historical and literary studies, the Harlem Renaissance is usually viewed either as the flowering of African-American culture or as a failed attempt to create great literature. The most influential studies of the movement have debated the quality of the texts, recovered important black women writers, and argued for the modernist dimension of the literary outpouring. In order to demonstrate the ways in which aspects of the Renaissance actually were shaped by the context of slumming, I want to divide the movement into two parts, poetry and novels, and then focus on the latter. Central to the discussion is this: although the novels varied in style and conventions, thematically the most popular, and important, works centered on Harlem. Scholars have noted the relations between city and literature, and specifically between Harlem and the authors who imagined it. Rather than being taken for authentic representations of life in the interzones, the Harlem novels ought to be seen as a kind of guide to urban exploration. More than two decades ago the historian Nathan Huggins argued that the Harlem Renaissance required the primitive black (read African) Others as the authentic inspiration for the New Negro. White authors also relied on blackness to draw distinctions, dramatize differences, and eroticize their contexts. Whether a form of leisure or a literary expedition, and usually both, "urban slumming" became critical to the rise of American sexual modernism. It delimited and defined the cultural shift from the private, quiescent, sexual reticence of the Victorians to the public, commercialized, ostentatious, even bawdy sexual expression that has become associated with the modern.

Slumming—traveling to "foreign," exotic, supposedly inferior cultures—gained popularity among several groups and served a range of purposes. Social reformers, intellectuals, sociologists, bohemians, white urban sophisticates—all can be understood as modern-day slummers. To understand the changing concepts of the slummer and of slumming, it is important to understand the changing concepts of the slum, for the practice of one remained contingent on the social definition of the other. The notion of the slum emerged simultaneously with reformers' efforts to understand the increasingly complex, heterogeneous, multilayered metropolis. As British urban historians have demonstrated, the classic Victorian city was increasingly defined by spatial contrasts between social classes. The key texts—Friedrich Engels's *The Condition of the Working Class in England*, Henry Mayhew's *London Labour and the London Poor*, and Charles Booth's *Life and Labour of the People in London*—explored the underworld of the West End and represented that world to the East End.[2] In the United States Jacob Riis's *How the Other Half Lives* presented the urban slum to middle-class reformers—and to a growing, popular audience. More important, Riis supplied a new kind of cultural narrative, the emerging genre of the social scientific study.[3] Through the numerical and illustrative methods of modern positivism—firsthand observations, photographs, detailed illustrations, maps, and tables—Riis acted as a kind of tour guide, escorting middle-class readers through areas of New York that few, if any, had traveled.[4]

How the Other Half Lives never actually provides a single, conclusive conception of the slum but rather offers several characteristics that identify areas of "pauperism."[5] In the English texts Mayhew and Booth drew on a colonial analogy to describe the "underworld." As Deborah Epstein Nord has argued, these urban explorers "developed the habit of comparing the English inhabitants of Victorian slums to Aborigines, South Sea Islanders and, most frequently, to African tribes."[6] In Chicago and New York urban explorers did not have to rely on an extended metaphorical comparison of colonialism but rather discussed race and ethnicity directly, sometimes simultaneously with, or even instead of, class concepts. In Riis's popular science, poverty itself is less a characteristic or category than a condition to be investigated and explained. Riis argued that the Italians were slum dwellers because they were "born gamblers" and "drinkers," and therefore suffered a condition of poverty caused by maladies of ethnic inheritance.

Beyond ethnic difference, Riis identified overcrowding, filth, odor, and general immorality as distinguishing features of the impoverished slum. In this respect Riis's analysis confirms the arguments of European theorists Peter Stallybrass and Allon White that the emergent social divisions organizing the city turned on the elaborated opposition between exalted top and the "low Other," between "the suburb and the slum, grand buildings and the sewer, the respectable classes and the lumpenproletariat." These in turn invoked distinctions between the pure and the polluted, the virtuous

★

and the immoral.[7] This high/low distinction certainly guided Riis's analysis of the slum, but the moral geography of New York and Chicago differed substantially from that of London. In the United States racial difference also shaped the urban terrain, and from the perspective of these urban geographers, their texts, and other narratives of city exploration, the low Other social space was to be classified through the incidence of interracial intimacy.

Riis's discussion of New York's Chinese population suggests the extent to which social scientists aligned ethnic mixture with generalized immorality. In his view, for example, Chinatown represented an especially wretched slum, because, unlike, "Jewtown" or the Italian slum, it was primarily a bachelor community, similar to Filipino communities in Chicago. "All kinds of men are met but not women—none at least with almond eyes." As Riis put it, "The 'wives of Chinatown' are of a different stock that comes closer from home."[8] Riis connected the incidence of Chinese/white marriage to the general problem of white slavery. In Chinatown one can easily find "the white slaves of its dens of vice and their infernal drug, that have infused into the Bloody Sixth Ward a subtler poison than ever the stale beer dives knew." For whereas the Italian beer dives encouraged laziness and drunkenness, within Chinatown there was Asian/white mixing in "houses, dozens of the them, in Mott and Pell streets, literally jammed from the 'joint' in the cellar to the attic with these hapless victims of a passion which, once acquired, demands the sacrifice of every instinct of decency."[9]

In a discussion of African-Americans, Riis again defined the slum by reference to the relative incidence of interracial sexual relations.[10] He points out that most African-Americans had been relegated to the areas of "unsavory reputation." Yet Riis attempted to portray the Negro in a positive light, stating that the "negro" was particularly neat: "There is no more clean and orderly community in New York than the new settlement of colored people that is growing up on the East Side from Yorkville to Harlem." Indeed, when it came to sanitation, Riis argued that African-Americans were "immensely superior of [the] lowest of whites, the Italians and Polish Jews." Historic because it assessed the virtues of black residents above certain white ethnic groups, Riis's analysis suggests a kind of late Victorian benevolent racial liberalism.[11]

Ultimately, however, Riis's efforts to exonerate the Negro relied on a distinction between the "Good Negro" and the "Bad Nigger," the latter defined as the black man who patronized the Black and Tans (such as Jack Johnson, who would become the archetypal quintessential "Bad Nigger"). Riis observes that the "colored citizen whom this Year's census man found in his Ninety-ninth Street flat is a very different individual from the 'nigger' his predecessor counted in the Black and Tan slums of Thompson and Sullivan Streets."[12] Later, although he persisted in defending recent black immigrants, he conceded that "the moral turpitude of Thompson street has been notorious for years, and the mingling of the three elements [Italian, black, and white] does not seem to have wrought any change for the better." Thus, although the predominately black areas of New York were clean, orderly, virtuous, Riis proclaimed that the "Borderland where the white and black races meet in common debauch, the aptly-named black and tan saloon, has never been debatable ground from the moral standpoint." According to Riis, "It has always been the worst of the desperately bad."[13]

As the professional sociological study of the city matured, both black and white scholars continued to align racial mixing with urban immorality. In his pioneering *Philadelphia Negro*, the black intellectual W.E.B. DuBois, like Riis, studied a variety of factors to understand the causes of poverty. Like Riis, DuBois drew distinctions between middle-class, working-class, and slum-dwelling African-Americans. The slum dweller—what DuBois termed, in contrast to his *talented tenth* of black leaders, the *submerged tenth* of the poverty-stricken—were characterized by moral laxity, specifically sexual promiscuity. DuBois most clearly defines his class distinctions in discussing the Seventh Ward, where at least thirty-three black/white married couples resided. Some were respectable, according to DuBois, but a certain class of couples were not. Unlike the middle- and working-class couples, this class or group "lived in slums" mostly. Feeding the general stereotype of the "white nigger lover," DuBois argued (without evidence) that "the women for the most part [were] prostitutes."[14]

In conceptualizing the black slums of South Side Chicago, E. Franklin Frazier borrowed the Park School model of dividing urban space into concentric circles. In this way he plotted not only personal background, home ownership, and family structure but also color difference, indicating that there were fewer black residents and more racially mixed people as the circles radiated outward. At the center were the newly arrived "Plantation Negroes" and within the outer rings resided the black middle class. The lighter the skin, the wealthier the resident. Most important, however, Frazier identified and then delimited the so-called Bright Light Areas of the Black Belt through marking out a demography of racial difference. In his moral map, he associated vice with the incidence of black/white sexual contact and the presence of racially mixed people.

In William Jones's study of amusements among African-Americans in Washington, D.C., a similar theory of racial mixture and vice guided sociological analysis. In Jones's analysis, dance and vice were the key factors. Dance halls were immoral because they "embraced an atmosphere in which the most powerful human impulses and emotions were released," resulting in a kind of social deterioration. But, according to Jones, one particular club, Andrew Thomas's Cabaret, was especially demoralizing and pathological because the "patronage consists of both Negroes and white persons."[15] Within the black urban sociological tradition, then, the implicit, unquestioned stigma of interracial relations was pervasive, virtually a foundation of the discipline.

It is difficult to measure precisely the social influence of socio-logical studies—to gauge the depth and extent of their dispersal and effects—but another competing narrative of the city drew from the sociological discourse and represented it to a broader audience. This narrative took the form of the modern travel manual or guidebook. In these texts of urban exploration, the original sociological concept of the slum persisted. Assuming the position of a tour guide, the manuals led the reader through the city, simultaneously translating and constructing the urban terrain, often warning the reader to be wary of poor areas or slums. Through a narrative strategy that attempted to place the reader within the urban context, race was almost always emphasized. In *Chicago in Seven Days*, the author offers a relatively mundane walking tour of the Chicago area. Speaking simultaneously to his companion and the reader, the guide described the various details of downtown Chicago: "When we arrived at State street," however, "it was unnecessary for me to tell my companion that we were in the heart of Chicago's large south-side 'Black-Belt' since colored folk were on every hand."[16] In New

York, guidebooks similarly described the sudden shock experienced by tourists who suddenly crossed racial boundaries. As the guide asserts, "If you are walking absent-mindedly up Fifth Avenue, and suddenly raise your eyes, you are surprised to notice, in the accustomed frame and low houses with brownstone fronts and door steps, a completely exotic picture. Within a few yards, within a few minutes, the New Yorkers have all turned black." Then, by characterizing Harlem as exotic, this guide moves in the direction of some of the English texts, which, as I have noted, conflated London's poor with distant, colonized African peoples. They racialized the English working class, drawing from a repertoire of imperialist culture to express the relations between economic or material groups, American discussions of poverty were less likely to extend the racial analogies to the working class, but popular descriptions of city life sometimes invoked Africa and even simianized African-American urbanites: "Clinging with long hooking hands to the leather straps, and chewing their gum, they remind one of the great apes of Equatorial Africa."[17] Comparing Harlemites to "Primitive" Others, another guide predicted that if the police disappeared, Harlem would quickly "revert to Haiti, given over to voo doo and the rhetorical despotism of a plumed Soulque."[18] Blackness had become a marker of city space, "coloring" the experience of readers taking imaginary walking tours through New York or Chicago.

In the guidebooks, as in the sociological discourse, the presence of black/white socializing signified the lowest slum, the most immoral vice. In 1904 tours of the "real" New York, for instance, one author offers a contrast between false and authentic slums, illustrating the early significance of black/white sexual relations. He recounts the story of a novice slummer, intent on locating vice. In this particular urban tour, however, the slummer was fooled into entering a false dive, filled with a "blameless collection of old newspapers, Civil War envelopes, wax casts of famous criminals and two or three slot machines."[19] Eventually the erstwhile urban explorer found a more "thrilling" area of New York, known as Hell's Kitchen. Yet, as the guide noted, "You would hardly know that you were in any place of especial wickedness." The urban tourist never reached the depths of vice, only the slumming surface, which was all-white. According to the authority, the degenerate and immoral saloons were marked by the mixing of "vicious Negroes and still lower white trash." Like reform tracts and sociological monographs, the guide-books conceived of black/white mixing as paradigmatic of vice and immorality.[20]

Through reform tracts, sociological monographs, and guide-books, the cultural map of the city had been reorganized. By the opening of the twentieth century, these naratives of urban explo-ration described the ways in which race "colored" the contours of the city, emphasized the sexualized and hence immoral characteris-tics of the slum, and consistently linked the most vicious of vice to the incidence of black/white sexual relations. As I made clear in the opening chapters, the origins of the interzones can be located in Progressive reform and the Great Migration, but the proliferation of slumming texts in turn reconstituted the texture and feel of inter-zone life. The point is historical and theoretical. I do not wish to exaggerate the analytical distinction between the material and cul-tural, suggesting that the "real" vice districts were created by failed reform and that the various cultural representations were secondary, somehow less historically significant. But my analysis of the making of the slum should be understood as theoretically distinct from my earlier discussion of the politics leading to the creation of black/white neighborhoods. The brothels, speakeasies, dance halls, sidewalks, corners, stoops: these were the infrastructure of the inter-zone. The prostitutes and their customers, the dancing couples, the homosexual men and women: they constituted the human geogra-phy of the interzones. As the vice districts attracted more white trav-elers, and as slumming texts dispersed, the experience of traveling—and living—in the interzones was also reshaped. Briefly, when slum-ming was in vogue, the interzone became in a sense a more discursive representational, relational phenomenon, one that became stable and intelligible through the contradistinction with geographies of wealth and pure whiteness. The *vice district* was the product of population movements, biased policing, failed reform, and sexually racist public policy. The *slum* was a representation, invented and popularized by social science, of the deteriorating neighborhoods, brothels, saloons. At some point, however, even this historical distinction between the material context and the cultural representation gradually blurred, and that blurred, complex inter-section between the cultural, social, and material can be captured, I suggest, by the concept of the interzone.

If a discussion of Riis suggests the extent to which the creation of cultural representation of the interzones originated in reform discourse, it should be noted that slumming likewise originated from social reform. In Chicago one authority noted, "Throughout the summer of 1911, Chicago was aflame with the fires of reform. Every night the segregated districts were 'slummed' by swarms of social and rescue workers from the missions." In New York, when temperance reformers invaded saloons, onlookers referred to the action as a "slumming run."[21] As everyday social reform work gave way to the professional sociological study of deviance, however, another kind of slumming developed. Rather than attempting to repress or "clean up" the slum, social analysts, specifically sociologists, produced detailed narratives purporting to advance a scientific approach to reform and uplift. In the 1920s an ethnographic mode of urban sociology had become a hallmark of the Chicago School of sociology, which emphasized the firsthand gathering of data, of which an excellent example is Nels Anderson's monograph on hoboes. He conducted his research by prolonged, daily immersion in the world of Chicago's "hobohemia," but Anderson's methodology was not, by definition, participant observation. As he described the process, "I did not descend into the pit, assume a role there, and later ascend to brush off the dust. The role was familiar before the research began."[22] In this case Anderson himself had been a hobo, and he conducted the study in order to earn a degree and begin his career.

Increasingly, University of Chicago graduate students employed Anderson's research methods, even if they did not necessarily originate from the communities they studied. As my earlier discussion of the taxi-dance hall might suggest, Paul Cressey's work, for instance, relied extensively on participant observation. He viewed himself as a "sociological stranger" who pretended to be a taxi-dance hall habitué, "mixing with the patrons on a basis of equality and concealment." To maintain the cover, the researcher had to invent "various fictions" and to learn and speak the language of the social insider. This methodology—of immersing oneself in an ostensibly foreign social world and participating as an insider to study its culture and advance particular academic projects—drew on, and in turn contributed to, the modern phenomenon of "slumming."[23]

Sociologists were not, however, white urbanites traveling to African-American neighborhoods for leisure and sexual amusement,

★

yet the increasing centrality of black spaces as sites of pleasure cannot be understood apart from an analysis of the shift in the definition of slumming from reforming—as the action of an outsider trying to make the margins more like the mainstream—to the practice of traveling to a different world not to eradicate but assimilate it. In the new sociology, there was a paradigmatic shift, I believe, from the value of objective, detached statistical analysis to the concept that experiencing the object of study was a valid method, perhaps even preferable to older research strategies. Slumming turned on the asymmetry between the slummer and its object, but remember that some slummers were sympathetic outsiders with a genuine sense of affinity whereas others were more concerned with exploitation than appreciation. The counterexample clarifies the latter kind of slumming: in African-American history, when a black person crossed racial borders and assimilated, the transgression was known as "passing." From escaping bondage through the slave underground to modern novels concerning fractured identities of racially mixed people, the cultural journey of "passing" represented an upward movement on the social hierarchy. Modern slumming was the opposite—social superiors temporarily exploiting people and institutions on the margins, usually for pleasure, leisure, or sexual adventure.

For the less affluent, spending a night on the town in Harlem might represent the cultural equivalent of taking a Cunard cruise to Africa, an exciting excursion into another social world. Although slumming never gained the public legitimacy of dancing, by the end of the 1920s many white urbanites were indeed traveling to enjoy jazz on the South Side of Chicago or to take in a show at the Cotton Club, which represented a sort of flagship nightclub of white slumming. In 1928 the New York Committee of Fourteen even published a report on the Cotton Club, located at 644 Lenox Avenue, describing it as a nightclub that "capitalizes on the white interest in colored resorts such as is described in Nigger Heaven." It is not mere coincidence that the investigator noted the novel *Nigger Heaven*.[24] Carl Van Vechten's popular story of Harlem, published in 1926, gained a wide audience among the avant-garde; in fact the novel served as a literary guidebook, first for bohemians and later for mainstream urbanites. In a history commissioned by the Federal Writers' Project in 1938, the section on Harlem emphasizes the significance of white modernist writers. There it mentions that "Gertrude Stein claimed a number of

Negro Adherents" and that the overall vogue of Harlem was "apotheosized in Carl Van Vechten's *Nigger Heaven,* a novel that New York read with avidity."[25] Another brief history even credited Van Vechten with "discovering Harlem."[26] Shortly after the publication of *Nigger Heaven,* the popular periodical *Vanity Fair* quipped that Van Vechten was getting a "tan," referring to the supposed bodily effect of his frequent taxi rides to the "African jungle" of Harlem. A well-known artist caricatured Van Vechten in blackface. And in a popular song about slumming, "Go Harlem," a lyric entreated adventurous New Yorkers to "Go Inspectin' like Van Vechten."[27]

At the center of Van Vechten's novel was the allure, and spectacle, of black/white sexual encounters. *Nigger Heaven* focused on a turbulent relationship between a black man and a black woman, Byron and Mary, but the scandalous interracial setting was at least as important as the romance. Harlem Renaissance scholars have by turns criticized or ignored *Nigger Heaven,* precisely because of its status as a slumming narrative. Nathan Huggins placed the novel within the tradition of white exploitation of the black "Heart of Darkness." David Levering Lewis dismissed Van Vechten as a dilettante and racial opportunist. Gloria Hull focused on Van Vechten's controversial lifestyle—"he frequented the transsexual floor shows, sex circuses, and marijuana parties along 140th Street"—more than on his novel.[28] In general the negative response to *Nigger Heaven* echoes critics of Van Vechten who expressed outrage at the novel's title.[29] The negative responses probably represent a generalized discomfort not merely with Van Vechten's racial position—a white man writing on black themes—but, more important, with the fact that his narrative seems to make implicit claims on insider status. *Nigger Heaven* presents an unmediated, racially neutral narrative of Harlem nightlife—its author could easily be read as African-American.

Despite all the controversy, Van Vechten intended the title *Nigger Heaven* not as an epithet against black people but rather as a critique of white participation in Harlem. Alluding to the title, the main character Byron exclaims: "Nigger Heaven, Nigger Heaven! That's what Harlem is." Byron invoked the metaphor of Harlem as a segregated theater. "We sit in our places in the gallery of the New York theaters and watch the white world sitting down below in the good seats in the orchestra. Occasionally they turn their faces up towards us, their hard, cruel faces to laugh and sneer, but then never beckon." Yet

Byron also asserts the potential for resistance: "It doesn't seem to occur to them either," he went on, "that we sit above them, that we drop things down on them and crush them, that we can swoop down from Nigger Heaven and take their seats."[30] In another scene critical of slumming, the black protagonist Mary converses with a white dancing partner: "I know what you're going to say: the Mecca of the New Negro!" Her partner replies: "To us on the outside, it seems magnificent, a dream come true. . . . You have everything here: ships and theaters and churches and libraries." Then, to underscore the extent to which leisure and sexuality were central to white definitions of Harlem, Mary retorts: "And Cabarets." The classic slummer replies: "You should have mentioned them first." In Nella Larsen's novel *Passing*, which can be taken as yet another slumming text, a character wonders about the pleasure that whites derive from slumming: "What do they come for?" As a partial answer, she replies: "A few purely and frankly to enjoy themselves. Others to get material." Then, in an interesting insight into the complex status hierarchies in the club: "More, to gaze on the great, and near great, while they gaze on the Negroes."[31]

Van Vechten's critique of slumming does not, however, mitigate the fact that his novel was a slumming text. First, like reform tracts and sociological studies, the novel as slumming text itself was produced through slumming. Van Vechten conceived of and wrote *Nigger Heaven* during an era when whites routinely patronized Harlem establishments. Van Vechten's close friend remembered, "After watching the winter sun rise over some Harlem cabaret, he would weave his way to a taxi, return to West Fifty-fifth Street, and start to work on the book."[32] More important, *Nigger Heaven* derives certain elements of its structure from the white travel narrative and from the modern guidebook. Van Vechten provides descriptions of the urban landscape, subtly comparing Harlem to a jungle, and constructs objectifying, frequently sexualized, portraits of the "natives." Like a standard guidebook, *Nigger Heaven* positions the reader as an outsider in need of guidance; it carefully describes Harlem's institutions and spatial dimensions, employing a kind of sociological realism by layering concrete details of streets, buildings, interiors. Like a travel guide, *Nigger Heaven* includes a "Glossary of Negro Words and Phrases," designed to initiate the foreigner into the customs and language of this "other" world of Harlem. Race signifies the "otherness" of Harlem; the majority of the terms in the glossary refer to color differences, such as "*buckra:* white person; *charcoal:* Negro; *ofay:* white person." Other terms—*hoof* and *cronch*—refer to dancing. Van Vechten even includes the term *Bulldiker:* which he interprets to mean "Lesbian." Certain highly sexualized expressions, such as the term *eel eater* to designate homosexual, were censored before publication. As should become clearer, in my interpretation of the Harlem novels, color and sexuality are the central characteristics of the slumming text. However exploitative this aspect of *Nigger Heaven* might now appear, it is probably worth noting that African-American writers also adopted the convention. Rudolph Fisher, in his 1927 Harlem novel, *The Walls of Jericho,* included a glossary entitled "An Introduction to Contemporary Harlemese, Expurgated and Abridged." It is significant that Van Vechten requested that Fisher read the galley proofs of *Nigger Heaven's* vocabulary, supposedly to check for authenticity. For his part, Fisher at least matches, if not surpasses, Van Vechten's portrayal of Harlem as both "foreign" (a culture requiring a translator) and as potentially "lewd and erotically immoral" (which must be censored, further arousing the reader).[33] Finally, in his memoir, entitled *White Women/Coloured Men,* the French explorer Henry Champly brought the slumming text as travel narrative full circle. In the tradition of de Tocqueville, Champly sets out to tour America to learn something of its distinctiveness, which he proposes to locate by exploring the black/white vice districts.

Perhaps the central distinguishing feature of the slumming narrative, beyond its derivation from the travel novel, was the sexualization of the space or geography that it explores. Van Vechten portrays Harlem as at once forbidden and lurid; in the final scene of the novel, Byron, after sacrificing both his writing and his lover, descends into the speakeasy scene of alcohol, drugs, and prostitutes. Drawing on his own experiences in that environment, Van Vechten portrays an underworld in which black women seductively dance the Charleston and the Camel Walk. Lasca, who represents Byron's illicit enchantress, lifts her "short skirt of champagne colored crepe high over her knees," while onlookers entreat her to "do that thing."[34]

The Harlem novel, more than any other slumming text of its era, dealt frequently and often explicitly with black male sexuality. Beginning at the turn of the century, some white males believed they were in the midst of a sexual crisis, caused by forces of modern civilization. To circumvent their sexual repression, some took up the strenuous life. Some white men, especially among the avant-garde, were fascinated with black male sexuality—an erotic fascination that becomes quite explicit in the slumming texts. In both the opening and closing scenes of *Nigger Heaven*, Van Vechten portrays hypersexual black men, entertaining a fantasy in which "authentic" black men are so virile and sexually attractive that they are "kept" by women. In *White Women/Coloured Men*, the French traveler Henry Champly demonstrates his obsession with color: "Among the men, every tone from light coffee to dark olive was represented." Invoking the fashionable cult of the primitive, Champly described a nearby, muscular man: "His white shirt emphasized his blackness as though he were wearing a mask made out of anthracite." It does not require a strained interpretation to read in these texts a kind of black/white homoeroticism.[35] Throughout Champly's narrative, the sexual prowess of black men is a central concern. In an urban journey with his guide into the Black Belt, Champly learned the story of a white woman who was in love with a black man. The guide entreated the black man, named White, to "show these fellows that letter from your latest white sweetie." Champly observed a letter written on "note paper in an artistic shade of mauve, in the flowing handwriting of a woman—an educated woman." It proclaimed that woman's devotion to White. After reading the note, Champly was stunned. Then, evincing a begrudging sexual admiration, he exclaims: "That Black Don Juan." Repeatedly Champly's discussion returns to black male (hyper)sexuality, especially in his discussion of "black Bullies," who, according to one of Champly's sources, were men "supported by several women, some White, others Black—[which was] quite common, both in Chicago and elsewhere."[36]

These and other narratives at the very least suggest white male admiration, if not erotic attraction, for a particular black male sexual aesthetic. This narrative phenomenon was unique to the era, a literary convention of key significance in the emergence of American modernism. The increasing centrality of black male sexuality—the move of focusing on and then celebrating black masculine appeal— should be conceived of as a discursive rupture from the Victorian culture of repression. The early Progressive response to Jack Johnson— who, rather than admired, was severely punished for his erotic appeal—represented a continuation of Victorian sexual racism. Bohemianism in particular and modern slumming texts in general therefore represented a conscious rebellion against the Victorians—against the suppression of black male sexuality. Some of these narratives rebelled to an extent that also suggests homosexual desire. But it would be wrong to assume that only white writers fantasized about the eroticized masculine black male of the vice districts. The central character of Claude McKay's popular slumming novel, *Home to Harlem*, is Jake, a "hypermasculine Africanized primitive." Likewise, Thurman's first novel of Harlem, *Blacker the Berry*, includes Alva, a hypermasculine, hypersexualized black gigolo (who ultimately turns to homosexual prostitution). Finally, in Thurman's *Infants of the Spring*, the homosexual potential of white slumming in vice districts becomes quite explicit in the relationship between the black protagonist, Ray, and the white slummer, Stephen.

As significant as the themes of slumming novels—the sexualized narrative of urban exploration—were the audiences. Van Vechten was a member of New York's literati. Urbane, intelligent, wealthy, Van Vechten's audience consisted of men and women in search of excitement, rebels challenging convention. Harlem was their mecca as well. In his 1930 novel, *Parties: Scenes from Contemporary New York Life*, the moderns take their anxious search for transcendence or stimulation to the clubs of the Black Mecca.[37] According to Van Vechten, the first wave of Harlem's white patrons were members of the avant-garde—a "clientele . . . [who] might be described as cosmopolitan. Perhaps bohemian—if one may revive a worn-out epithet that once meant a great deal."[38]

Both *Nigger Heaven* and *Parties* represent slumming novels—they are inspired by slumming expeditions, invoke the conventions of travel narrative, and are informed by the genre of the guidebook. I suggest, however, that these texts provide an important historical distinction between bohemian exploration and writing and white mainstream "slumming." Thus Van Vechten was critical of slumming, but he softened his critique in the case of the genuine bohemian. In my view Van Vechten was justified in doing so, since the bohemian, in certain respects, was more like the homosexual—a socially repressed cultural outsider—than like the mainstream white urbanite. Thus, among white bohemians as among white homosexuals, one of the most important features of the black/white urban speakeasy was dancing. In *Parties*, for instance, black dancing became a kind of spectacle for white bohemians who in fact appreciated the movements for more than its putative sexual appeal. In effect they looked for artistic or aesthetic quality and inspiration. In so doing, Van Vechten's characters attempt, perhaps out of a genuine admiration, to elevate the status of certain African-American cultural forms. As one character asserts, for instance, "Nearly all the dancing now to be seen in our musical shows is of Negro origin." Unlike the typical vice investigator or moralist, the bohemian endeavors to "appreciate" the Lindy Hop, not merely as an "imitation" of sexuality but as an aesthetic, artistic expression. "To observe the Lindy Hop being performed at first induces gooseflesh, and second, intense excitement, akin to religious mania, for the dance is not of sexual derivation, nor does it include its hierophants towards pleasures of the flesh." Yet, in the final analysis, the book's careful, appreciative description of the Lindy Hop betrays a fetishistic fascination with skin color and an underlying sexual fantasy: "Their lithe African beauty, shading from light tan, through golden bronze, to blue-black, these boys and girls with woolly hair, these boys and girls with hair ironed out and burnished." Eventually, in describing the dance, the observer (unwittingly?) returns to a kind of primitivism.[39] Both groups felt affinity, but there is an important difference between the bohemian appreciation of black dance and the (white) homosexual participation and performance.

In the end Van Vechten vacillates between portraying the bohemian as being above the typical slummer, someone who appreciated Harlem on an artistic level, but also someone who succumbed to the impulse to sexualize and sensationalize black Harlemites. In *Parties*, for example, Van Vechten's bohemianism was explicitly sexual. Always in search of the transgressive, urban bohemians sought even to break with the conventions of the New Morality. A central female character emphasizes her sexual promiscuity, and then, as if that alone were not transgressive enough, indicates that she routinely has sexual relations with black men. "I woke up in the morning with a start to see a black head on my pillow, Noma was saying to David. I was so amazed, she continued in her baby voice. Je croyais que c'était un Nègre. I never sleep twice with the same person anymore and I have such a frightful memory, she went on."[40] Van Vechten seems determined to shock us with black/white sexual situations; he himself indulges in the kind of bohemian exoticism he critiques. Wallace Thurman directly attacked such tendencies through his portrayal of Stephen, a white character in *Infants of the Spring*; at first, although Stephen is genuinely attracted to Harlem, he becomes bored by Harlem and its residents. In the end Stephen admits as much: I am one of "Gertrude Stein's Lost Generation or rather post-lost generation. Why not revolt? There's really very little to revolt against since the Victorians have been so thoroughly demolished. And it's too soon to rebel against the present regime of demolition."[41]

As the bohemian enthusiasm for slumming to Harlem waned, mainstream slumming increased. Before the late 1910s Harlem was neither a popular nightspot nor a common destination of tourism; even among New Yorkers it was not notable in the ways that Times Square or Broadway had become. In a popular guide to New York City, published before *Nigger Heaven*, Harlem was not mentioned.[42] By the late 1920s uptown nightlife had become so popular that, in 1927, the Committee of Fourteen investigators reported that Harlem had "become a 'slumming ground' for certain classes of whites who are looking for picturesqueness, 'thrills,' and too frequently a place to go on a 'moral vacation.'"[43]

The very terms the committee used to describe the slumming situation—picturesqueness, thrills, and moral vacation—suggest that urban slumming was closely connected to the modern notion of travel as invigorating leisure. In the 1920s black areas of the city were attracting an increasing number of mainstream white urbanites. In Chicago, for instance, an investigator for a juvenile protective agency reported on an all-white club, where he had arrived around 12:30 A.M. Only seven people were present, and he asked the waiter about the small crowd; the waiter told him that the club was losing business. "I asked him why, and he replied, 'Oh, I don't know. They get big crowds over at the black and tan joints on the South Side.'"[44] In New York, too, Harlem was overtaking several other entertainment districts in popularity. According to one nightlife observer, "Long after the cascading light of Times Square flickered out, the boulevards [of Harlem] were ablaze."[45] In both cities the allure of black entertainment and the sexual appeal of black/white socializing was radiating outward, from the original black/white interzones through the bohemian avant-garde into the white leisure class.

Harlem had now become a standard destination on the itineraries of the Broadway denizens. Rian James, in a popular guide to New York, observed that "when the downtown theatre closes and the nightclubs decide to call it a night, the sportier element of Manhattan turns north to Harlem and Uptown Seventh Avenue becomes what midtown Broadway has just been."[46] The interest extended beyond the wealthy and into the middle class. A popular history noted that white middle-class urbanites "found Harlem exotic and colorful." Of the slumming expeditions, another observer recalled that "you saw throngs on Lenox and Seventh Avenues, ceaselessly moving from one pleasure resort to another." Indeed, Harlem's appeal—by which I mean Harlem's sexual appeal—was fast becoming legendary worldwide: "The legend of Harlem by night—exhilarating and sensuous, throbbing to the beating of drums and the wailing of saxophones, cosmopolitan in peculiar sophistication—crossed the continent and the ocean."[47]

Although more and more white urbanites followed bohemians to Harlem, they ultimately arrived at very different destinations, patronizing the new slumming clubs built for tourists. Clubs such as the Cotton Club probably were "capitalizing" on the interest generated by *Nigger Heaven*, but they were not in fact the establishments described in Van Vechten's novels. As the committee observed of the Cotton Club, the "place is operated by white men who provide colored entertainment," catering to a decidedly different crowd from the one at a typical black speakeasy. Reports indicate that members of organized crime frequented the Cotton Club, Connie's Inn, or the Plantation Café in Chicago: "The gangsters rub elbows with visitors from Park Avenue in evening dress and from other smart residential sections of the city." Another source indicated that several clubs had begun to draw crowds away from Times Square and Broadway, but the source maintained that the Cotton Club was "attracting a clientele of wealthy whites—theatrical folk, professional people, and socialites."[48] The major New York guides also included Connie's Inn at 131st and Seventh.[49] These clubs shared at least one common characteristic. African-Americans were employed to perform but were not admitted to the club itself. Yet, as one source noted, "it was the goal of every Negro entertainer, whether singer, tap dancer, or band leader, to appear on stage at these establishments."[50] In remembering the vogue of Harlem, one popular history noted the irony of clubs like the Cotton Club that employed a black "massive doorman" to bar the entrance to African-Americans. Many popular memories of the era of the black nightclub tended to elide the distinction between bohemian and more mainstream slumming. By 1943 a history of Harlem attributed the continuing "vogue" of the "Black Metropolis" to Van Vechten,[51] but in reality, the nature of slumming had changed dramatically since the days of Van Vechten's expeditions into underground speakeasies.

Despite the differences between the early black/white clubs and late 1920s slumming, sexuality continued to be central, especially in the entertainment realm. Some of the early black/white dives included small-scale, often quite lurid erotic shows. In Chicago an establishment on Halsted provided black/white sexual entertainment for white patrons, including a performance "in which the most popular guide was a midget named Julie Johnson. She gave erotic exhibitions with a Negro nearly three times her height and more than twice her weight." Chicago also featured "peep shows" that "catered especially to boys, and provided entertainment for stag parties. . . . which featured white women and black men."[52] Another popular form of sexual entertainment were the burlesque shows. In Chicago one well-known establishment charged ten cents for admission. The "women sang, then gradually undressed themselves before their audiences, and, once naked, shimmied in that most suggestive way."[53] As in the urban experience of slumming, the spectacle of black/white sexuality also defined the genre of the slumming narrative. In his exploration of Chicago and New York, Champly recounts the visual experience of slumming, obsessed with the differing shades of color of those he was observing. After enlisting the services of a "roper" to act as tour guide, Champly reminds the guide of his singular interest: "You remember what especially interests me, Arsense—Black men, White women?" The roper replies, "You want to see the brothels where the girls are White, and the clients Black, the bullies Black and the proprietors a Negress, don't you?"[54] Whether in the form of surreptitiously viewing a peep show, enjoying a performance of burlesque, or clandestine taxi rides, slumming was an exceedingly visual event. It was a matter of leisurely sightseeing, or thickly descriptive, realist prose.

The entertainment offered in mainstream slumming clubs, although in some sense derivative of the marginal peep shows and burlesque performances, nonetheless reflected a decidedly different set of racial and sexual politics. In the original dives the black male/white female dyad predominated. The prostitutes were African-American, but the more highly paid and desirable positions for dancers or burlesque performers were held primarily by white women. Mainstream slumming spots offered the sexual display of African-American women for the visual pleasure of white men. The Cotton Club advertised by using an electric sign reading: "Tall, Tan, Terrific Gals."[55] Another guide proclaimed that in Harlem one could easily find "High Brown Babies." To a much greater extent than in the world of prostitution, light-skinned women were elevated above dark-skinned women in the so-called black reviews staged for white slummers.[56] The highly charged sexual taboo of black men consorting with white women—the defining taboo of the margin— had, by the time it reached the Cotton Club, been ideologically reversed, and thus the sexualized color line so central to bohemian slumming had been marginalized.

Slumming to white clubs located in black neighborhoods did not signal the actual decline of the black/white clubs. Moreover, the black middle class gradually increased its participation in the speakeasy scene and dance halls. They attended the Sugar Cane Club, operated by Edwin Small, which was typical of the era's off-the-beaten-path joint. It was a damp, dimly lit cellar, with two dozen tables surrounding a tiny dance floor.[57] Another club, the Savoy on Lenox Avenue, was popular with "middle-class Harlem." Black writers and artists also congregated at Tillie's. And by the 1930s Gladys Bentley, once relegated primarily to the underground speakeasies, was enjoying a receptive audience at the popular Clam House, even though it was acknowledged that her songs were "far too torrid to please respectable folk."[58] Members of the black middle class had caught on to the speakeasy club craze.

Nevertheless, by the late 1920s there was a growing sense that the erotic edge of Harlem and South Side Chicago had been dulled by the rise of nightspots like the Cotton Club and Connie's Inn. The "primitive" sexuality of the Harlem experience, it was believed, had been lost. Indeed, by 1938 a standard travel guide directed its readers to skip the Cotton Club and attend instead some of the black clubs along Lenox Avenue, such as the Savoy Ballroom. Another popular club, according to the guide, was the Apollo Theater, whose appeal derived in large part because it "puts on a colored review and is patronized by everybody."[59] Similar sentiments appear in McKay's *Home to Harlem*, when the main character returns from abroad to find that his favorite clubs were now catering to "ofay trade." Avoiding the Black and Tans, Jake preferred the "Congo," which "was the real throbbing little Africa in New York. No white person was admitted there. High Yallers were scarce."[60] The vogue of black/white mixing detracted from the transgressive thrill to be had from slumming. In his intimate guide to New York, for instance, an urban traveler reported on locating that rarest of spaces: "At last—a Harlem unknown to Americans!" He then describes a black working-class atmosphere but ultimately despairs over the changes wrought by the continuing vogue of black/white socializing. According to the guide: "These Negroes were so much taken up with the glory of being seen with a white man that they showed me nothing, but showed all round. Already I could see the Cotton Club looming up again."[61] It is probably true, as one guide estimated, that "the apex of night-time Harlem came in 1926 and 1927. By 1929 its reputation was waning." Part of the problem with this vogue of Harlem revues was the inevitable decline into banality—because the kind of (re)invigoration stimulated by transgression seemed to thrive more on novelty than any other quality. The formula of black revues—black music for white people, black bodies for the white gaze—actually represented quite unique shows, very different from the shows staged at speakeasies, which were informal and improvisational. Nevertheless, slumming turned on the novelty of its object—and novelties can easily become routine and predictable.[62]

Since the opening of the twentieth century white participation in black spaces had changed significantly. Throughout the history of black urban vice districts, the white people who participated were relegated to the social margins. With the rise of bohemian slumming, and the deployment of a slumming narrative, a partic-

ular version of Harlem was articulated. In effect, there were competing representations of the black urban underworld. Nothing
expressed the nature of that competition as clearly as the scene in
Nigger Heaven where the protagonist, Byron, is summoned to the
offices of a famous white publisher. Byron had submitted a story
concerning an interracial affair, dealing with the racial double
standard of the 1920s—the cultural rule that white men were
allowed access to black women whereas black men who dared
cross the color line were routinely punished. But the white editor
rejects Byron's writings. In the editor's view Byron failed to create
a convincing portrait of a prostitute, of Harlem nightlife, and suggests that Byron write a story about gambling, vice, and speakeasies.[63] Ironically Byron, the Harlem insider, was being instructed
by a white outsider on how to create "authentic" representations of
African-American culture. Somehow, somewhere, black writers
and creators had lost control of their subjects and with them, some
of the Harlem Renaissance.

Within and outside the vice districts the meaning of Harlem
changed over time. In the world of leisure and entertainment the
meaning of Harlem was fiercely contested, and white mainstream
slummers gained dominance. The story of the Harlem Renaissance is that there were in effect two Harlems—one black, the
other white. Black establishments, and black/white socializing,
continued throughout the decade, but the emergence of new
nightclubs and their popularization through guidebooks had created another, virtually all-white leisure zone within Harlem.
Through the social practices of slumming, another concentric circle had emerged—a zone not of deeply marginalized black/white
sexual and cultural interchange but rather a zone of asymmetrical
cultural appropriation. The large-scale, virtually all-white clubs,
capable of paying top wages, lured some of the most talented black
musicians and performers away from black audiences. Elaborate
African-American revues were staged in clubs like Connie's Inn,
the Cotton Club, and the Plantation Café, but black people were
frequently prohibited from gaining entrance. Slumming steadily
increased throughout the 1920s, attracting white urbanites with
exhortations that "Harlem is a great place, a real place, an honest
place, and a place that no visitor should even think of missing."[64]
Yet the publicity itself, by both drawing on and feeding the vogue,

had made Harlem less real and less honest. What could be more false than a Harlem slumming spot that prohibited the entrance of black people? Finally, by the end of the 1930s, the white middle-class appropriation of "Harlem" found symbolic completion: the premier club of the area, the Cotton Club, moved downtown to 48th Street and Broadway.

9

RACIAL REACTIONS

Prohibiting Miscegenation in the 1920s

By the 1920s scientific experts, social critics, and newspaper reporters were proclaiming that in the realm of manners, morals, and public comportment, Americans were in the midst of a cultural revolution. As I have tried to demonstrate, when white urbanites spent a night on the town, they did more than fashion new forms of entertainment. The New Woman, Companionate Marriage, the New Morality — in cities such as Chicago and New York, through new modes of leisure and consumption, they transformed the sex/gender system. In the rebellious and conservative era between Prohibition and repeal, the respectable white mainstream crossed the color line. Slumming became the conduit through which interracial cultural practices dispersed ever further into the imaginations, and intimacies, of more mainstream urban Americans.

To an extent the slumming impulse can be seen as a response to progressive moral reform. Moderns defined themselves through rebellion against perceived Victorian prudishness of moral reformers. More than a Foucauldian matter of repression inciting desire, however, antivice had quite specific and racially particular effects —

for example, relocating prostitution in predominately African-American neighborhoods. Similarly, antivice reformers constructed a racialized subject worthy of uplift—the white slave—and in the process erased the black prostitute. If they did not tacitly approve of black prostitution, they did create the moral conditions for black prostitution to thrive. Prohibition also represented a kind of moral reaction that inspired a modernist, progressive response. As commentators observed, the passage of the Volstead Act did not eliminate drinking; it increased criminal activity and weakened the legitimacy of American legal institutions. In retrospect the 1920s can in fact be seen as an era of a dynamic sexual revolution, to the extent that revolution indicates dramatic and decisive transformation; however, it must also be viewed as an era of intense moral conservatism. Undoubtedly the two social trends were connected, shaped by a perhaps uniquely American dynamic in which the more radical modernist impulse surfaces and then a reactionary, conservative tide sweeps through the cultural mainstream. As the previous chapters have demonstrated, the centers of modernism were primarily urban—and it was the modern avant-garde who were most critical of the contemporary conservatism. As one *American Mercury* commentator put it, "The Espionage Act cases, the labor injunction cases, the deportation cases, the Postal Act cases, the Mann Act cases, and now the Prohibition cases . . . will rob them [the judges] of all their old dignity." More serious, these commentators argued that prevailing conceptions of liberty and justice had been gravely compromised. Throughout the 1920s, urban bohemians and artistic self-styled moderns challenged Prohibition on every front, caricaturing its supporters and transforming the elusion of liquor authorities into a rebellious form of sociability.[1] In some cases the rebellion was connected to a political program, in some to forms of artistic achievement, and in others merely to pleasure. Whatever the scenario, the avant-garde or modernist critique of conservatism did in fact reveal the prejudice that fueled prohibitionism.

In connecting Prohibition to ethnic conservatism, these critics developed an analysis of the era that historians would do well to consider. The cultural conservatism that was symbolized by the Volstead Act not only was a matter of "repressing" white ethnic, working-class spheres of male sociability; prohibitionism also stemmed from deeper anxieties toward the changing norms of sexual propriety and

★

gender comportment. All these concerns over morality frequently focused on urban vice, which in turn had become closely connected to black/white sex districts. To make sense of various reactions against black/white marriage, one has to assume that for a considerable group of Americans intermarriage represented a kind of ultimate moral boundary—the last vestige of a system that gave order and ideological coherence not only to racial matters but to systems of sexuality, gender, and ultimately to the very concept of "Americanness." When Jack Johnson was brought down, there was little in the way of substantial white dissent—a consensus of sexual racism prevailed. By the 1920s the rise of slumming suggested a weakening of the consensus: the forces of repression were faltering and impropriety was ascending. In response to the perception of cultural change, some Americans, specifically rural Americans, became part of a cultural movement to reassert an older moral system, to commence a search for a kind of Great White Hope, this time for immutability in an era of tremendous social change.[2]

Nowhere is the search for control and the desire for a return to an older system of race relations more evident than in the conflicted history of D. W. Griffith's film *Birth of a Nation*. Conceived as a grand epic, the film recounted the story of the Civil War and Reconstruction through blatantly racist characterizations. *Birth of a Nation* can be understood as the cultural opposite of *All God's Chillun'*. In Griffith's version of history Reconstruction represented an era in which black people captured the seat of government, bankrupted the South, and displaced white southern common people. Reconstruction was characterized as a threat because it represented the sharing of political power—which resulted in social equality and racial intermarriage. (As will become clearer, most commentators believed in a causal relationship between intermarriage and social equality—and that tolerating racial crossings diminished white social status.) Indeed, perhaps the most provocative scene in the film concerns a black man in sexual pursuit of the white heroine, played by Lillian Gish (a celebrity known for her New Woman style). Rather than succumb to the Black Beast Rapist, she attempts suicide but is eventually rescued by her father. This is the white slave trope—the racial world turned upside down. Immediately upon its release, the film stirred controversy, as much if not more than O'Neill's production of *All God's Chillun' Got Wings*. In this case, however, leading black reform organizations, particularly the NAACP, led the movement of repression and protested the screening of *Birth of Nation* in major cities. They were unsuccessful, and the feature attracted the largest audiences in the history of silent film. Rather than viewing *Birth of a Nation* as an original milestone in silent film, we should understand Griffith's classic as a quintessential white slavery film, and as a drama constructed around the motif of moral decline, collapsing social order, and white female vulnerability to social outsiders. The innovation of *Birth of a Nation* was to make race more explicit: it replaced the dark and sinister White Slaver (his immigrant ethnic identity barely concealed) with the full-blown black villain—the Black Beast Rapist. Thus *Birth of a Nation* stands as a kind of cinematic summary of more than a decade of northern urban reaction against black/white intimate relations. What had changed was that the reactionary discourse had to compete with the vogue of black/white texts, and with the popularity of black entertainment, discussed in the previous chapter.

If Griffith's film signaled a more general social trend, it was that the vogue of interracial representations was only temporary and supported by a minority of Americans. In the older era of white slavery, there was something of a consensus on the issue of black/white sex—Jack Johnson's fight films were legally banned—but by the 1920s, the release of *Birth of a Nation* suggested a shift in the politics of representation. There was more conflict. Griffith's film is an angry polemic against social change, an attempt to use historical narrative to champion an older system and warn people of the dangers of racial change. It was precisely because of liberalization that some Americans joined together in a conservative backlash. Inspired by Griffith's portrayal of the southern Ku Klux Klan as the heroes of the Reconstruction and the protectors of white virtue, a new, primarily northern KKK movement emerged. Using *Birth of a Nation* as a promotional film, the KKK traveled across the country to give screenings to sympathetic audiences, gathering support for their cause. The melodramatic narrative, with its romantic concept of a pastoral America under attack from the evil forces of immorality, fit perfectly with the ideological currents of the Red Scare. Fears of impurity were strong—whether of foreigners threatening to corrupt American politics or of black people threatening to dilute Nordic virtue and integrity. Certainly the modern KKK was never as popular or powerful as in the late-nineteenth-century South, and many members were isolated extremists; it is worth pointing out, however, that once again the representation of black male access to white women was central to the symbolic politics of conservative reaction in America. And again, prohibiting miscegenation seemed to many a necessary measure in the fight for social order and white hegemony.[3]

At its core, white resistance to black/white marriage reflected the predominant northern response to the increase in black population resulting from the Great Migration. Conservative northerners believed that black/white sexual relations led inevitably to intermarriage and, by their definition, to a kind of "social equality." As the Jack Johnson case had demonstrated, black male sexual access to white womanhood had to be strictly controlled. Between 1913 and the 1920s the cluster of symbols revolving around black/white sexual relations had expanded beyond a concern with the Woman Adrift to a more generalized fear of racial decline. The new reaction represented a different group of voices—those of conservative intellectuals responding to the rise of liberal intellectuals. At the same time, the reaction shifted location, with some of the strongest dissent emanating not from northern cities but from the Midwest and rural America more generally. By the late 1920s the antimiscegenation taboo seemed as powerful in Green Bay, Wisconsin, as it was in New York, as strong in rural areas far removed from both the Great Migration as it was in 1919, on a beach on Chicago's near North Side.

The resurgence of antimiscegenation sentiment in part explains the increase in popular and scientific discussions of the so-called mulatto. Throughout the 1920s periodical articles discussing the topic appeared; novels on the "mulatto" proliferated; newspaper coverage increased. If the increase in discourse is any measure, a kind of fear or concern with not just sexual relations but "racially procreative" relations and the racially mixed progeny had escalated. This anxious discourse actually heightened general awareness of the "racially mixed subject," dispersing ideas that "mulattoes" would racially pass, infiltrate the white race, and diminish the quality of white stock. Even in remote rural areas black/white couples intending to marry were often discouraged and sometimes harshly punished. Why did Americans, virtually untouched by racial diversity, protest intermarriage?

In part, the answer can be located in the changing social context of the urban North. Between 1900 and 1930 American cities became increasingly diverse and, more significant, "multicolored." From the perspective of "Anglo-Saxons," southern and Eastern Europeans were distinctive, not the least because of perceived bodily differences. The so-called new immigrants posed a serious threat to "100 percent Americanism."[5] In both cases white northerners worried about the effects of ethnic diversity on the state of white civilization. In the case of southern and Eastern Europeans, however, "Nordic nationals" could prevent racial decline by restricting immigration. Comparatively, however, by the 1920s, white supremacists were less able to regulate African-Americans.[6]

Conservative whites understood the Great Migration as a racial threat, not because of some primordial racist impulse but in part because of ideological conditions in the North. As Rayford Logan has argued, the era between 1890 and 1910 can generally be seen as the "nadir of black history"; over the next twenty years a kind of liberalism emerged. But the forces of reaction were equal to the challenge of liberalism and probably became stronger because of it.[7] An analysis of a particular kind of pseudoscience illustrates the motif of the racial backlash. In 1890 the United States census indicated that black fertility rates gradually declined, a trend that must have reassured white supremacists observing changes in racial population. Proponents of Darwinism argued that the development was an inevitable feature of evolution: Negroes, "the weaker race," were dying out.[8] However, by the 1900s, scientists focused on white fertility rates, which had declined more steeply. This decline led to widespread discussions of "race suicide," the theory that native stock white women were not producing enough citizens to maintain Anglo-Saxon hegemony. If race suicide discourse encouraged one kind of reproduction, the eugenics movement worked to stop undesirable unions. For them, one of the most important tasks was to stop mixture among "disparate types," whether between the intelligent and the feebleminded, the wealthy and the poor, or white and black.[9] Espoused by politicians, scientists, and eugenicists, one key trend in racial thought linked the survival of civilization to encouraging reproduction between civilized whites and, conversely, discouraging all intimate contacts between blacks and whites.

★

In retrospect, given the racial statistics, northern fears of declining numbers of Anglo-Saxons seem difficult to fathom. Yet several white nationalist texts gained a formidable reading audience. Lothrop Stoddard's *The Rising Tide of Color* and Madison Grant's *The Passing of the Great Race* illustrate the direction of the new discourse.[10] Stoddard's and Grant's works explored the "world system of race" and analyzed the impact of "miscegenation" on the supposed racial integrity of white Nordics.[11] Although historians often read these tracts as nativist attacks on Southern and Eastern European immigrants, it is worth noting that each contains significant discussions of racial mixture.[12]

These trends in white thought coincided with a pronounced shift against intermarriage within black social thought. In the 1890s Frederick Douglass, T. Thomas Fortune, and Charles Chesnutt each advocated racial intermarriage as a solution to racial inequality.[13] At the opposite end of the spectrum, Booker T. Washington, in his famous Atlanta Compromise speech, implicitly rejected black/white marriage. He argued for total social separation between white and black people.[14] By roughly 1910 W.E.B. DuBois had articulated the classic black liberal position on interracial marriage. DuBois, James Weldon Johnson, and other black leaders argued that African-Americans did not wish to marry across the color line and in fact should not do so. But black liberals also stressed that the NAACP must oppose all laws banning intermarriage, because such legislation was unconstitutional and stigmatized black Americans.[15] In sexual matters, black women were more vocal about southern lynching than they were about white resistance to northern intermarriage. Anna Julia Cooper stated that the "blending of races in the aggregate is simply an unthinkable thought." Most black women in the leadership probably supported DuBois. Hallie Q. Brown, for example, served as a conduit between the NAACP and the National Association of Colored Women, and urged female reformers to oppose a 1923 federal marriage bill that included an anti-intermarriage clause.[16]

As Frederick Douglass's amalgamation position declined, the two most significant schools of thought were the traditional DuBoisian liberals and a new incarnation of Washingtonian social separation, propagated by Marcus Garvey. Like Washington, Garvey directly opposed social mixture between whites and blacks, but his innovation was to use intermarriage as a political issue. Garvey focused on intermarriage to discredit the black members of the NAACP, particularly DuBois. He referred to DuBois as "an unfortunate mulatto," who wanted "a black and white admixture which will ultimately produce new types which are neither black nor white."[17] Garvey can be seen as a "radical antimiscegenationist," distinguished from previous opponents of intermarriage by his support for the legal prohibition of mixture.[18] Although most African-Americans probably rejected legal prohibition, by the 1920s Garvey had a phenomenal following among southern and working-class black people. His political manipulation of the intermarriage issue converged with white supremacist rhetoric against "social equality," aggravating the already volatile racial climate for couples who intermarried.[19]

[Fears of intermarriage probably intensified when famous cases of black/white marriage surfaced, such as the Jack Johnson–Lucille Cameron union. The year Johnson was indicted, ten states attempted to pass antimiscegenation statutes. The ideological lesson was clear: black male access to white women should be strictly prohibited.[20] By the 1920s, however, intermarriage had become both increasingly visible and statistically probable. Unlike the response to Johnson, then, by the late 1920s the fears of racial pollution and black dominance were ascendant, overshadowing concerns with sexual immorality and gender security, as indicated in the scientific and popular discourse. Another, less well-known scenario should also be included in an analysis of northern perceptions of racial mixture: the case of racially indeterminate divorces, in which white men sued their white wives because of reputed black ancestry. As in the case of the Filipino dance hall patron who dated the white hostess, black/white marriage posed a challenge to fundamental ideologies concerning citizenship and racial prerogative, again reflecting the foundational presumption that intermarriage led inevitably to the erosion of racial distinction and hierarchy.

Of the various divorce cases challenging commonsense notions of "race," the most famous was the Alice and Kip Rhinelander controversy. In 1925 Kip, from one of New York's oldest and wealthiest families, married Alice Jones, a biracial chambermaid. The two met and carried on an affair for several months; eventually they eloped and were married. Roughly a month later Kip's family forced him to file for divorce. Their legal brief alleged that Kip had only recently learned of Alice's black ancestry and therefore wanted the marriage annulled because of fraud. At first, defense attorneys denied that Alice was black, but eventually they argued that Kip was fully aware of her racial ancestry when they married. The ensuing trial grabbed the headlines. To demonstrate that Kip must have known her racial identity, Alice partially disrobed, exposing her legs and back to the white, all-male jury. They inspected her for ten minutes and decided in favor of Alice. Kip Rhinelander must have known of his wife's ancestry. Alice received a small settlement and alimony, but she lost her husband and the trial had been humiliating.[21]

These divorce cases served to challenge beliefs that race was self-evident, readily observable to all reasoned individuals. Indeed, one problem courts faced was determining the actual "social race" of the people involved. In some divorce cases the wife was asked to prove her racial identity. In others, experts on race were summoned to classify women charged with racial passing.[22] The anthropologist Franz Boas was "called in to declare whether a woman was actually white." According to the anthropologist, however, there was "no way to prove it." He observed that "it is easy to decide whether this woman has any black characteristics, but the lack of them would not on the other hand prove that she has no negro blood in her veins."[23] In another case a white husband charged that his wife was illegitimate and possessed black ancestry. The wife admitted illegitimacy but not blackness. The court was forced to bring in a "racial expert."[24]

These and other cases served to underscore two fundamental points: the process and rules of racial classification were contradictory, and some people exploited the contradictions through racial passing.[25] Indeed, many women accused of possessing black ancestry challenged the prevailing racial system. For example, a white husband charged his wife with fraud because she allegedly "had forgotten to supply him with her family genealogical tree." In this case, however, the wife did not deny she had black ancestry but argued that it was insignificant. In the process her trial raised the possibility that many seemingly respectable and content white couples were in fact involved in black/white marriages. One judge went so far as to claim that "if every wife and every hubby with at least a drop of negro blood in their veins were sued for separation," the court would be inundated with cases. In effect, the judge, and these cases in general, raised the specter of concealed blackness. As the judge concluded,

"Thousands of light-colored people are at present passing for white and marrying."[26] Indeed, one U.S. senator argued in a speech to the Judiciary Committee that "America was about 50% Negroid. From the White House down, through every strata and ramification of our 'pure white' social fabric, there are Negroes."[27] Another authority stated that "the white and black races are becoming so mixed here the question is to be asked, 'Is White America to become a Negroid Nation?' "[28] It seems a huge leap to move from the random case of racial passing to predictions of imminent white decline. But such was the logic of moral panic in the 1920s.

The diversification of northern urban populations, the changing currents both of white and black racial thought, the continuing contradictions of racial classification, and the threat of racial passing combined to intensify the anxiety and panic in the North.[29] Caught in the swirling current of sexual racism, some northern states formulated and passed anti-intermarriage laws. Between 1910 and 1940 almost all northern and midwestern states, including states whose black populations were statistically negligible, conducted hearings on "antimiscegenation" statutes.[30] The circumstances surrounding the introduction of many of the intermarriage bills remain largely unknown, but several general trends can be identified. In addition to the random bills introduced almost every year, there were also waves of "antimiscegenation" bills, not only in 1913 but again in 1927 when state legislators in seven states introduced antimiscegenation bills into committees on the floor.[31] In at least four states the NAACP had reason to believe that "the Klan and allied groups [were] behind these measures."[32] The NAACP suppressed intermarriage legislation through lobbying, but their actions were not necessarily popular. They were vulnerable to the accusation that they were a "miscegenation" society.[33] So negative was the general view of intermarriage that their key legislative strategy was to stop the bills in committee, before the initiatives could attract public attention, stir controversy, and hence become law.[34]

Although it is possible to plot the general trends of intermarriage law by looking at NAACP records, it is difficult to understand the origins of these bills.[35] A close look at a Wisconsin case provides some insight. In 1917 J. Henry Bennet, a state senator from rural, all-white Viroqua, Wisconsin, introduced legislation to prohibit intermarriage.[36] The Madison branch of the NAACP learned of the senator's intentions and contacted the national headquarters of the NAACP. After the association offered advice on how to block the legislation,[37] local black political and religious leaders planned to protest the bill. Three men actually testified before the Judiciary Committee; one was Lucius Palmer of Milwaukee, who in 1908 had served in the state legislature (the first black person to do so). The black speakers met each argument for the bill with persuasive counterarguments, refuting the theory that the progeny of black/white marriages were inferior and defending interracial couples from attacks on their integrity. In turn no sponsors of the bill emerged to testify on its behalf, perhaps because few, if any, committed antimiscegenationists were aware of the hearings.[38] The NAACP blocked the legislation.

The role of the NAACP in defeating these and other intermarriage bills can be viewed either optimistically or pessimistically. The failure of the legislation to pass the statutes speaks to the growing power of the association, as well as to the gradual rise of white liberalism in the North. Indeed, roughly forty years ago Rayford Logan argued that the historical significance of the northern intermarriage laws was not their introduction but their defeat. His point was that there were many antiblack bills put before state and federal legislatures, but very few became law. Logan's argument was that legislation did not win approval because the early twentieth century, when compared with the nadir of the 1890s, was an era of relative tolerance during which African-Americans made social gains.[39]

Before recognizing northern liberals for accepting NAACP arguments against the legislation, our inquiry ought to focus on the introduction of the statutes in the first place. Of critical importance is that some of the legislation emanated from virtually all-white areas. That a state senator from Wisconsin, Iowa, or Idaho could even entertain the idea of introducing antimiscegenation legislation strikes me as significant. In my view these were the actions of people caught in a racial or moral panic. Another, related geographical trend suggests the connection between urban cultural change and the rural response to black/white marriage. In several states antimiscegenation statutes made it through the committee, entered debate on the legislative floor, and passed in one house of the legislature. It was significant that the two states involved, Kansas and Ohio, both had cities with substantial black populations, and that in both states were located notorious, highly visible black/white vice districts. It is a stunning fact that legislators in virtually all-white states introduced anti-miscegenation bills and that in states with a small but concentrated black population these bills passed in one chamber of the legislature. Miscegenation in the cities was a telling test of Northern liberalism.

If the Great Migration in general and interracial relations in particular generated a kind of panic in the North, as evinced by the incidence of efforts to pass intermarriage laws, then it would follow that in states with the largest black populations, antimiscegenation statutes would become law. This was not the case, however. In Chicago and New York, laws to ban intermarriage either were never introduced or failed to make it out of committee. One possible explanation for the failure is that the laws were unnecessary because powerful social mechanisms already regulated black/white marriages.

This unofficial regulation of intermarriage operated through a variety of channels. In some cases couples were stopped from marrying by ministers. For example, an Episcopalian clergyman, after being approached by an interracial couple, refused to perform the ceremony at their wedding, and then "announced himself as favoring a law prohibiting marriage between persons of white and Negro ancestry." In a similar case, after a black/white couple asked a minister to perform at their ceremony, he reported their intention to marry to the local sheriff, as if they were in violation of a law.[40] In other cases couples had to confront the norms against intermarriage in a given community, which might become violent in its defense of the racial status quo. Here the imagery and importance of *Birth of a Nation* become undeniable. For example, not far from the interzones of New York City, in Connecticut, a black man, Clarence Kellem, who intended to marry a young white woman, indicated that he had been threatened by mail and telephone. Then, just before their marriage, "a fiery cross was burned on a hill near their home."[41] In 1903 in Sandusky, Ohio, not far from the interzones of Cleveland, a prosperous white farmer and a black woman announced plans for a traditional marriage ceremony, and their neighbors responded by trying to stop the wedding. At first a few people verbalized their feelings against the marriage, and then local residents threatened the couple. According to the press, "A mob of masked and armed men attacked their house." They "riddled the house with bullets." Both the husband and wife were wounded.[42] In

Fond du Lac, near Milwaukee, the *New York Times* reported on
another controversy surrounding intermarriage. Apparently the
young bride was "well developed, rather pretty." They described the
groom as a "full-blooded African, and as black as a kettle." They predicted "that the usually sleepy town of Fond du Lac will become
wild with excitement when the story becomes known."[43]

More than vigilante actions served to regulate intermarriage. In
states where there were no laws prohibiting "miscegenation" and in
cities with large black populations, judges and bureaucrats, often
through clandestine actions, prevented couples from intermarrying.
In Illinois Gladys Jones, a white woman, applied for a license to
marry Frank Michener, a black man. Even though no laws prohibited racial intermarriage, the couple was denied the license. In this
case, "the woman was declared mentally incompetent and removed
to the Vineland Home for the feeble-minded."[44] In Minneapolis, a
city in which black/white marriages were statistically overrepre-
sented, police arrested a white woman for carousing with Bert
Green, a black man who allegedly was the woman's chauffeur. The
judge sentenced the young woman to ten days in the workhouse and
then to an institute for the insane.[45] In the case of the statistically
probable black/white dyad—that of black men and white women—
the woman was seen not merely as corrupt or delinquent but as
intrinsically immoral and mentally incapacitated.[46]

Black men who attempted to marry white women faced a different set of unofficial obstacles, many of which were also deployed by
city or state government institutions. Some of these were general
morality laws that could double as racial/sexual controls. Such was
the case of Jack Johnson's persecution under the Mann Act.[47]
When the Mann Act could not be applied, local authorities relied
on age of consent laws or morality charges. For example, the *New
York Times* reported on a trial concerning intermarriage that had
just ended in Detroit, another city known for its black/white vice
districts. According to the report, the couple, charged with lewd and
lascivious cohabitation, "have been married for some time and
lived together as man and wife." They lost the trial, and even
though intermarriage was perfectly legal in Michigan, one newspaper headline was nonetheless accurate: "Couple Was Convicted of
Miscegenation."[48]

In 1913, when the most famous black man in America, Jack Johnson, was forced into exile for intermarrying, the country was in the midst of a national hysteria over the virtue of white women. It was no accident that Johnson's legal trial and popular persecution were in Chicago, a city notorious for interracial socializing. Johnson's persecutors, like many Progressive reformers in general, expressed fears about morality and sexual danger in the cities. The same year that Johnson returned to the United States and began serving his sentence, Olin Caver, an obscure black man living in a rural, isolated, overwhelmingly white town, was sentenced to prison for the same transgression. Much, of course, had transpired in the decade or so between Jack Johnson's and Olin Caver's fall. When Johnson was arrested the black/white sex districts were just beginning to gain popularity among the avant-garde white urbanites. Now it seemed some of the most strident "antimiscegenation" sentiments could be found in rural Wisconsin, Connecticut, Pennsylvania, or Rhode Island. From the era of Johnson's exile, of course, the black/white taboo had become a staple of American culture, whether urban or rural, but the changing racial climate, and the brief vogue of slumming, combined to heighten awareness of racial diversity in America. By the time mainstream urbanites could guiltlessly spend a night on the town at the Cotton Club, rural Americans responded by denouncing race mixing and asserting the necessity of white superiority and white purity. In the era of the Great Migration black/white marriage represented not only a symbolic target—and its repression not only conservative symbolic protest. Rural attacks on black/white couples were very real attempts to prohibit the perceived decline of the white race.

A comparison between Johnson and Caver suggests another trend worth noting. The legal history of antimiscegenation reveals that rather than improving over the decades between roughly 1870 to 1930, prejudice against black/white couples probably intensified. Examples of official antimiscegenation demonstrate that public and private interference with intermarriage did not follow the pattern of the liberalization of sexual mores. Periodic attempts to pass anti-intermarriage laws or bureaucratic interference with the rights of couples to intermarry or the misapplication of antiprostitution or morality laws indicates a climate of increasing repression. The statistical evidence of intermarriage suggests that in cities such as Boston and Philadelphia, the numbers of black/white marriages actually declined, even though the black population was steadily increasing.[49] In part this reflects the decrease in opportunities for couples to meet since segregation had become more rigid, but the growing reaction against racial mixing was also brought on by the increased visibility and knowledge of black/white sexual relations. What was vice had become vogue, as an analysis of slumming suggests, and now the vogue was eliciting a negative response.[50] Although the cultural legacy of the vice districts remains with us today, in the form of jazz or certain dances, the specific practice of white slumming seemingly faded. The cultural institutions and practices of black/white sexual relations—speakeasies, nightclubs, and brothels—had fostered cross-cultural exchange. They also fomented a reaction, and black/white marriage represented an easy target.

★

EPILOGUE

Sexual Racisms

The story of black/white sexual relations—from the persecution of Jack Johnson to the creation of sex districts to episodes of social repression—should not be understood as merely another in the many instances of racial reaction that pervaded the 1920s. Yet the temptation to do so is great, in part because of the ways in which historians have conceptualized racial conflict. Throughout my study, I have tried to suggest that the history of sexuality must be introduced into any sustained analysis of urban black/white relations, because urban culture and commercialized sex were so central to the era. Studying the intersection of race/sexuality, however, is more complex than simply including the sexual. To understand the intersection of race and sexuality, one must interrogate not only the traditional modes of racism—the repressive, punitive, negative policies and actions that subordinate people because of their social ancestry and color—but also the productive aspects of racism, and, more important, the ways in which the ideological mode racism/sexism operates to reshape historical realms ranging from urban social policy to everyday intimacies.

Epilogue

In the introduction to this book I suggested that we need new perspectives on the history of black/white sexual relations—innovative conceptual frameworks, creative discourses, carefully applied theories. After completing the research and writing for this study, I have not come to the point of rejecting narratives, as have many postmodern critics of current historiographical practice, but I now feel uncomfortable with the kinds of strategies through which I conceive of historical events and social phenomena. I think I tried to make a narrative that could be described as something like minimalist superrealism. Mine is a story comprising purposeful actors, episodes that get defined as historical events, strategically arranged demographics, and recorded statements. Within each chapter or essay, it is true that events follow one another—and I attempt to interpret the meanings of their succession—but the study is less concerned with the chronological than with the diachronic. I am more concerned, therefore, with relations between areas of the city, areas of experience, realms of culture, groups of people, kinds of leisure institutions. All of this is to say that when considering histories of race or sexuality, the central goal seems to be to consider relational points of historical overlap, but the problem is that one can then lose sight of the larger questions of historical change and causation.

Over the past decade, scholars have debated and analyzed the changing historical and cultural meanings associated with race and racial difference. Literary scholars influenced by theories emphasizing language and textual interpretation suggested some of the contradictions that inhered in race. In the early 1980s, historians were influenced by several important essays on the origins of race, specifically an emergent Marxist tradition that criticized liberal race relations scholarship for its ahistoricity. They argued for the primacy of class and invoked the Marxian concept of false consciousness to explain the historical persistence of racism. Race relations scholars responded to the new Marxism by arguing for something like the autonomy of racism from material or class interests, and they pointed out that *class* too was a matter of construction, ideology, and cultural perception. As one school of thought downplayed racism in favor of class, another school concentrated on demonstrating the extent to which racism resulted in residential segregation or antimiscegenation laws or social violence—historical events that seemed

★

174

clearly to demonstrate the relative "autonomy" of white supremacy. One problem with this debate was that, theoretically, it polarized two categories of analysis that historically have almost always been interrelated.[1] Another problem arising from the debate was that race, and particularly class, remained undertheorized, and, more significantly for our purposes, that race was not clearly distinguished from racism. Historians and social theorists argue that when one is discussing race, the category ought to conjure up images of science — or, to be more precise, pseudoscience. These scholars argue that people cannot be divided biologically or genetically into stable, measurable categories known as "races." Scholars have become increasingly critical of institutions or works that invoke race, whether in the law, science, statistics, or literature. Now we have a broad, sophisticated literature that, in a generalized sense of the term, *deconstructs* the making of "race."

If the new thought effected a transformation in scholarly thinking about race, it also elicited a vigorous response from thinkers critical of the theoretical methods, in part because of political implications. The new approaches seemed to imply that race was unreal — and experiences of oppression, therefore, figments of our imagination. The problem was that the theorists did not distinguish carefully enough between *race,* which does seem to be a matter of pseudoscience, and *racism,* which can be seen as a historical force supported by various and changing social contexts. Thus it is now more widely understood that although people cannot accurately, and certainly not neutrally, be divided into "races," racism certainly exists.

The problem with the first wave of scholarship was its tendency to lead scholars to downplay the significance of racism in American culture and politics. The problem with the second wave was that, although it asserted the salience of racism, it did not provide sufficiently concrete historical examples. This book has tried to show the modes through which race as a category of social analysis could, and often did, have deleterious consequences for social groups relegated to the margins and stigmatized by social discourses. At the same time, it has tried to explore the ways in which social racism, at least in part, is responsible for the production of geographies and institutions and cultures, which sometimes have the peculiar tendency of circling back to reshape the dominant culture. The second feature of this book has been to explore the operation of racism on the individual level, in the everyday lives of the people most affected by ideologies of white supremacy, and particularly sexual racism.

Let me reflect on my historical theses to illustrate these theoretical points. Perhaps the most important contribution of the Marxist literature was to force scholars to criticize the scholarship whose implicit theoretical framework was in fact racialist. There is a difference between racialism and racism, however, and I want to illustrate the distinction. In the early twentieth century, an example of racialism was the white slavery discourse, and an example of sexual racism was the Jack Johnson episode. As I have argued, both historical events made a significant impact in the realm of symbols, but they can nevertheless be analyzed as distinct aspects of the ideology of white supremacy. The white slavery scare, as traditionally understood, mobilized public sentiment and resources against prostitution. It also provided the ideological tools necessary to restore fallen women to white womanhood, serving as a kind of ideology of respectability. My contribution, the discursive, critical race analysis, was to demonstrate that white slavery represented a white movement, erasing black women from social scientific analysis and therefore removing them from Progressive reform agendas that had come to depend on social science data to create and administer policy. In the Jack Johnson controversy, a kind of sexual racism rather than *racialism* operated. Thus in the opening story, and in the closing essay on the populist movements to stop miscegenation, my analysis reveals the extent to which broad-based social movements exerted power to stop people from pursuing their desire to cross the sexual color line and marry, date, or engage in sexual relations.

In the history of antiprostitution reform as well, racialism effected a discriminatory social policy. Throughout the early twentieth century, social reformers had worked to rescue and uplift fallen women. As the Great Migration continued and as more black women became prostitutes, the ideology of the movement changed decisively. Prostitutes were not seen as worthy of uplift and were more likely to be stigmatized as biologically degenerate. That this ideology emerged at approximately the same time that black women were disproportionately represented in the ranks of prostitution was not a coincidence. Neither was the transformation of the vice districts. Here again it is possible to analyze the ways in which racialism—the uncritical use of the category of race—fosters sexual racism and thereby produces segregation and unequal opportunity. By (unconsciously and sometimes consciously) constructing the deserving prostitute as white, the antiprostitution movement tacitly approved the internal migration of prostitution from white to black neighborhoods. Once the migration was completed—and again this is not a coincidence—Progressive reformers turned their attention away from the issue of prostitution. As in the white slavery scare, by the beginning of the 1920s elite philanthropists, social workers, and members of the fledgling state removed the black prostitute from the social reform agenda.

If the creation of the vice zones revealed the consequences of racialism, the social history of the vice zones themselves reveals still more dimensions of sexual racisms. The plight of the Filipino patron stranded between his native country and the United States provides an excellent example of how sexual racism (operating as a kind of ritual of assimilation) shaped the lives of people living on the margins. As I have argued, the vice districts were the products of the newly created antimiscegenation taboo, which to a large extent structured relations within the vice zones (even if one can locate important moments of resistance from the margins). Hence conflict between Filipino and white men over the favors of white dance hall hostesses took on some of the cultural forms associated with black/white relations. In the Jack Johnson case, white men experienced Johnsons's victory and, more important, his sexual relations with white women as a threat to their cultural or status privilege. Inside the dance halls, the operation of sexual racism served to leverage white ethnic males' access to "Americanness" through white women. As I try to suggest in my discussion of masculinity, sexual racism must also be seen as a psychological phenomenon through which identities were interpolated. In other words, both white and Filipino men invested so much energy in winning the attention of white, native-stock women because it was precisely at the level of the dance hall, standing around and waiting to choose a partner, that the general ideology of race directly shaped the perceptions and experiences of the patrons. To be rejected by a dance hall hostess was painful, but to be rejected because of color was to learn through the most intimate experiences that Filipino, Chinese, or African-American heritage was devalued and subordinated.

In the realms of prostitution as well, sexual racism shaped the everyday lives of women in concrete and consequential ways. Excluded from most forms of "legitimate" labor and abandoned by reformers, black prostitutes were subordinate on the social hierarchy operating in the black/white vice districts. They were less likely to be connected to brothels and more likely to be arrested and convicted for streetwalking. All black women were believed to be sexually immoral—potential prostitutes—and so were white women who accepted black men as customers. In the end, the ideological prohibition against black/white sexual relations not only subordinated black women and some white women within the culture of the vice districts, but also supplied a negative ideal against which the mainstream middle class defined the New Woman of the 1920s. Significantly, sexual racism operated to restrict opportunity for one group while it helped to "liberate" another group.

Men and women who desired sexual relations with members of their own gender were also relegated to the urban social margins. Recent scholarship demonstrated the ways in which a gendered, "gay" subculture developed, but race has not played a significant role in these discussions. If viewed from the relative effect of leisure institutions on sexual identities, it is possible to demonstrate that the predominant form of same-gender desire was influenced by the culture of the Black and Tans. Likewise, African-American culture, and black/white sexual relations in particular, influenced the emergence of a recognizably "homosexual" identity. One can push the interpretation too far, given the great extent to which gender shaped early-twentieth-century urban homosexuality, but we must take account of the ways in which race might have structured these formations. Racism and then sexual repression from without helped to forge cultural bonds between subordinated groups. It is also worth pointing out an obvious parallel between sexual racism and homophobia, even if ideologically the axes of oppression originate from two different social systems. In both sexual racism and homophobia, the center of the oppression is the stigmatization of people because of the nature or direction of their sexual desire.

By the 1920s, such figures as Carl Van Vechten had taken up the topic of black/white sexual relations, representing it to an ever-expanding audience. The gradual dispersion and circulation of ideas about black/white sexuality ushered in a new era of black artistic achievement. Tenuously connected to the new wave of white, van-guard elite artists and writers, black writers absorbed the interracial subculture and presented certain cultural forms and practices to an expanding audience. Such popular novels as *Nigger Heaven* and *Infants of the Spring* can be seen as literary guidebooks to the inter-zone. Indeed, they drew from and contributed to the structure of the modern travel guidebooks sold over the counter at drug stores and rental libraries. The sudden surge of interest in the Harlem books suggests a discursive departure in the trajectory of sexual racism. In the 1910s, the ideology of sexual racism operated to marginalize black/white sexual relations. Nonracist or racially liberal representa-tions were repressed. By the 1920s, however, as the popularity of *All God's Chillun'* demonstrates, such representations gained favor among elites, and then, with the rise of slumming, among more mainstream urbanites. In this instance, however, there was a kind of sexual racism involved in the production of black/white sexual cul-ture. What I am terming *pleasurable appropriation* through slum-ming represented a moment of circling back — of the original repres-sive sexual racism that created the zones transformed into produc-tive sexual racism. As the explosion of African-American culture bears witness, the subaltern responded — not simply surviving the oppression, but resisting through the creation of cultural practices. The quintessentially *modern* innovation in sexual racism was the sex-ualized appropriation — not the appreciation — of those practices. The modern (imperialist?) move, then, was to create the material conditions for the black/white vice zones and then to return to appropriate the formations that had been created within the urban colonies.

The increasing visibility of black/white sexual relations resulting from the modern appropriations, therefore, does not reveal racial progress (though it probably is true that for a minority of black peo-ple and intermarried couples involved with the forward-thinking modernists, the quality of life did improve). But the concluding chapter nevertheless demonstrates that social conservatism remained largely unchanged during the 1920s — that the era of Prohibition, despite the radical critiques from the margins, was pro-foundly reactionary. And, once again, social reaction in America turned to its cultural repertoire of interracial sexual imagery and symbols. If taken out of its historical context, the random effort to stop an intermarriage in an all-white town, or the lapse into prohibitive legislation, remains almost impossible to understand. Why so much effort to stop something that either never occurred or, if it did, was not a significant social threat? The answer can only be understood by examining the possible motives of the racial oppressors. And their motives can only be understood by examining the ideological conditions of 1920s America. The fact is that renewed fear of racial dilution and impurity represented a generalized reaction against urban cultural change. For some people, the absolute evil of black/white marriage was the last bastion of moral consensus.

More than the occasional symbolic protest, the modern antimiscegenation impulse illustrated a significant historical trend in black/white relations since the turn of the century. On the whole, most black/white marriages were between black men and white women. It should not be a surprise, then, that when asked about their experiences with prejudice, black/white couples reported that white men and black women were hostile to their relationships. White people did not want to risk racial dilution—and, hence, cultural and economic privilege—through intermarriage. So they attempted to stop it.

The black response requires a different historical explanation, one provided implicitly by the stories retold in this book. By the 1920s, black/white marriage had become a politicized social issue in black communities. Intermarriage was strenuously discouraged. But African-American rejection of intermarriage also reflected resistance to black/white sexual relations in general—and, by the late 1920s, black/white relations in Harlem or South Side Chicago actually represented a form of cultural imperialism. It may well be that the internal regulation of interracial marriage derives from a specific community memory. The movement of prostitution, gambling, and saloons to black neighborhoods was the result of a particular reform politics, a specific racist policy on regulating vice. The nightly parade of wealthy and avaricious whites traveling to Harlem to take in a show was but another spectacle of sexual racism. Relying on this community memory of violation, some African-Americans resented black/white sexual relations and intermarriage. The unfortunate problem is that such anger, when vented at intermarried couples, was misdirected, and the concept of *misdirection* does not adequately describe the phenomenon, because the African-American response was culturally overdetermined. Black/white sexuality became the surface imagery in a cultural system that African-Americans did not create. At moments of racial crisis—when Americans were poised on the precipice of a battle over political, material, and cultural resources—engaging the intermarriage issue probably only served the interests of white people in power.

And for the stigmatized and dispossessed, life in the interzones continued.

★

NOTES

Introduction

1. James Hugo Johnston, "Race Relations in Virginia and Miscegenation in the South," Ph.D. diss., University of Chicago, 1937, p. 37; David M. Fowler, *Northern Attitudes Toward Interracial Marriage: Legislation and Public Opinion in the Middle Atlantic and States of the Old Northwest, 1780–1930* (New York: Garland, 1988); Albert Ernest Jenkes, "The Legal Status of Negro-White Amalgamation in the United States," *American Journal of Sociology* 21 (Winter 1928): 667–70; Robert Sickels, *Race, Marriage, and Law* (New York: Basic Books, 1972), p. 32; Joel A. Rogers, *Sex and Race: History of White, Negro, Indian Miscegenation in the Two Americas,* 3 vols. (New York: J. A. Rogers Publ., 1940-42); Louis Wirth and Herbert Goldhammer, "The Hybrid and the Problem of Miscegenation," in Otto Kleinberg, ed., *Characteristics of the American Negro* (New York: Harper and Brothers, 1944); Carl Degler, *Neither Black Nor White: Slavery and Race Relations in Brazil and the United States* (New York: Oxford University Press, 1971); Harry Hoetnik, *Slavery and Race Relations in the Americas: An Inquiry in Their Nature and Nexus* (New York: Oxford University Press, 1973); George Fredrickson, *White Supremacy: A Comparative Study of*

American and South African History (New York: Oxford University Press, 1982); Joel Williamson, *The New People: Miscegenation and Mulattoes in the United States* (New York: The Free Press, 1980); John German Mencke, "The Mulatto and Race Mixture, 1877–1914," Ph.D. diss., University of North Carolina, 1976; Leonard Lemple, "The Mulatto and Race Relations in the United States, 1800–1940," Ph.D. diss., Syracuse University, 1982; Paul Spickard, *Mixed Blood: Ethnic Mixture and Identity in Twentieth-Century America* (Madison: University of Wisconsin, 1989); Patricia Morton, "From Invisible Man to 'New People': The Recent Discovery of American Mulattoes," *Phylon* (1985): 106–22; James Kinney, *Amalgamation!: Race, Sex, and Rhetoric in the Nineteenth-Century Novel* (Westport, Conn.: Greenwood, 1985); Judith Berzon, *Neither White Nor Black: The Mulatto Character in American Fiction* (New York: Garland, 1975); Bruce Payton Adams, "The White Negro: The Image of the Passable Mulatto Character in Black Novels, 1853–1954," Ph.D. diss., University of Kansas, 1976; Robert Brent Toplin, "Between Black and White: Attitudes Toward Southern Mulattoes, 1830–1861," *Journal of Southern History* 45, 2 (1979): 185–200.

2. St. Clair Drake and Horace Cayton, *Black Metropolis: A Study of Negro Life in a Northern City* (New York: Harcourt, Brace, 1945); Gunnar Myrdal, *An American Dilemma* (New York: Harcourt, Brace, 1942), p. 57.

3. Myrdal, *American Dilemma*, p. 59; James Weldon Johnson, *Along This Way* (New York: New American Library, 1987); Winthrop Jordan, *White Over Black: American Attitudes Toward the Negro, 1550–1812* (New York: Oxford, 1968); Calvin Hernton, *Sex and Racism* (New York: Oxford, 1967); Charles Stember, *Sexual Racism: An Emotional Barrier to an Integrated Society* (New York: Greenwood, 1972).

4. On constructionist historiography more generally, see John D'Emilio and Estelle B. Freedman, *Intimate Matters: A History of Sexuality in America* (New York: Harper and Row, 1988); Joan Scott, *Gender and the Politics of History* (New York: Columbia University Press, 1990); Joan Scott, "The Evidence of Experience," in Henry Abelove et al., eds., *The Lesbian and Gay Studies Reader* (New York: Routledge, 1992).

5. Cornel West, "New Cultural Politics of Difference," in Russell Ferguson et al., *Out There: Marginalization and Contemporary Cultures (Cambridge: MIT Press, 1990)*; Barbara J. Fields, "Ideology and Race in American History," in J. Morgan Kousser and James M. McPherson, eds., *Region, Race, and Reconstruction* (New York: Oxford, 1982); George M. Fredrickson, *The Arrogance of Race: Essays on Slavery, Racism, and Social Inequality* (Middletown, Conn.: Wesleyan University Press, 1988); Henry Louis Gates, Jr., ed., *Race, Writing, and Difference* (Chicago: University of Chicago Press, 1986); Werner Sollors, *Beyond Ethnicity: Consent and Descent in American Culture* (New York: Oxford, 1986).

6. Once the notion of the construction of race gained favor, numerous studies on the science and literature of race appeared. I take ideology to be those ideas that, first, attain relatively high levels of dispersion and, second, ideas that get enforced. The rise of racial biology is a discursive event; the production of the Mann Act and prosecution of Jack Johnson, and the media coverage, is an ideological event. The resulting panics are psychological results of ideological phenomena.

7. Alan H. Spear, *Black Chicago: The Making of a Negro Ghetto, 1890–1920* (Chicago: University of Chicago Press, 1967), p. 16; James R. Grossman, *Land of Hope: Chicago, Black Southerners, and the Great Migration* (Chicago: University of Chicago Press, 1989); Gilbert Osofsky, *Harlem: The Making of a Ghetto; Negro New York, 1890–1930* (New York: Harper, 1965), pp. 18, 130; Kenneth Kusmer, *A Ghetto Takes Shape: Black Cleveland, 1870–1930* (Urbana: University of Illinois Press, 1976), pp. 37–39.

8. Daniel Scott Smith, "The Dating of the American Sexual Revolution: Evidence and Interpretation," in Michael Gordon, ed., *The American Family in Social and Historical Perspective* (New York: St. Martin's, 1973); Christina Simmons, "Modern Sexuality and the Myth of Victorian Repression," in Kathy Peiss and Christina Simmons, eds., *Passion and Power: Sexuality in History* (Philadelphia: Temple University Press, 1989), pp. 157–77; Kevin J. Mumford, " 'Lost Manhood' Found: Male Sexual Impotence and Victorian Culture in the United States," *Journal of the History of Sexuality* 3 (July 1992): 33–57.

1. Jack Johnson and the Abolition of White Slavery

1. Wisconsin Teasdale Commission, Milwaukee, Wis., Investigator Report, box 18, p. 10.

2. Benjamin Savitch, "The Well-Planned Riot of October 21, 1835: Utica's Answer to Abolitionism," *New York History* 50 (3): 251–63; Linda Kerber, "Abolitionists and Amalgamators: The New York City Race Riots of 1834," *New York History* 48 (1967): 28–39; William S. McFeely, *Frederick Douglass* (New York: Norton, 1991), pp. 380–82; Waldo E. Martin, Jr., *The Mind of Frederick Douglass* (Chapel Hill: University of North Carolina Press, 1984), p. 221.

3. On repeal of laws in the North in the nineteenth century, see David M. Fowler, *Northern Attitudes Toward Interracial Marriage: Legislation and Public Opinion in the Middle Atlantic and the States of the Old Northwest, 1780–1930* (New York: Garland, 1988); Martin, *The Mind of Frederick Douglass*, p. 217.

4. The best treatment of Johnson and issues of racial mixture is Al-Tony Gilmore, *Bad Nigger!: The National Impact of Jack Johnson* (Port Washington, N.Y.: Kennikat Press, 1975); Randy Roberts, *Papa Jack: Jack Johnson and the Era of White Hopes* (New York: Free Press, 1983); Finnis Farr, *Black Champion: The Life and Times of Jack Johnson* (London: Macmillan, 1965); for focused studies of the social response to Johnson, see Raymond Wilson, "Another White Hope

Bites the Dust: The Jack Johnson–Jim Flynn Heavyweight Fight of 1912," *Montana: The Magazine of History* 29 (1979): 30–39; Randy Roberts, "Heavyweight Champion Jack Johnson: His Omaha Image, a Public Reaction Study," *Nebraska History* 52 (1976): 226–41.

5. On Gans, see Gilmore, *Bad Nigger!*, pp. 10–13.

6. Ibid., p. 88. Riots broke out across the country, including New York City, Little Rock, Philadelphia, Cincinnati, St. Louis, Houston, Pittsburgh, St. Joseph, Charleston, Roanoke, and New Orleans. See *St. Paul Pioneer Press*, July 5, 1910, p. 2.

7. *St. Paul Pioneer Press*, June 23, 1910, p. 7.

8. *St. Paul Pioneer Press*, November 27, 1910, p. 3.

9. Gilmore, *Bad Nigger!*, p. 15; *Chicago Defender*, November 23, 1912; on Johnson's ostentatious and brash manner, see *Pittsburgh Courier*, October 14, 1911, p.1.

10. *Chicago Defender*, September 14, 1912, p. 1.

11. Gilmore, *Bad Nigger!*, p. 89. Also see Adam Clayton Powell's response: "The overwhelming majority of colored people have no sympathy whatever with Johnson in his inordinate and persistent desire to seek female companionship with the whites" (quoted in ibid., p. 100).

12. *St. Paul Pioneer Press*, October 19, 1912, pp. 1, 3, reported for Chicago, October 18, 1910; *Chicago Defender*, August 24, 1913, p. 2; Finnis Farr, *Black Champion*, p. 86.

13. *Chicago Defender*, October 26, 1912, p. 1; *The New York Age* (November 30, 1912) argued that there was "no evidence against Jack Johnson. The whole thing was a frame up on account of color."

14. Jack Johnson, *Jack Johnson—In the Ring and Out* (Chicago: National Sports, 1927), p. 68; *Chicago Defender*, July 13, 1912.

15. *Baltimore Afro-American*, November 23, 1912, p. 6; *Chicago Defender*, July 13, 1912, p. 1; in his own words, the Café de Champion was a "place where the races had an opportunity to come in contact." See Johnson, *In the Ring and Out*, p. 68.

16. Gilmore, *Bad Nigger!*, p.106; NAACP Collection on "Intermarriage," file 1913.

17. The states were Illinois, Indiana, Iowa, Ohio, Kansas, Nebraska, New York, Pennsylvania, Washington, and Wisconsin. See Albert Ernest Jenkes, "The Legal Status of Negro-White Amalgamation in the United States," *American Journal of Sociology* 21 (Winter 1928): 669. According to Johnson, "Countless other efforts were made to charge me with various crimes by Mrs. Cameron and others who were interested in the situation." See Johnson, *In the Ring and Out*, p. 80.

18. Gilmore, *Bad Nigger!*, p. 118.

19. Charges included prostitution, debauchery, unlawful sexual intercourse,

and crimes against nature. See Finis Farr, *Black Champion: The Life and Times of Jack Johnson* (London: Macmillan, 1964), p. 68.

20. Johnson, *In the Ring and Out*, p. 161.

21. Gilmore, *Bad Nigger!*, p. 112.

22. See, for example, *Chicago Defender*, May 10, 1913, p. 1.

23. *Chicago Defender*, May 31, 1913.

24. *Chicago Defender*, July 15, 1913, p. 1.

25. Johnson, *In the Ring and Out*, p. 83.

26. Al-Tony Gilmore, "Jack Johnson and White Women: The National Impact," *Journal of Negro History* 58 (1973): 18–38.

27. *The Pittsburgh Courier*, September 15, 1923, p. 1.

28. *Chicago Defender*, March 4, 1920, p. 3.

29. Mary Ellen Odem, "Delinquent Daughters: The Sexual Regulation of Female Minors in the United States, 1880–1920" (Ph.D. diss., University of California at Berkeley, 1989).

30. NAACP Collection, Correspondence, January 7, 1921, Intermarriage File.

31. *Milwaukee Sentinel*, December 11, 1920, p. 1.

32. NAACP Collection, Intermarriage File, Correspondence from Charles Bentley, 1921.

33. NAACP Collection, Intermarriage File, from C. G. Martin, file 1920, December 31, 1920.

34. Martha Hodes, "The Sexualization of Reconstruction Politics: White Women and Black Men after the Civil War," in John C. Fout and Maura Shaw Tantillo, eds., *American Sexual Politics: Sex, Gender, and Race Since the Civil War* (Chicago: University of Chicago Press, 1992), pp. 68–69.

35. On white slavery, see Ernest A. Bell, ed., *Fighting the Traffic in Young Girls, or War on the White Slave Trade* (New York: G. S. Ball, 1910); "The White Slave Decision," *Literary Digest* 46 (1913): 500–502; "White Slave Revelations," *Current Literature* 47 (December 1909): 594–98; "White Slaves," *Outlook* 103 (1913): 569–70; "The White Slave Traffic," *Outlook* 95 (1910): 544–46; Brand Whitlock, "The White Slave Trade," *Forum* 51 (1914): 193–216; "The Futility of the White Slave Agitation as Brand Whitlock Sees It," *Current Opinion* 56 (1914): 287–88; Emma Goldman, "The Traffic in Women," in *The Traffic in Women and Other Essays on Feminism* (New York: Times Change Reprint, 1970); Edward Janney, *The White Slave Traffic in America* (New York: National Vigilance Committee, 1911); Clifford Roe, *The Girl Who Disappeared* (Chicago: American Bureau of Moral Education, 1914); Clifford Roe, *Panders and Their White Slaves* (New York: Fleming Revell, 1910).

36. An excellent treatment of white slavery in England is Judith Walkowitz, *City of Dreadful Delight: Narratives of Sexual Danger in Late-Victorian London* (Chicago: University of Chicago Press, 1992), pp. 102–15, 132–34.

37. The evil procurer of white slaves often were cast as "racial others," dis-

tinguished by their dark complexions and foreign manners. To an extent, these images were probably meant to represent recently arrived immigrants from Eastern and southern Europe. Connelly compares the structure of the white slave narrative with Indian captivity tales. See Connelly, *Response to Prostitution*, pp. 60–63, 149; for significance of white slave tracts to prostitution, see Ruth Rosen, *The Lost Sisterhood: Prostitution in America, 1900–1918* (Baltimore: The Johns Hopkins University Press, 1982), p. 117; Timothy Gilfoyle, *City of Eros: New York City, Prostitution, and the Commercialization of Sex, 1790–1920* (New York: Norton, 1992), pp. 270–83.

38. Katherine Lineham, "Vicious Circle: Prostitution Reform and Public Policy in Chicago, 1830–1930," Ph.D. diss., Notre Dame University, 1991, p. 150.

39. For examples see the *New York Times*, July 4, 1926, p. 2; the *Pittsburgh Courier*, July 16, 1923, p. 1.

40. *Social Evil in Chicago: A Study of Existing Conditions*, Vice Commission of Chicago, 1911, pp. 38–39, 41, 219.

41. *The National Purity Congress* (1896; reprint, New York: Arno, 1969), pp. 328–31.

42. Ibid.

43. Ibid., pp. 174–75.

44. Ibid., p. 178.

45. George Kneeland, *Commercialized Prostitution in New York City* (New York: Century, 1913), pp. 118, 123.

46. Kneeland, *Commercialized Prostitution in New York City*, p. 199.

47. *Chicago Defender*, November 16, 1912.

48. *Chicago Defender*, December 14, 1912.

49. Quoted in Gilmore, *Bad Nigger!*, p. 122.

50. *Chicago Defender*, December 14, 1912.

51. David J. Langum, *Crossing over the Line: Legislating Morality and the Mann Act* (Chicago: University of Chicago Press, 1994).

2. Interzones 1: Transforming Urban Geography

1. *Annual Report of the Committee of Fourteen*, 1911, p. 2; *Annual Report of the Committee of Fourteen*, 1912, p. 14; on the end of Raines Law hotels, see *Annual Report of the Committee of Fourteen*, 1914, p. 12; for background, see Jeremy P. Felt, "Vice Reform as a Political Technique: The Committee of Fifteen in New York, 1900–1901," *New York History* 54 (1973): 24–51; New York City, Research Committee of the Committee of Fourteen for the Suppression of "Raines Law Hotels." *The Social Evil in New York City: A Study in Law Enforcement* (New York: Andrew H. Kellog, 1910).

2. *Annual Report of the Committee of Fourteen*, 1914, p. 5.

3. Ibid., 1916, p. 9; for an overview of Committee of Fourteen history, see ibid., 1924, pp. 7–9. Historians argue that St. Louis was the only city to accept

★

formal regulation, which meant the registration of prostitutes. Informal regulation—the toleration of prostitution within the boundaries of specific neighborhoods—characterized police policy toward prostitution before the rise of the antiprostitution movement (see Lineham, "Vicious Circle," p. 14).

4. Roland R. Wagner, "Virtue Against Vice: A Study of Moral Reformers and Prostitution in the Progressive Era," Ph.D. diss., University of Wisconsin, 1971, p. 214; Lineham, "Vicious Circle," pp. 205, 265; Willoughby Waterman, *The Repression of Prostitution in New York, 1900–1931* (New York: Columbia University Press, 1932), p. 95; New York Committee of Fourteen, ms., correspondence, box 96.

5. Herbert Asbury, *Gem of the Prairie: An Informal History of the Chicago Underworld* (DeKalb: Northern Illinois University Press, 1941), p. 286.

6. Vice districts were closed in cities around the country: Atlanta, 1912; Baltimore, 1915; Bay City, 1913; Bridgeport, 1915; Chicago, 1912; Cleveland, 1915; Denver, 1913; Elmira, 1913; Grand Rapids, 1912; Hartford, 1912; Honolulu, 1917; Kansas City, 1913; Lancaster, 1914; Lexington, 1915; Little Rock, 1913; Minneapolis, 1913; Newark, 1917; New York City, 1916; Philadelphia, 1913; Pittsburgh, 1914; Portland, 1915; Richmond, 1914; St. Louis, 1914; Shreveport, 1917; Springfield, 1915; Syracuse, 1913; and Toledo, 1913.

7. *Annual Report of the Committee of Fourteen*, 1924, p. 10.

8. Asbury, *Gem of the Prairie*, p. 310; Committee of Fourteen, manuscript copy of *Annual Report*, box 96, 1916; quoted in Waterman, *Repression of Prostitution in New York*, p. 135; Lineham, "Vicious Circle," p. 40.

9. *Annual Report of the Committee of Fifteen*, 1923, p. 23; on Chicago, see Richard Linberg, *To Serve and Collect: Chicago Politics and Police Corruption from the Lager Beer Riot to the Summerdale Scandal* (New York: Praeger, 1991), pp. 129–30; on legal repression of streetwalking, see Waterman, *Repression of Prostitution in New York*, p.55.

10. Wagner, "Virtue Against Vice," p. 65.

11. On the scattering to middle-class areas in mid-nineteenth-century New York, see Gilfoyle, *City of Eros*, pp. 116–18; Lineham, "Vicious Circle," p. 43; Wagner, "Virtue Against Vice," p. 83.

12. *Annual Report of the Committee of Fifteen*, 1918–19, p. 14. Some prostitution reemerged in the Chicago suburbs of Cicero and Burnham (Linberg, *To Serve and Collect*, p. 134). On roadhouses, see Walter Reckless, *Vice in Chicago* (Chicago: University of Chicago Press, 1933), pp. 126–28, 134–35.

13. On segregated vice in northern cities, see Julius F. Nimmons, "Social Reform and Moral Uplift in the Black Community: Social Settlements, Temperance, and Social Purity," Ph.D. diss., Howard University, 1991, p. 238; Wagner, "Virtue Against Vice," p. 265.

14. Waterman, *Repression of Prostitution in New York*, p. 123. According to Wallace Thurman, "The first place in New York where Negroes had a segregated community was in Greenwich Village, but as the years passed and their

numbers increased they soon moved northward into the twenties and lower thirties west of South Avenue until they finally made one big jump and centered around West Fifty-third Street" (*Negro Life in Harlem*, pp. 13–14).

15. Thurman, *Negro Life*, pp. 141, 124. In the 1950s Times Square had become a full-fledged tourist attraction. See Lloyd Morris, *Incredible New York: High Life and Low Life of the Last Hundred Years* (New York: Random House, 1951), p. 295.

16. Asbury, *Gem of the Prairie*, p. 102.

17. William Howland Kenney, *Chicago Jazz: A Cultural History, 1904–1930* (New York: Oxford University Press, 1993), p. 14; Asbury, *Gem of the Prairie*, p. 247.

18. Kenney, *Chicago Jazz*, p. 14; Asbury, *Gem of the Prairie*, p. 299; John Drury, *Chicago in Seven Days* (New York: McBride, 1928), p. 149; Reckless, *Vice in Chicago*, p. 194.

19. On racial segregation of neighborhoods, see Thomas Lee Philpott, *The Slum and the Ghetto: Neighborhood Deterioration and Middle-Class Reform, Chicago, 1880–1930* (New York: Oxford University Press, 1978), pp. 122–23; Gilbert Osofsky, *Harlem: The Making of a Ghetto, 1890–1930* (New York: Harper, 1965); E. Franklin Frazier, *The Negro Family in Chicago* (Chicago: University of Chicago Press, 1932), p. 95. In 1914 white leaders had mounted a campaign to wipe out vice in St. Louis. However, Reverend Brandt (a black community leader) "discovered that a number of these lewd women had taken up residence in the fashionable West End, in the neighborhood of their church." In response, several black leaders initiated a "Campaign Against Vice." According to an article that appeared in the *Chicago Defender*, the reverend and his congregation "began a systematic campaign to rid the district of the undesirable characters." In the process they learned that "some of them (white prostitutes) have secured flats in and bordering on portions of the city where members of the race live." The most alarming development, however, was their "invasion of the quasi-questionable resorts, 'buffet flats,' where they nightly pl[ied] their trade" (*Chicago Defender*, October 14, 1916, p. 3).

20. Wagner, "Virtue Against Vice," pp. 80, 134, 166; *Annual Report of the Committee of Fourteen*, 1914, p. 19: "The problem of the negro resorts is still a pressing one, there being a considerable number located in the heart of the colored colony at 135th Street [Harlem]." Another excerpt also acknowledges black clubs but then distinguishes them from the few black/white clubs: "The negroes, too, had their resorts. On 37th Street, the most popular being known as 'Digg's' and 'Herbert's' while on 28th over a stable was the infamous 'Douglas Club.' On 35th street was 'Baron Wilkin's,' catering to both races and sexes while on Cornelia and Bleeker were places which had not as yet been entirely closed and whose chief attraction was perversion."

21. Some black leaders apparently protested Committee of Fourteen interference with local establishments (*Annual Report of the Committee of Fourteen*

[1914], p. 15); increasingly, however, committee members set up meetings with local community leaders to allay these and other concerns (*Annual Report of the Committee of Fourteen*, 1916, p. 58).

22. Two studies in particular have shaped my understanding of prohibition: John Allen Krout, *The Origins of Prohibition* (New York: Knopf, 1925); John J. Rumbarger, *Profits, Power, and Prohibition: Alcohol Reform and the Industrializing of America, 1800–1930* (Albany: State University of New York, 1989); on prostitution and alcohol, see Waterman, *Repression of Prostitution in New York*, p. 134.

23. Quoted in Timothy J. Gilfoyle, *City of Eros: New York City, Prostitution, and the Commercialization of Sex, 1790–1920* (New York: Norton, 1992), p. 38. Residents reported observing white women in bed with black men, especially in Five Points.

24. Ibid., p. 41.

25. David Nasaw, *Going Out: The Rise and Fall of Public Amusements* (New York: Basic Books, 1993), p. 118.

26. Luc Sante, *Low Life: Lures and Snares of Old New York* (New York: Farrar Straus Giroux, 1991).

27. *New York Age*, May 30, 1915, p. 4.

28. *Pittsburgh Courier*, November 17, 1923, p. 1.

29. William H. Jones, *Recreation and Amusement among Negroes in Washington D.C.* (Washington, D.C.: Howard University Press, 1928), p. 194.

30. Quoted in Kenney, *Chicago Jazz*, p. 19.

31. *Pittsburgh Courier*, October 17, 1923, p. 1; J. A. Rogers, *Sex and Race: A History of Miscegenation in the Two Americas*, vol. 2 (New York: J. A. Rogers Publ., 1942), pp. 289–90.

32. *Baltimore Afro-American*, April 10, 1920.

33. Ernest Burgess Collection, box 6, folder 8, June 11, 1934.

34. *New York Age*, March 8, 1924, p. 4.

35. *Baltimore Afro-American*, April 10, 1920.

36. *Annual Report of the Committee of Fifteen*, 1923, p. 12. Black dancing was seen as synonymous with sexuality; see, for example, Committee of Fourteen, ms., Investigative Report, box 31, July 9, 1921, p. 2.

37. Quoted in *Annual Report of the Committee of Fifteen*, 1923, p. 12.

38. *Pittsburgh Courier*, January 18, 1923, p. 1.

39. *New York Age*, July 4, 1923, p. 1.

40. *Pittsburgh Courier*, January 18, 1923, p. 1.

41. Kenney, *Chicago Jazz*, p. 26.

42. *New York Age*, July 4, 1923, p. 1.

43. *Pittsburgh Courier*, October 4, 1925.

44. *Pittsburgh Courier*, October 26, 1929, p. 1.

45. *Pittsburgh Courier*, August 13, 1927, p. 3.

46. *Annual Report of the Committee of Fifteen*, 1922, pp. 6–7.

47. Even before Prohibition, local attempts to control liquor had the "contrary effect" on prostitution (Waterman, *Repression of Prostitution in New York*, p. 31; *Annual Report of the Committee of Fourteen*, 1924, p. 24).

48. *Annual Report of the Committee of Fourteen*, 1928, p. 13.

49. Committee of Fourteen, ms., Summary of Investigations, box 96, July 22, 1931.

50. Police used the technique of entrapment before World War I (see Hobson, *Uneasy Virtue*, p. 160; Committee of Fourteen, ms., Investigative Report, box 30, April 29, 1916).

51. Morris, *Incredible New York*, pp. 324–26. Because of the secretive nature of speakeasies, investigators reported difficulties in investigating various establishments (Committee of Fourteen, ms., Investigative Report, box 27).

52. Committee of Fourteen, box 29, Investigative Report, November 21, 1915.

53. Committee of Fourteen, ms., Investigative Report, box 30, August 31, 1916.

54. *Annual Report of the Committee of Fourteen*, 1926, p. 24. Waterman noted that in every case of eighty-five speakeasies visited, black and white customers were present (*Repression of Prostitution in New York*, p. 129). In New York, for example, the clubs passed from black to Italian ownership during Prohibition. I have not found extensive evidence detailing Mafia or criminal underworld involvement in the underground, interracial speakeasy scene (see Federal Writers' Project, *New York Panorama: The American Guide* (New York: Random House, 1938), p. 140).

55. *Annual Report of the Committee of Fourteen*, 1929, p. 13.

3. Interzones 2: Reform and Representation

1. Committee of Fourteen, ms., unpublished report of Women's Court, box 89, June 1924.

2. Ibid.

3. Walter Reckless, *Vice in Chicago* (Chicago: University of Chicago Press, 1933), p. 47.

4. Lineham, "Vicious Circle," p. 294.

5. Committee of Fourteen, ms., unpublished report of Women's Court, box 89, June 1924.

6. Ibid.

7. Waterman, *Repression of Prostitution in New York*, p. 57. On black soliciting in Chicago, see correspondence from Charles Miner to Committee of Fifteen, Ernest Burgess Collection, box 6, folder 6, April 10, 1930; on police difficulty in monitoring Harlem, see *Annual Report of Committee of Fourteen*, 1928, pp. 3–5. These statistics must be interpreted through the lens of race because evidence indicates that black women were more likely to be convicted of prostitution than white women. In 1922, for example, the Committee of Fourteen compared conviction rates for that year among three groups of women

and found that 79 percent of native white women, 74 percent of immigrant women, and 81 percent of black women were convicted of prostitution (*Annual Report of the Committee of Fourteen*, 1922, p. 16).

8. Joan Scott, *Gender and the Politics of History* (New York: Columbia University Press, 1990), p. 115.

9. *Annual Report of the Committee of Fourteen*, 1927, p. 21.

10. William Acton, *Prostitution* (1857; reprint, New York: Praeger, 1968), pp. 117–18, 136–37; William Sanger, *History of Prostitution* (1859; reprint, New York: Arno, 1972); Jane Addams, *A New Conscience and an Ancient Evil* (New York: MacMillan, 1913), p. 68; Rosen, *The Lost Sisterhood*, pp. 143, 162.

11. Julius Rosenwald Collection, correspondence from Alfred K. Stern to Charles Miner, October 17, 1930, box 11, folder 10.

12. *Annual Report of the Committee of Fifteen*, 1928, p. 14; *Annual Report of the Committee of Fourteen*, 1923, p. 12; Clinton P. McCord, "One Hundred Female Offenders: A Study of the Mentality of Prostitutes and 'Wayward' Girls," *Journal of the American Institute of Criminal Law and Criminology* 6 (1915–16): 385–407; Lineham, "Vicious Circle," p. 288; Waterman, *Repression of Prostitution in New York*, p. 119; Nimmons, "Social Reform and Moral Uplift," p. 237.

13. Juvenile Protective Agency, ms., file 128, Louise De Koven Bowen, *The Colored People of Chicago* (1913).

14. Reckless, *Vice in Chicago*, p. 29; Waterman, *Repression of Prostitution in New York*, p. 128; E. Franklin Frazier, *The Negro Family in Chicago* (Chicago: University of Chicago Press, 1930).

15. Quoted in Waterman, *Repression of Prostitution in New York*, p. 130; Rosen, *The Lost Sisterhood*, p. 141.

16. Hobson, *Uneasy Virtue*, pp. 35, 40, 88–91; Lineham, "Vicious Circle," p. 117.

17. Marilyn Wood Hill, *Their Sisters' Keepers: Prostitution in New York City, 1830–1870* (Berkeley: University of California Press, 1993), pp. 53–54; Lineham, "Vicious Circle," p. 39.

18. Lineham, "Vicious Circle," p. 171.

19. Ibid., pp. 22–26; Hobson, *Uneasy Virtue*, chap. 4; Regina G. Kunzel, *Fallen Women, Problem Girls: Unmarried Mothers and the Professionalization of Social Work, 1890–1945* (New Haven: Yale University Press, 1993), p. 11; Judith Lee Vaupen Joseph, "The Nakfeh and the Lady: Jews, Prostitutes, and Progressives in New York City, 1900–1930," Ph.D. diss., State University of New York, Stony Brook, 1986, p. 15; Edward Bristow, *Prostitution and Prejudice: The Jewish Fight against White Slavery, 1870–1939* (New York: Schocken Books, 1983).

20. *Annual Report of the Committee of Fourteen*, 1928, pp. 3–5; Committee of Fourteen, ms., box 7, September 18, 1929, from Bascom Johnson, Director of Legal and Protective Measures, American Social Hygiene Association (ASHA), to George Worthington; Committee of Fourteen, ms., box 7 September 28, 1929,

correspondence, from George Worthington, to Bascom Johnson; on ASHA, see Estelle B. Freedman, " 'Uncontrolled Desires': The Response to the Sexual Psychopath, 1920–1960," in Kathy Peiss and Christina Simmons, eds., *Passion and Power: Sexuality in History* (Philadelphia: Temple University Press, 1989).

21. Peggy Pascoe, *Relations of Rescue: The Search for Moral Authority in the American West, 1874–1939* (New York: Oxford University Press, 1990), pp. 198, 201, 207; Lineham, "Vicious Circle," p. 128.

22. Kunzel, *Fallen Women, Problem Girls*, pp. 17–18; for the evidence on the Salvation Army and the Juvenile Protection Agency, see *Chicago Tribune*, January 25, 1923, p. 3.

23. Kunzel, *Fallen Women, Problem Girls*, p. 13.

24. Nimmons, "Social Reform and Moral Uplift," pp. 104–5, 109, 247; on black settlements, see Thomas Lee Philpott, *The Slum and the Ghetto: Neighborhood Deterioration and Middle-Class Reform, Chicago, 1880–1930* (New York: Oxford University Press, 1978), pp. 316, 320–24.

25. Nimmons, "Social Reform and Moral Uplift," pp. 61, 95, 101, 105, 212, 222; Philpott, *The Slum and the Ghetto*, pp. 320–21.

26. Nimmons, "Social Reform and Moral Uplift," p. 115.

27. Christina Simmons, "African Americans and Sexual Victorianism in the Social Hygiene Movement, 1910–1940," *Journal of the History of Sexuality* 4, no. 1 (1993): 59.

28. Dorothy Salem, *To Better Our World: Black Women in Organized Reform, 1890–1920* (Brooklyn, N.Y.: Carlson, 1990), pp. 139, 140, 141, 182.

29. Nimmons, "Black Moral Reform," pp. 48, 240–44; Simmons, "African Americans and Sexual Victorianism," p. 61; National Association of Colored Women, *Lifting as They Climb*. Phyllis Wheatley homes, founded first by Jane Edna Hunter in Cleveland, reportedly served as a model of black female reform, and could be found in other cities. We do not know yet how they operated—and there is no evidence that they extended their services to prostitutes. On black female reform or philanthropy, see Darlene Clark Hine, " 'We Specialize in the Wholly Impossible': The Philanthropic Work of Black Women," in Clark Hine, *HineSight: Black Women and the Reconstruction of American History* (Brooklyn, N.Y.: Carlson, 1994), p. 120.

30. Salem, *To Better Our World*; Simmons, "African Americans and Sexual Victorianism," pp. 51–75; Evelyn Brooks Higginbotham, "African-American Women's History and the Metalanguage of Race," *Signs* 17, no. 2 (1992): 271–73; Dorothy Sterling, *We Are Your Sisters: Black Women in the Nineteenth Century* (New York: Norton, 1984), p. 352.

4. Leisure and Sexual Racism: In-between Men in the Dance Halls

1. Paul Cressey, *The Taxi-Dance Hall* (Chicago: University of Chicago Press, 1932), pp. ix–x.

★

2. The classic statement of dance halls as pluralistic institutions is in Russell B. Nye, "Saturday Night at the Paradise Ballroom: Or Dance Halls in the Twenties," *Journal of Popular Culture* 7 (Summer 1973): 14–22.

3. On institutionalized racism, see Robert Blauner, *Racial Oppression in America* (New York: Harper and Row, 1972), pp. 184–93.

4. For sketches of the concert saloon, see Luc Sante, *Low Life: Lures and Snares of Old New York* (New York: Farrar Straus Giroux, 1991), pp. 104–40; in 1873 the first concert saloon appeared in Chicago, in the black vice district (Asbury, *Gem of the Prairie*, p. 102).

5. Kathy Peiss, *Cheap Amusements: Working Women and Leisure in Turn-of-the-Century New York* (Philadelphia: Temple University Press, 1986); David Nasaw, *Going Out: The Rise and Fall of Public Amusements* (New York: Basic Books, 1993); Nye, "Saturday Night at the Paradise Ballroom," pp. 14–22; *Annual Report of the Committee of Fourteen*, 1930, p. 20; *Annual Report of the Committee of Fourteen*, 1927, p. 27.

6. Peiss, *Cheap Amusements*, p. 65; Cressey, *The Taxi-Dance Hall*, pp. 12–16; in turn, many of these clubs derived certain features from West Coast establishments. See Herbert Asbury, *The Barbary Coast* (New York: Knopf, 1933); Lewis Erenberg, *Steppin' Out: Leisure and the Transformation of New York City Nightlife* (Westport, Conn.: Greenwood, 1982), p. 45.

7. I want to thank Robert Orsi for this insight.

8. *Annual Report of the Committee of Fourteen*, 1927, p. 24.

9. Ibid., pp. 21–23, 25–27; Jessie Binford, "The Taxi-Dance Halls," *Journal of Social Hygiene* (December 1933): 502–509.

10. Cressey, *The Taxi-Dance Hall*, p. 210.

11. *Annual Report of the Committee of Fourteen*, 1930, p. 29.

12. In 1929 the committee noted the existence of halls catering "almost exclusively to Oriental." By 1930 the committee stated that the conditions in the dance halls "rivals anything existing in New York for a score of years." They refrained from describing the activities because such a description would be "pornographic." The incidence of Asian/white mixing and the new view of the taxi-dance hall clearly seem connected (*Annual Report of the Committee of Fourteen*, 1929, p. 48).

13. Cressey, *The Taxi-Dance Hall*, p. 109.

14. Ibid., pp. 181–86.

15. For an important analysis of treating in saloons as an example of worker consciousness, see Roy Rosenzweig, *Eight Hours for What We Will: Workers and Leisure in an Industrial City, 1870–1920* (Cambridge: Cambridge University Press, 1983).

16. Ernest Burgess Collection, box 192, folder 6, ca. 1925.

17. Ibid.

18. On the construction of whiteness as a social practice, see Mumford, "'Lost Manhood' Found," p. 89; David Roediger, *Wages of Whiteness: Race and the Making of the American Working Class* (London: Verso, 1991).

19. B. T. Catapusan, "Filipino Social Adjustment in the United States" Ph.D. diss., University of Southern California, 1940, p. 22.

20. Honorante Mariano, "Filipino Immigrants in the United States," Ph.D. diss., University of Oregon Press, 1933, pp. 18–23.

21. Ernest Burgess Collection, box 137, folder 1, January 1932.

22. Mariano, "Filipino Immigrants," p. 38. Mariano derived these and several other key theoretical concepts from the Chicago School.

23. Ernest Burgess Collection, box 129, folder 2, ca. 1930s.

24. Ibid., box 137, folder 1, January 30, 1932.

25. Cressey, *The Taxi-Dance Hall*, p. 123.

26. Ernest Burgess Collection, box 192, folder 6, 1925.

27. For the social history of Filipinos and the dance halls in California, see Ronald Takaki, *Strangers from a Different Shore: A History of Asian Americans* (Boston: Little, Brown, 1989), pp. 329–34.

28. Ernest Burgess Collection, box 192, folder 6, 1925.

29. Ibid. A white woman told an interviewer: "Even right here on the L if you were with a Filipino they'd all be staring at us. Now, nobody pays any attention to us" (Ernest Burgess Collection, box 134, folder 2, May 1, 1926).

30. Cressey, *The Taxi-Dance Hall*, p. 126; on Filipinos in Harlem, see Committee of Fourteen, mss., box 36, 1927; Ernest Burgess Collection, box 192, folder 6, February 20, 1926; Ernest Burgess Collection, box 192, folder 2.

31. Cressey, *The Taxi-Dance Hall*, p. 35.

32. For a good example of leisure and gender in historical perspective, see Peiss, *Cheap Amusements*, chap. 2; for a good overall analysis of capitalism and women's labor, see Susan Porter Benson, *Counter Cultures: Saleswomen, Managers, and Customers in American Department Stores, 1890–1940* (Urbana: University of Illinois Press, 1986).

33. The veteran dancers "played the racial prejudices against each other" (Cressey, *The Taxi-Dance Hall*, p. 99).

34. Ibid., pp. 44, 43.

35. Committee of Fourteen, ms., box 35 (November 17, 1924).

36. Ibid., box 36.

37. Ibid.

38. Catapusan, "Filipino Social Adjustment," p. 72.

39. Cressey, *The Taxi-Dance Hall*, p. 44.

40. Ernest Burgess Collection, box 134, folder 2, May 1, 1926; other examples include a statement from a woman comparing white and Filipino patrons: "She says that she will always stick up for the Filipinos, that they are about the only decent high class fellows that come to the hall" (see Ernest Burgess Collection, box 192, folder 6, April 17, 1926).

41. On the construction of nationalism, see Benedict Anderson, *Imagined Communities: Reflections on the Origin and Spread of Nationalism* (London: Verso, 1983).

★

42. On the social reception of Italians and the significance of color, see Robert Orsi, "The Religious Boundaries of an In-between People: Street *Feste* and the Problem of the Dark-Skinned Other in Italian Harlem," *American Quarterly* 44, no. 3 (September 1992): 313–47.

43. For a synthesis of shifts from a communal to continence to expression models of masculinity, see Kevin J. Mumford, " 'Lost Manhood' Found: Male Sexual Impotence and Victorian Culture in the United States," *Journal of the History of Sexuality* 36 (July 1992). For a more detailed discussion of mainstream masculinity, see Anthony Rotundo, *American Manhood: Transformations in Masculinity from the Revolution to the Modern Era* (New York: Basic Books, 1993).

44. David Roediger, *Wages of Whiteness*; Orsi, "Italian Harlem," p. 318.

45. For an excellent theorization of masculinity, race, and citizenship, see Eric Lott, *Love and Theft: Blackface Minstrelsy and the American Working Class* (New York: Oxford University Press, 1993), pp. 64–84, 105–7, 138–58. The dance hall hostesses were most often from the more Nordic areas, including Sweden, Holland, Germany, Belgium, and France. In Chicago there were also a significant number of Polish dance hostesses who had less prestige than the northern European, second-generation women (Cressey, *The Taxi-Dance Hall*, p. 56). A survey of case studies indicates that the majority of hostesses had northern European backgrounds (Cressey, *The Taxi-Dance Halls*, pp. 54–106).

46. Cressey, *The Taxi-Dance Hall*, p. 111. On Italian sexual hierarchy, see William Foote Whyte, "Sex Code of the Slums," *American Journal of Sociology* 49, no. 1 (July 1942): 25–27.

47. On Italian and Polish men wanting to assimilate, see Cressey, *The Taxi-Dance Hall*, pp. 112–14. Cressey generalized about the motives guiding Italian and Polish patrons. Given the "handicaps of language and culture," the immigrant "may become romantically interested in a taxi-dancer who is identified in his own mind as an 'American' " (ibid., p. 114). On Italian intermarriage in Chicago, see Humbert S. Nelli, *Italians in Chicago: A Study in Ethnic Mobility, 1880–1930* (New York: Oxford University Press, 1970).

48. Cressey, *The Taxi-Dance Hall*, p. 148.

49. Ibid., pp. 218–19.

50. Ibid.

51. Quoted in Kobena Mercer and Isaac Julien, "Race, Sexual Politics, and Black Masculinity: A Dossier," in Rowena Chapman and Jonathan Rutherford, eds., *Male Order: Unwrapping Masculinity* (London: Lawrence and Wishart, 1988), p. 112.

52. Richard Majors and Janet Mancini Billson, *Cool Pose: The Dilemmas of Black Masculinity* (New York: Lexington, 1992), p. 84.

53. Catapusan, "Filipino Social Adjustment," p. 74.

54. Cressey, *The Taxi-Dance Hall*, p. 244; Catapusan, "Filipino Social Adjustment," p. 75.

55. Stuart Hall and Tony Jefferson, eds., *Resistance Through Rituals: Youth Subcultures in Post-War Britain* (London: Hutchinson, 1976); Dick Hebdige, *Subculture: The Meaning of Style* (London: Methuen, 1979).

56. Cressey, *The Taxi-Dance Hall*, p. 219.

57. Ibid., p. 9.

5. Interracial Intersections:
Homosexuality and Black/White Relations

1. Blair Niles, *Strange Brother* (1931, London: GMP, 1990).

2. "Homosexual Interview," Ernest Burgess Collection, box 127, folder 8.

3. Although the *New York Times* reviewed some fourteen of Niles's previous novels, they refused to review *Strange Brother*, probably because of its sympathetic treatment of homosexuality. See Jonathan Ned Katz, *Gay/Lesbian Almanac: A New Documentary* (New York: Harper & Row, 1986), p. 468; on the survey of rental libraries, see Ernest Burgess Collection, ms., box 89, folder 11.

4. Ernest Burgess Collection, box 145, file 10 (ca. 1930s).

5. Greg Sprague, "On the 'Gay Side' of Town: The Nature and Structure of Male Homosexuality in Chicago, 1890–1935," p. 7 (unpublished manuscript); Jonathan Katz, *Gay American History: Lesbians and Gay Men in the U.S.A.* (New York: Thomas Crowell, 1976), pp. 80–81.

6. The Vice Commission of Chicago, *The Social Evil in Chicago* (Chicago: 1911), p. 127; Havelock Ellis quoted in Katz, *Gay American History*, pp. 80–81.

7. Katz, *Gay/Lesbian Almanac*, p. 307

8. Quoted in Katz, *Gay American History*, pp. 66–67.

9. Sprague, "On the 'Gay Side' of Town," pp. 13–15; Margaret Otis, "A Perversion Not Commonly Noted," *Journal of Abnormal Psychology* 8 (1913): 113–17; Katz, *Gay American History*, p. 75.

10. On interchange between racial and sexual science, see Siobhan Sommerville, "Scientific Racism and the Emergence of the Homosexual Body," *Journal of the History of Sexuality* 5, no. 2 (1994): 243–67.

11. Thus, in a discussion of public sexual activity, one Washington, D.C., authority reported that "under the very shadow of the White House," one could find inverts searching for partners. "Both white and black were represented among these moral hermaphrodites, but the majority of them were negroes" (see Katz, *Gay/Lesbian Almanac*, p. 234). William Jones argues that in Washington, D.C., commercial amusements and presumably sexual relations were strictly segregated. This was not the case with regard to same-sex relations; much of the evidence on such practices in Washington, D.C., indicates extensive racial mixing (see William H. Jones, *Commercial Amusements among Negroes in Washington, D.C.* [Washington, D.C.: Howard University Press, 1927]).

12. "Leo," Ernest Burgess Collection, box 98, folder 11, pp. 1, 12–15.

13. See Katz, *Gay American History*, pp. 66–67, 75; also see Sprague, "On the 'Gay Side' of Town," pp. 13–15.

14. Katz, *Gay American History*, pp. 101–2; also see George Henry, *Sex Variants: A Study of Homosexual Patterns*, vol. 1 (New York: Paul B. Hoeber, 1941), pp. 350–51, 425–26, 438–45.

15. George Chauncey, Jr., "From Sexual Inversion to Homosexuality: Medicine and the Changing Conceptualization of Female Deviance," in Kathy Peiss and Christina Simmons, eds., *Passion and Power: Sexuality in History*, (Philadelphia: Temple University Press, 1989), pp. 93–98. In European scholarship the debate turns on the work of Foucault, with several influential British historians arguing for the persistence of the inversion or queen model from the eighteenth through the twentieth century. For a review of the literature, and an incisive critique of the tendency of overgeneralization, see Gert Hekma, "The Homosexual, the Queen and Models of Gay History," *Perversions*, no. 3 (Autumn 1994): 119–38.

16. In Philadelphia there is evidence of homosexuality near vice districts. "Fairies" congregated in the tenderloin area. See Vice Commission of Philadelphia, 1913, pp. 64–81.

17. Quoted in Sprague, "On the 'Gay Side' of Town," p. 9.

18. Harvey Warren Zorbaugh, *The Gold Coast and the Slum* (Chicago: University of Chicago Press, 1929, 1976), pp. 96, 102, 100; quoted in Sprague, "On the 'Gay Side' of Town," p. 19; Randolph and State, near the Navy base, was another site of public sex activity, particularly among sailors who solicited "fairies" for money (see Ernest Burgess Collection, location unknown, June 29, 1933).

19. On the unique sexual practices of the hobo subculture, see interview with J. P. Smith, Ernest Burgess Collection, box 134, folder 2, October 13, 1934, 9 pp.; see also Sprague, "On the 'Gay Side' of Town," pp. 15–16.

20. Walt Lewis, "My Story of Fags, Freaks, and Women Impersonators," Ernest Burgess Collection, mss., box 98, file 11, p. 2; quoted in Sprague, "On the 'Gay Side' of Town," p. 20; "Mr. K.," Ernest Burgess Collection, ms., box 98, file 11. In an interview, one African-American man stated that while at a North Clark Street club, another women approached his female date and asked her to dance.

21. Ernest Burgess Collection, ms., box 145, folder 10, 1930s.

22. Katz, *Gay American History*, pp. 76–77; Katz, *Gay/Lesbian Almanac*, p. 307.

23. Mabel Hampton, interview five, with the kind permission of Joan Nestle.

24. Committee of Fourteen, Investigator Report, box 85, June 21, 1928.

25. Committee of Fourteen, mss., box 37, June 8, 1928; Committee of Fourteen, ms., box 37, May 16, 1928; *Annual Report of the Committee of Fourteen*, 1928, pp. 31–34.

26. Committee of Fourteen, Investigator Report, box 37, 1928.

27. Ibid.

28. Committee of Fourteen, Investigator Report, box 37, June 8, 1928.

29. Committee of Fourteen, ms., box 85, 1928.

30. Lillian Faderman, *Odd Girls and Twilight Lovers: A History of Lesbian Life in Twentieth-Century America* (New York: Penguin, 1992), p. 76. "Sex Circuses" were often discussed in connection with homosexuals and lesbians, but an interview with a young black man about Chicago's sexual underground reveals that there were also heterosexual "sex circuses" (see Lewis, "Fags, Freaks, and Women Impersonators," Ernest Burgess Collection, box 98, file 11). On lesbian circuses, see Eric Garber, "A Spectacle in Color: The Lesbian and Gay Subculture of Jazz Age Harlem," in Martin Duberman, Martha Vicinus, and George Chauncey, eds., *Hidden from History: Reclaming the Gay and Lesbian Past* (New York: New American Library, 1990), pp. 322–23.

31. Ernest Burgess Collection, box 121, folder 6. The black gay artist Richard Nugent pointed out that not only ethnic difference but also class diversity was a feature of some establishments. He recalled a certain club where men could find "rough trade" (see Garber, "Spectacle in Color," p. 323).

32. Langston Hughes, *The Big Sea: An Autobiography* (1940; reprint, New York: Thunder's Mouth, 1986), p. 273.

33. Ernest Burgess Collection, box 127, folder 8. The German Freudian psychoanalyst Wilhelm Stekel was influential in American discussions of sexuality. See, for instance, Wilhelm Stekel, *Impotence in the Male*, 2 vols. (New York: Boni and Liveright, 1927), especially vol. 2, chaps. 18, 20, for a detailed discussion of homosexuality.

34. Glen Carrington Papers, correspondence from Glen Carrington to David, box 5, February 8, 1926.

35. Committee of Fourteen, Investigative Report, ms., box 36, May 25, 1928; Committee of Fourteen, Investigative Report, box 37, ms., n.d.; also "pervert practices" in majority heterosexual black/white speakeasy, Committee of Fourteen, ms., Investigative Report, box 36, "Lenox Avenue Club," investigated in February, March, and June 1928.

36. Committee of Fourteen, Investigative Report, box 36, May 28, 1928; Committee of Fourteen, Investigative Report, box 37, June 8, 1928. Investigators reported sexualized dance in heterosexual speakeasies as well (Committee of Fourteen, Old Kid Morris Dance Hall, June 22, 1928). The evidence here is limited: we do not know the precise movements of each dance.

37. Lynne Fauley Emery, *Black Dance in the United States from 1619 to 1970* (Palo Alto, Calif.: National Press Books, 1972); Katrina Hazzard-Gordon, *Jookin': The Rise of Social Dance Formations in African-American Culture* (Philadelphia: Temple University Press, 1990).

38. Faderman, *Odd Girls and Twilight Lovers*, pp. 76–78; Eric Garber,

★

"T'Ain't Nobody's Business: Homosexuality in 1920s Harlem," in Michael J. Smith, ed., *Black Men, White Men: A Gay Anthology* (San Francisco: Gay Sunshine, 1983), pp. 7–16; Garber, "A Spectacle in Color," p. 320.

39. Ernest Burgess Collection, "Observations by Earle Bruce," box 127, file 8.

40. Ernest Burgess Collection, "Harold, age twenty-one," box 127, folder 8, p. 5.

41. M. Hampton, Joan Nestle's possession, interview 5; for use of the term *jazz* by a black man in a homosexual context, see Lewis, "Fags, Freaks, and Women Impersonators," Ernest Burgess Collection, box 98, file 11, p. 1; for white prostitutes' use of the term, see Chicago Committee of Fifteen, Investigative Reports, mss., vol. 12, pp. 340–41.

42. Lewis, "Fags, Freaks, and Women Impersonators," Ernest Burgess Collection, box 98, file 11 (ca. 1930s); "Lester," Ernest Burgess Collection, box 98, file 11 (ca. 1930s); "Leo," Ernest Burgess Collection, box 98, file 11.

43. Chauncey, "From Sexual Inversion to Homosexuality," pp. 93–98; Michel Foucault, *The History of Sexuality*, vol. 1: *An Introduction*, trans. Robert Hurley (New York: Random House, 1980); on inverts, see George Chauncey, Jr., "Christian Brotherhood or Sexual Perversion? Homosexual Identities and the Construction of Sexual Boundaries in the World War I Era," in Duberman, Vicinus, and Chauncey, eds., *Hidden from History*, pp. 294–317.

44. I was influenced by D. Halperin's essays on Foucault. I thank him for a conversation on the construction of intercourse that always stuck with me.

45. For the importance of the straight-queer distinction in defining public homosexual contacts, see Chauncey, "Christian Brotherhood or Sexual Perversion?" pp. 294–317.

46. For a discussion of class, see Jeffrey Weeks, "Inverts, Perverts, and Mary-Annes: Male Prostitution and the Regulation of Homosexuality in England during the Nineteenth and Early Twentieth Centuries," in Duberman, Vicinus, and Chauncey, eds., *Hidden from History*, pp. 195–211; on the persistence of "trade" in New York in the 1950s, see Martin Duberman, *Cures: A Gay Man's Odyssey* (New York: Dutton, 1991), pp. 75–92.

47. Committee of Fourteen, Investigative Report, box 36, May 25, 1928; another example of male and female homosexual prostitution can be found in a report on the Blue Ribbon Chile Parlor, Committee of Fourteen, Investigative Report, box 37, May 16, 1928. I want to thank Katie Gilmartin for drawing my attention to the implications of this dialogue.

48. Committee of Fourteen, Investigative Report, box 36, November 10, 1928; for a similar conflation of male with female prostitution, see Committee of Fourteen, Investigative Report, box 36, February 9, 1927.

49. See contents of Committee of Fourteen, mss., full typed reports, boxes 36, 37.

50. Mumford, " 'Lost Manhood' Found," p. 98.

51. A good example is the description of a "Colored Pervert," which blurs the

distinction between public sex and prostitution (see Committee of Fourteen, Investigative Report, box 36, May 19, 1927.

52. Committee of Fourteen, box 36, May 19, 1927.

53. Correspondence from Wallace Thurman to William Rapp, James Weldon Johnson Collection, Beineke Library at Yale University, box 1, file 7, ca. 1926.

54. Ibid., June 1, 1929; ibid., ca. 1926; on Thurman's divorce and marriage, see correspondence from Wallace Thurman to Claude McKay, ibid., box 5, October 4, 1928.

55. Wallace Thurman, *Infants of the Spring* (1932; reprint, Boston: Northeastern University Press, 1992).

56. Ibid., p. 34.

57. The majority of homosexual restaurants in Chicago presumably were all white, since they were middle-class, located in predominately white areas, and no mention of racial mixture appears in descriptions of them (see Sprague, "On the 'Gay Side' of Town," pp. 13–14). On Dill, see Garber, "A Spectacle in Color," p. 320.

6. New Fallen Women: Black/White Prostitution

1. Asbury, *Gem of the Prairie*

2. In addition to statistics cited in chapter 2, see Committee of Fourteen, mss., box 89, June 1924; Rosen, *Lost Sisterhood*, p. 80.

3. De Koven Bowen, *Colored People of Chicago*, p. 13; Waterman, *Prostitution and Its Repression in New York*, p. 17.

4. In 1913 black women represented approximately a third of arrested prostitutes; in 1924 they represented 46 percent of arrested prostitutes. The Women's Court stated: "Of the recidivists, but a fifth of whites were given the maximum sentence (parole commission or 180 days) while over half of the blacks were." Black women were less successful on probation (Committee of Fourteen, mss., Women's Court Records, box 89 June 1924).

5. Deborah Gray White, *Ar'n't I A Woman: Female Slavery in the Antebellum South* (New York: Norton, 1985); Elizabeth Fox-Genovese, *Within the Plantation Household: Black and White Women of the Old South* (Chapel Hill: University of North Carolina Press, 1988); Bryan Turner, *The Body and Society* (New York: Oxford University Press, 1984); Hazel Carby, "Policing the Black Woman's Body in an Urban Context," *Critical Inquiry* 13 (Summer 1993): 739–52; Norma Burgess and Derrick Horton, "African American Women and Work: A Socio-Historical Perspective," *Journal of Family History* 8 (1993): 53–63; Eleanor Smith, "Black American Women and Work: A Historical Review, 1619–1920," *Women's Studies International Forum* 8, no. 4 (1985): 343–49.

6. De Koven Bowen, *The Colored People of Chicago*, p. 25. I am indebted to conversations with Debra Satz for the notions of bodily autonomy and labor.

7. Faye E. Dudden, *Serving Women: Household Service in Nineteenth Century America* (Middletown, Conn.: Wesleyan University Press, 1983), pp. 32–35, 63–65, 222–26.

8. For New York, see George Edmund Haynes, *The Negro at Work in New York City: A Study in Economic Progress*, vol. 49, no. 3 (New York: Columbia University Press, 1912), pp. 26, 72; for Chicago, see U.S. Bureau of the Census, *Negro Population in the United States, 1790–1915* (New York: Arno, 1968), p. 512.

9. Kneeland, *Commercialized Prostitution in New York City*, pp. 212, 6; De Koven Bowen, *The Colored People of Chicago*, p. 25; for the preponderance of black women as servants in brothels in Philadelphia, see Vice Commission of Philadelphia, *Annual Report for 1913*, p. 65.

10. *Pittsburgh Courier*, May 8, 1912, p. 1; *Chicago Defender*, October 26, 1912, p. 1.

11. On the limitations of black employment agencies, see Theodore Cowgill, "The Employment Agencies of Chicago," M.A. thesis, University of Chicago, 1928, pp. 33, 66, 87.

12. Anne Butler, *Daughters of Joy, Sisters of Misery: Prostitutes in the American West, 1865–90* (Urbana: University of Illinois Press, 1985), p. 4.

13. Lucie Cheng Hirata, "Free, Indentured, Enslaved: Chinese Prostitutes in Nineteenth-Century America," *Signs: Journal of Women in Culture and Society* 5, no. 1 (July 1980): 13; Beth Bailey and David Farber, "Hotel Street: Prostitution and the Politics of War," *Radical History Review* 52 (1992): 54–77.

14. Committee of Fourteen, mss., Investigative Report, box 36; *Annual Report for the Committee of Fourteen*, 1929, pp. 13–14; Committee of Fourteen, mss., memorandum, box 89, 1927.

15. Committee of Fourteen, mss., Investigative Report, box 36, February 9, 1927. "The usual charge is a flat rate of $15, although some charge on an hourly basis. Of this the dance manager receives from 50 to 60 percent" (*Annual Report of the Committee of Fourteen*, 1930, p. 22).

16. Committee of Fourteen, mss., Investigative Report, box 31, February 9, 1921.

17. Committee of Fourteen, mss., box 37, Investigative Report, May 15, 1928; on working-class "treating," see Peiss, *Cheap Amusements*, pp. 53–55, 108–9. For general prices, see Committee of Fourteen, mss., box 37, Hostess File, 1931.

18. Committee of Fourteen, mss., Investigative Report, box 34; instead, these hostesses were described as American, which meant white only. For example, one bulky folder of Committee of Fourteen manuscripts consisted of approximately a hundred reports on hostesses, but none of the material concerned a dance hall hostess who was black (see Committee of Fourteen, mss., box 37, Investigative Reports, 1927). For the construction of the white hostess, see *Annual Report of the Committee of Fourteen*, 1927, pp. 22–23.

19. *Baltimore Afro-American*, October 29, 1920, p. 1.

20. Kneeland, *Commercialized Prostitution in New York*, pp. 105–7; Gilfoyle, *City of Eros*, pp. 289–90; Dudden, *Serving Women*, pp. 66–67, 84, 219–22; on black women's wages as domestics, see David Katzman, *Seven Days a Week: Women and Domestic Service in Industrializing America* (New York: Oxford University Press, 1978), pp.303–14; Elizabeth Clark-Lewis, "'This Work Had No End': African-American Domestic Workers in Washington, D.C., 1910–1940," in Carol Groneman and Mary Beth Norton, eds., *"To Toil the Livelong Day": America's Women at Work, 1780–1980* (Ithaca, N.Y.: Cornell University Press, 1987), pp. 196–212.

21. Juvenile Protective Agency, mss., "Parlor House," file 95b.

22. Committee of Fourteen, mss., Investigative Report, box 36, May 28, 1928.

23. Committee of Fourteen, mss., Investigative Report, box 37, May 13, 1928; Committee of Fourteen, mss., Investigative Report, box 33, 1928. In this white brothel for black men, liquor cost approximately fifty cents and the price for room and sexual exchange was seven dollars. Also see Committee of Fourteen, mss., box 36, Investigative Report, May 28, 1928.

24. Committee of Fourteen, mss., Investigative Report, box 37, 1928; Committee of Fourteen, mss., Investigative Report, box 36, May 29, 1928.

25. Juvenile Protective Agency, "Cabaret," file 93, 1928; also see Juvenile Protective Agency, file 95b, "Parlor House."

26. Juvenile Protective Agency Collection, file 93, Investigative Report, November 25, 1922.

27. Juvenile Protective Agency, mss., file 108; for a view of Filipino men and white women, see Juvenile Protective Agency, file 104, October 12, 1928.

28. Ruth Rosen, *The Lost Sisterhood: Prostitution in America, 1910–1918* (Baltimore: The Johns Hopkins Press, 1982), pp. 107, 148, 171–72; Louise White, *The Comforts of Home: Prostitution in Colonial Nairobi* (Chicago: University of Chicago Press, 1990). pp. 6–9.

29. Ernest Burgess Collection, box 129, folder 2, Cynthia Cohen, Graduate Student Essay, ca. 1930, p. 5.

30. Ibid., p. 3.

31. Ruth Rosen argues that streetwalking was the least preferred form of prostitution among prostitutes themselves (see Rosen, *Lost Sisterhood*, chap. 3). White argues for the greater autonomy of streetwalking (see *Comforts of Home*, introduction).

32. Cohen, Graduate Student Essay, p. 5

33. Bureau of Social Hygiene Collection, Series 3, reel 4, bureau memo, September 20, 1930.

34. *Annual Report of the Committee of Fourteen*, 1929, p. 9.

35. Bureau of Social Hygiene Collection, Series 3, reel 4, bureau memo, October 20, 1932.

36. *Annual Report of the Committee of Fifteen*, 1927, p. 21.

37. Committee of Fourteen, mss., box 31, Summary of Reports, 1927; Ernest

★

Burgess Collection, mss., Correspondence, box 12, file 8, February 13, 1929; Juvenile Protective Agency, mss., Investigative Report, file 92.

38. Ernest Burgess Collection, box 6, folder 8, Confidential Memorandum, June 6, 1934.

39. Committee of Fourteen, mss., Investigative Report, box 37, April 14, 1928.

40. Ibid.

41. Committee of Fourteen, mss., Investigative Report, box 37, 1927–28.

42. Ibid.

43. This is particularly true of the advertisements appearing in the *New York Age* and the *Baltimore Afro-American*, but all of the black press I surveyed indicated extreme color consciousness.

44. Committee of Fourteen, mss., Investigative Report, box 36, May 22, 1928.

45. Ibid.

46. Committee of Fourteen, mss., Investigative Report, box 37, October 31, 1928.

47. Bureau of Social Hygiene, Series 3, reel 4, October 20, 1932.

48. Ibid., September 6, 1932.

49. According to one report, for example, the "colored" women "accosted the men very boldly" (see Committee of Fourteen, mss, box 37, 1927–28; Committee of Fourteen, mss., Investigative Reports, Nicholas Avenue resorts, box 36, 102–4).

50. Quoted in Peiss, *Cheap Amusements*, p. 66.

51. Rosen, *The Lost Sisterhood*, p. 107.

52. Asbury, *Gem of the Prairie*, pp. 97, 318.

53. Quoted in Estelle B. Freedman, "The New Woman: Changing Views of Women in the 1920s," *Journal of American History* 61 (June–September 1974): 373.

54. Mary P. Ryan, *Womanhood in America: From Colonial Times to the Present*, 2nd ed. (New York: New Viewpoints, 1979), pp. 153–58.

55. In portraying the New Woman of the 1920s, for example, Smith-Rosenberg largely confines her analysis to modernist writers (see *Disorderly Conduct*, pp. 281–93). For a similar emphasis, see Esther Newton, "The Mythic Mannish Lesbian: Radclyffe Hall and the New Woman," in Martin Duberman et al., eds., *Hidden from History: Reclaiming the Gay and Lesbian Past* (New York: New American Library, 1990), pp. 281–93.

56. William O'Neill, *Everyone Was Brave: The Rise and Fall of Feminism in America* (Chicago: Quadrangle Books, 1969), p. 297.

57. Meyerowitz, *Women Adrift*, chap. 6.

58. Committee of Fourteen, mss., Investigative Report, box 37, March 29, 1928; Committee of Fourteen, mss., Investigative Report, box 36, February 9, 1927; *Annual Report of the Vice Commission of Philadelphia*, 1913, p. 64.

59. New Woman styles in France reflected a blurring of distinctions

between men and women, and reflected the social turmoil caused by World War I (see Mary Louise Roberts, *Civilization Without Sexes: Reconstructing Gender in Postwar France, 1917–1927* [Chicago: University of Chicago Press, 1994], pp. 63–88).

60. Barbara Meil Hobson, *Uneasy Virtue: The Politics of Prostitution and the American Reform Tradition* (New York: Basic Books, 1987), pp. 166–67; Mary Ellen Odem, "Delinquent Daughters: The Sexual Regulation of Female Minors in the United States, 1880–1920," Ph.D. diss., University of California-Berkeley, 1989, p. 196.

61. Robert E. Riegel, "Changing American Attitudes Toward Prostitution, 1800–1920," *Journal of the History of Ideas* 29, no. 3 (July–September 1968): 437–53; Ruth Rosen, *Lost Sisterhood*, chap. 2; Egal Feldman, "Prostitution, the Alien Woman, and Progressive Imagination, 1910–15," *American Quarterly* 19 (1967): 192–206; Sylvia D. Hoffert, "This 'One Great Evil,'" *American Historical Illustrated* 112, no. 2 (1977): 37–41; Marion Goldman, *Gold Diggers and Silver Miners: Prostitution and Social Life on the Comstock Lode* (Ann Arbor: University of Michigan Press, 1981); Thomas Mackey, "Red Lights Out: A Legal History of Prostitution, Disorderly Houses, and Vice Districts, 1870–1917," Ph.D. diss., Rice University, 1984; Larry Shumsky, "Tacit Acceptance: Respectable Americans and Segregated Prostitution, 1870–1910," *Journal of Social History* 9 (1986): 665–79.

62. *Annual Report of the Committee of Fourteen*, 1927, p. 18.

63. Ibid., p. 18.

64. Nancy F. Cott, *Bonds of Womanhood: "Woman's Sphere" in New England, 1780–1835* (New Haven: Yale University Press, 1977); Katherine Kish Sklar, *Catherine Beecher: A Study in American Domesticity* (New York: Oxford University Press, 1977); Mary P. Ryan, *Cradle of the Middle Class: The Family in Oneida County, New York, 1790–1865* (New York: Cambridge University Press, 1982); Estelle B. Freedman, *Their Sisters' Keepers: Women's Prison Reform in America, 1830–1930* (Ann Arbor: University of Michigan Press, 1981); on space and fallen women, see Margaret Wyman, "The Rise of the Fallen Woman," *American Quarterly* 3 (1951): 167–76; Walkowitz, *City of Dreadful Delight*, chap. 2; Nancy F. Cott, "Passionlessness: An Interpretation of Victorian Sexual Ideology, 1790–1850," *Signs* 4 (1978): 219–36; on public/private distinctions and class, see Christine Stansell, *City of Women: Sex and Class in New York, 1789–1860* (New York: Knopf, 1986), pp. 190–92.

65. Walter Reckless, *Vice in Chicago* (Chicago: University of Chicago Press, 1933; repr. 1969), pp. 54–56.

66. Ibid., p. 55.

67. Ibid.

68. Kunzel, *Fallen Women, Problem Girls*, p. 55.

69. Earl Richard Moses, "Community Factors in Negro Delinquency," Ph.D. diss., University of Chicago, 1932, p. 184.

70. *Annual Report of the Committee of Fourteen*, 1928, pp. 31–34.

71. Deborah Gray White, *Ar'n't I A Woman: Female Slavery in the Antebellum South* (New York: Norton, 1985); Hazel Carby, "Policing the Black Woman's Body in an Urban Context," *Critical Inquiry* 13 (Summer 1993): 739–52.

72. Reckless, *Vice in Chicago*, p. 59.

73. Cressey, *The Taxi-Dance Hall*, p. 34.

74. Ernest Burgess Collection, mss., box 193, folder 6, February 20, 1926.

75. Cressey, *The Taxi-Dance Hall*, pp. 92–94, 124.

76. Quoted in Elaine Tyler May, *Great Expectations: Marriage and Divorce in Post-Victorian America* (Chicago: University of Chicago Press, 1980), p. 110.

77. *Pittsburgh Courier*, September 8, 1923; on racial jealousy in Washington, D.C., see Leona Ann Herbert, "A Study of Ten Cases of Negro-White Marriages in the District of Columbia," Ph.D. diss., Catholic University, 1939, pp. 33, 74.

78. Robert Edward Thomas Roberts, "Negro-White Intermarriage: A Study of Social Control," M.A. thesis, University of Chicago, 1940, p. 89.

7. On Stage: The Social Response to All God's Chillun' Got Wings

1. Eugene O'Neill, *All God's Chillun' Got Wings*, in *Nine Plays by Eugene O'Neill* (New York: The Modern Library, 1941), p. 91.

2. *New York Times*, February 16, 1924, p. 2.

3. O'Neill, *All God's Chillun'*, p. 91.

4. Ibid., p. 94

5. Ibid., p. 95.

6. Ibid., p. 98.

7. Ibid., p. 102.

8. Ibid., p. 105.

9. Ibid., p. 110.

10. Ibid., p. 113.

11. Ibid., p. 125.

12. Ibid., p. 126.

13. Ibid., p. 129.

14. Ibid., p. 130.

15. Ibid., p. 132.

16. *Nation*, March 5, 1924.

17. Correspondence to NAACP, Miscegenation File, March 5, 1924, p. 1.

18. *New York Sentinel*, March 3, 1924.

19. *Union*, Cincinnati, Ohio, March 1, 1924.

20. Ibid.

21. *Greensboro Daily News*, North Carolina, February 22, 1924, p. 1.

22. *North Carolina Herald*, Durham, February 24, 1924, editorial.

23. *New York Herald*, Rochester, February 23, 1924, p. 5.

24. *New York American*, March 18, 1924.

25. *North Carolina Herald*, Durham, February 24, 1924, editorial.

26. *New York American*, March 15, 1924.

27. Martin Duberman, *Paul Robeson: A Biography* (New York: Ballantine, 1989), p. 59.

28. *New York American*, March 11, 1924.

29. Ibid., March 17, 1924, p. 1.

30. Ibid., March 15, 1924, p. 34.

31. Duberman, *Paul Robeson*, p. 66.

32. *New York World*, March 20, 1924, p. 4.

33. *New York Herald*, Rochester, February 23, 1924, p. 5.

34. *New York American*, March 11, 1924.

35. *New York World*, March 9, 1924.

36. *North Carolina Herald*, Durham, February 24, 1924, editorial.

37. Correspondence to NAACP, March 3, 1924.

38. *Age-Herald*, Birmingham, Alabama, March 18, 1924.

39. *New York Herald*, March 17, 1924, p. 2.

40. *Age-Herald*, Birmingham, Alabama, March 18, 1924.

41. *New York Times*, May 16, 1924, p. 1.

42. NAACP Files, "Statement Made by Eugene O'Neill."

43. O'Neill statement, p. 3.

44. Ibid.

45. *Tampa Florida Tribune*, February 23, 1924, p. 2.

46. *New York Times*, May 16, 1924.

47. Duberman, *Paul Robeson*, p. 67.

8. *Slumming: Appropriating the Margins for Pleasure*

1. On American modernism, see Ann Douglas, *Terrible Honesty: Mongrel Manhattan in the 1920s* (New York: Farrar, Straus and Giroux, 1995); Roberts, *Civilization Without Sexes*, pp. 12–16; Mary Louise Pratt, "Scratches on the Face of the Country; or, What Mr. Barrow Saw in the Land of the Bushmen," in Henry Louis Gates, Jr., ed., *Race, Writing, and Difference* (Chicago: University of Chicago Press, 1985), pp. 138–62.

2. Friedrich Engels, *The Condition of the Working Class in England*, trans. and ed. W. O. Henderson and W. H. Caholoner (Stanford: Stanford University Press, 1958); Henry Mayhew, *London Labour and the London Poor*, 4 vols. (New York: Dover, 1968); Charles Booth, *Life and Labour of the People of London*, 9 vols. (London: Macmillan, 1891–1897).

3. Jacob A. Riis, *How the Other Half Lives: Studies among the Tenements of New York* (New York: Scribners, 1920); James B. Lane, *Jacob Riis and the American City* (Port Washington, N.Y.: Kennikat, 1974); Roy Lubove, *The Professional Altruist: The Emergence of Social Work as a Profession* (Cambridge,

★

Mass.: Harvard University Press, 1965); and his *The Progressives and the Slums: Tenement House Reform in New York City, 1890–1917* (Cambridge, Mass.: Harvard University Press, 1962).

4. Riis, *How the Other Half Lives*, p. 2

5. Ibid., p. 17.

6. Deborah Epstein Nord, "The Social Explorer as Anthropologist: Victorian Travellers among the Urban Poor," in William Sharpe and Leonard Wallock, eds., *Visions of the Modern City: Essays in History, Art, and Literature* (Baltimore: The Johns Hopkins University Press, 1987), pp. 118–30.

7. Ibid., p. 56; Peter Stallybrass and Allon White, *The Politics and Poetics of Transgression* (Ithaca, N.Y.: Cornell University Press, 1986), pp. 2–5, 125–27.

8. Riis, *How the Other Half Lives*, p. 95.

9. Ibid., pp. 95–96. For each social problem Riis identified, he formulated a solution. In general, he was part of the sanitation movement, which proposed to clean up slums and restore the neighborhoods as a method for containing pauperism. But for Chinatown, Riis proposed that immigration authorities "make it a condition of his [the Chinese] coming or staying that he bring his wife with him" (ibid.).

10. Ibid., p. 148.

11. Ibid., p. 152.

12. Ibid.

13. Ibid., p. 156.

14. W.E.B. DuBois, *The Philadelphia Negro: A Social Study* (1899; reprint, New York: Kraus-Thompson, 1973), pp. 46, 166, 304, 365.

15. William H. Jones, *Recreation and Amusement among Negroes in Washington D.C.* (Washington, D.C.: Howard University Press, 1928), pp. 122, 132.

16. John Drury, *Chicago in Seven Days* (New York: McBride, 1928), p. 161.

17. Walter Burrows, *New York: An Intimate Guide* (New York: Knopf, 1931), p. 268.

18. Niles Hogner, *Cartoon Guide of New York* (New York: Augustin, 1938), pp. 34–35.

19. Rupert Hughes, *The Real New York* (New York: Smart Set, 1904), p. 353.

20. Ibid., pp. 356–57, 363.

21. Asbury, *Gem of the Prairie*, p. 295; Luc Sante, *Low Life: Lures and Snares of Old New York* (New York: Farrar Straus Giroux, 1991).

22. Martin Bulmer, *The Chicago School of Sociology* (Chicago: University of Chicago Press, 1984), p. 92.

23. Ibid., p. 104

24. Committee of Fourteen, Investigative Report, ms., box 85, 1928.

25. Federal Writers Project, *New York Panorama: The American Guide* (New York: Random House, 1938), p. 143.

26. Lloyd Morris, *Incredible New York: High Life and Low Life of the Last Hundred Years* (New York: Random House, 1951), p. 337.

27. Bruce Kellner, *Carl Van Vechten and the Irreverent Decades* (Norman: University of Oklahoma Press, 1968), p. 198; Edward Lueders, *Carl Van Vechten and the Twenties* (Albuquerque: University of New Mexico Press, 1955).

28. Gloria Hull, *Color, Sex, and Poetry* (Bloomington: Indiana University Press, 1987), p. 9.

29. W.E.B. DuBois, "Books," *Crisis* (December 1926); James Weldon Johnson, "Romance and Tragedy in Harlem," *Opportunity* 4 (October 1926): 316–17, 330; Louis Kronenberger, "*Nigger Heaven,*" *International Book Review* (October 1926); Abbe Niles, "Aunt Haggar's Children," *New Republic* 48 (September 29, 1926): 162; "*Nigger Heaven,*" *Independent* 117 (August 28, 1926): 248.

30. "*Nigger Heaven,*" p. 154.

31. Ibid., p. 107; Nella Larsen, *Quicksand and Passing,* ed. by Deborah McDowell (New Brunswick, N.J.: Rutgers University Press, 1986), p. 198.

32. Kellner, *Carl Van Vechten,* p. 219.

33. Ibid., p. 211.

34. Ibid., p. 242.

35. Ibid., pp. 109. 112.

36. Ibid., p. 113.

37. Carl Van Vechten, *Parties: Scenes from Contemporary New York Life* (New York: Knopf, 1930), pp. 8, 68.

38. Ibid., pp. 68, 174.

39. Ibid., p. 186.

40. Ibid., p. 71.

41. Ibid., p. 220.

42. J. George Frederick, *Adventuring in New York* (New York: Brown, 1923).

43. Committee of Fourteen, ms., box 85, 1928.

44. Juvenile Protective Agency, Investigative Report, box 92, 1923.

45. Lloyd Morris, *Incredible New York: High Life and Low Life of the Last Hundred Years* (New York: Random House, 1951), p. 333.

46. Rian James, *All about New York: An Intimate Guide* (New York: John Day, 1931), p. 249.

47. Morris, *Incredible New York,* p. 333.

48. Committee of Fourteen, Investigative Report, box 36, January 13, 1928.

49. James, *All about New York,* p. 249.

50. Morris, *Incredible New York,* p. 333.

51. Roy Ottley, *A New World a Coming* (Boston: Houghton Mifflin, 1943), p. 67.

52. Asbury, *Gem of the Prairie,* pp. 103, 246.

53. Henry Champly, *White Women, Coloured Men* (London: John Long, 1936), p. 96.

54. Ibid., p. 95.

55. George Seaton, *Cue's Guide to New York City* (New York: Prentice-Hall, 1940), p. 95.

★

56. Wils Hogner and Guy Scott, *Cartoon Guide to New York City* (New York: Augustin, 1938).

57. Ottley, *A New World a-Coming*, p. 62.

58. Morris, *Incredible New York*, p. 334.

59. Ibid.

60. Hogner and Scott, *Cartoon Guide of New York City*.

61. Burrows, *New York: An Intimate Guide*, p. 271.

62. Ibid., p. 270. At the same time, guides routinely listed the Cotton Club alongside the most exclusive entertainment spots in the city, including the Persian Room at the Plaza Hotel, located on Fifth Avenue and 59th Street; the Stork Club, located on 53rd Street; and the Rainbow Room, in the RCA Building.

63. Van Vechten, *Nigger Heaven*, p. 107.

64. James, *All About New York*, p. 249.

9. Racial Reactions: Prohibiting Miscegenation in the 1920s

1. *American Mercury* 1, no. 2 (February 1924): 163; *American Mercury* 3, no. 11 (November 1924).

2. Don S. Kirschner, *City and Country: Rural Responses to Urbanization in the 1920s* (Westport, Conn.: Greenwood, 1970), pp. 118–121.

3. D. W. Griffith, *Birth of a Nation*, ed. Robert Lang (New Brunswick, N.J.: Rutgers University Press, 1994), p. 291.

4. For evidence that illicit sexual relations actually increased during black migration, see Joel A. Rogers, *Sex and Race: A History of White, Negro, and Indian Miscegenation in the Two Americas*, vol. 2 (New York: J.A. Rogers Publ., 1942), p. 288. For an excellent summary of *early* northern response to black migration expressed through intermarriage anxiety, see St. Clair Drake and Horace Cayton, *Black Metropolis: A Study of Negro Life in a Northern City*, vol. 1 (1945; reprint, New York: Harper, 1962), pp. 133–36.

5. John Higham, *Strangers in the Land: Patterns of American Nativism, 1860–1925* (New York: Atheneum, 1965), pp. 271–73, 290–91; see also John Higham, *Send These to Me: Immigration in Urban America* (Baltimore: The Johns Hopkins University Press, 1984), pp. 29–65, 117–44. For background on hostility to immigrants, see Theodore Hershberg, ed., *Philadelphia: Work, Space, Family, and Group Experience in the Nineteenth Century* (New York: Oxford University Press, 1981); John Bodnar, Roger Simon, and Michael Weber, *Lives of Their Own: The Changing Face of Inequality: Urbanization, Industrial Development, and Immigrants in Detroit, 1880–1920* (Urbana: University of Illinois Press, 1981).

6. On convergence between anti-immigrant and antiblack racism, see Thomas F. Gosset, *Race: The History of an Idea in America* (New York: Schocken, 1963), pp. 287–309.

7. Rayford Logan, *The Betrayal of the Negro: From Rutherford B. Hayes to Woodrow Wilson* (New York: Collier, 1965), pp. 218–41; Higham, *Strangers in the Land*, pp. 264–99.

8. George M. Fredrickson, *The Black Image in the White Mind: The Debate on Afro-American Character and Destiny, 1817–1914*, 2nd ed.(Middletown, Conn.: Wesleyan University Press, 1987), pp. 245–55; Gosset, *Race*, pp. 145–46, 159–60.

9. Linda Gordon, *Woman's Body, Woman's Right: Birth Control in America* (New York: Grossman, 1976), p. 139; Mark Haller, *Eugenics: Hereditarian Attitudes in American Thought* (New Brunswick, N.J.: Rutgers University Press, 1963); Donald Pickens, *Eugenics and Progressives* (Nashville: Vanderbilt University Press, 1968); Caleb William Saleby, *The Progress of Eugenics* (New York: Funk and Wagnalls, 1914); C. P. Blacker, *Eugenics: Galton and After* (Cambridge, Mass.: Harvard University Press, 1952).

10. Theodore Lothrop Stoddard, *The Rising Tide of Color Against White World Supremacy* (New York: Scribner, 1920), p. 302. He did argue explicitly against racial mixture: "And of course the more primitive a type is the more potent it is. This is why crossings with the negro are uniformly fatal" (Madison Grant, *The Passing of the Great Race* [New York: Scribner, 1916]).

11. Higham refers to Grant as "the most important nativist in recent American history" (Higham, *Strangers in the Land*, p. 156).

12. According to Higham, Grant's book "had caused no considerable comment when first published in 1916. New editions appeared in 1921 and 1923, bringing total sales to about sixteen thousand copies" (see Higham, *Strangers in the Land*, p. 221).

13. Waldo E. Martin, Jr., *The Mind of Frederick Douglass* (Chapel Hill: University of North Carolina Press, 1984), pp. 219–22; for Charles Chesnutt on amalgamation, see *New York Age*, July 20, 1905, p. 7.

14. Louis R. Harlan, *Booker T. Washington: The Wizard of Tuskegee, 1901–1915* (New York: Oxford University Press, 1983), pp. 33, 129, 205, 250.

15. W.E.B. DuBois, "Miscegenation," ms., Schomburg Center for Black Culture, New York City, p. 3. James Weldon Johnson writes, "We are not here considering the advisability, either pro or con, of intermarriage. We are simply questioning the justice of spreading such a law upon the national statute books" (see *New York Age*, January 21, 1915, p. 1). For outlines of the NAACP position, see *Crisis* 5 (February 1913): 18; 11 (April 1916): 306; 24 (May 1922): 8; 23 (December 1921): 56; 19 (January 1920): 337; 12 (May 1916): 30.

16. Ann Julia Cooper, *A Voice from the South* (1892; reprint, New York: Negro Universities Press, 1969), p. 221; NAACP Collection, Intermarriage File, 1923, correspondence from Hallie Q. Brown to officers of the National Association of Colored Women, February 1, 1923.

17. *The Marcus Garvey Papers and Universal Negro Improvement Association Papers*, vol. 4 (Berkeley: University of California Press, 1989), p. 41.

★

18. Evidence indicates that some black people supported legalized restrictions on intermarriage. For example, in 1907 one black paper reported that "three colored men introduced a bill to the House to prohibit intermarriage" (Bill H.R. 24539) (see *New York Age*, March 21, 1907, p. 1).

19. Judith Stein, *The World of Marcus Garvey: Race and Class in Modern Society* (Baton Rouge: University of Louisiana Press, 1986), pp. 4–6, 38–60; also see Marcus Garvey, "The Negro's Greatest Enemy," *Current History* 19 (March 1921): 951–58.

20. Gilmore, *Bad Nigger!* See also Randy Roberts, *Papa Jack: Jack Johnson and the Era of White Hopes* (New York: Free Press, 1983); Finnis Farr, *Black Champion: The Life and Times of Jack Johnson* (London: Macmillan, 1964); for focused studies of the social response to Johnson, see Raymond Wilson, "Another White Hope Bites the Dust: The Jack Johnson–Jim Flynn Heavyweight Fight of 1912," *Montana: The Magazine of History* 29 (1979): 30–39; Randy Roberts, "Heavyweight Champion Jack Johnson: His Omaha Image, a Public Reaction Study," *Nebraska History* 52 (1976): 226–41.

21. *Pittsburgh Courier*, November 14, 1925, p. 1; *New York Times*, December 6, 1925, p. 27; *New York Times*, November 27, 1925, p. 3; Claude Barnett Collection, #887; Mark Madigan, "Miscegenation and the 'Dicta of Race and Class': The Rhinelander Case and Nella Larsen's *Passing*," *Modern Fiction Studies* 36, no. 4 (Winter 1990): 523–29.

22. *Chicago Defender*, August 9, 1919, p. 6; see also *Pittsburgh Courier*, January 2, 1911, p. 2.

23. *New York Age*, December 31, 1914, p. 3; a similar case occurred a decade later, in which a Michael Mallio claimed that his wife was actually of "negro parentage" (see *Pittsburgh Courier*, May 17, 1924, p. 4).

24. *Pittsburgh Courier*, March 8, 1924, p. 1.

25. Connections between intermarriage and racial passing were common (see Barnett Collection, "Racial Classifications and Intermarriage," nos. 890, 935, 997, 1130; for an extensive discussion, see St. Clair Drake and Horace Cayton, *Black Metropolis: A Study of Negro Life in a Northern City*, vol. 1 (1945; reprint, New York: Harper, 1962), pp. 131–43.

26. *New York Amsterdam News*, December 6, 1922, p. 3.

27. As the NAACP pointed out, "If any measure prohibiting racial inter-marriage ever comes to a vote in either house of the Congress, it would probably pass by an overwhelming majority" (see NAACP Collection, Intermarriage File, Speech by Wendell P. Dabney to U.S. Judiciary Committee, March 3, 1925).

28. *Pittsburgh Courier*, February 13, 1916, p. 2. However, the legislature rejected the system because it "designated as colored at least a dozen members of the General Assembly, and not less than 20 percent of the most distinguished members of Congress."

29. Throughout the 1920s the panic reached into several southern states. Attempts were made to install more stringent systems of racial classification. In

Notes

Kentucky the State registrar of Vital Statistics advocated a national system of compulsory racial registration. The registrar had identified "great peril in the inability of the members of the white race to distinguish between colored people of light complexion and white people" (see *New York Age*, December 21, 1916, p. 2). In addition, the Virginia registrar, William Plecker, advocated a national racial registration system (see *Baltimore Afro-American*, March 14, 1922, p. 3).

30. During the late nineteenth century, several northern states repealed anti-intermarriage laws. However, between 1890 and 1930 sentiments against intermarriage intensified, as evidenced by no states repealing their statutes. See Michael Grossberg, *Governing the Hearth: Law and the Family in Nineteenth-Century America* (Chapel Hill: University of North Carolina Press, 1985), p. 138.

31. The states were Illinois, Indiana, Iowa, Ohio, Kansas, Nebraska, New York, Pennsylvania, Washington, and Wisconsin. See Albert Ernest Jenkes, "The Legal Status of Negro-White Amalgamation in the United States," *American Journal of Sociology* 21 (Winter 1928): 669.

32. The states were Connecticut, Iowa, Idaho, Maine, Massachusetts, New Jersey, Pennsylvania, and Rhode Island. See NAACP Collection, Intermarriage File, 1927; NAACP Collection, Intermarriage, correspondence from the NAACP to Kansas City Branch, March 12, 1927; also see NAACP Collection, Intermarriage, February 22, 1927: "The national office has evidence that this effort is being put forth by the Ku Klux Klan."

33. NAACP Collection, Intermarriage, 1918, anonymous interoffice memo; NAACP Collection, Intermarriage, December 10, 1913, correspondence to the editor of *Omaha Bee*, Victor Rosewater.

34. NAACP Collection, Intermarriage, April 12, 1921, correspondence to the Detroit branch.

35. Many of the bills died in congressional committee, so the records contain little evidence about the arguments either for or against the legislation. Even when the bills were debated on the floors of state senates, the record is often incomplete.

36. *History of Wisconsin*, vol. 5 (State History of Wisconsin, 1990), pp. 122–25. The bill was to create a section 4582 of the statutes, relating to intermarriage of white persons and Negroes and providing a penalty. On January 12, 1917, the bill was referred to committee; on February 1, 1917, it was posted for hearing; on February 7, 1917, the hearing was held.

37. NAACP Collection, Intermarriage, February 20, 1913, correspondence from William Miller to director of branches, NAACP.

38. *Wisconsin State Journal*, February 8, 1917, p. 1; NAACP Collection, Intermarriage, May 19, 1929, correspondence to W. Andrews from Les Robinson, secretary of Madison, Wisconsin, branch of the NAACP.

39. Logan, *Betrayal of the Negro*, p. 364.

40. *Hartford Connecticut Times*, February 9, 1928, p. 1; *New York Times*, February 6, 1928, p. 1; *New York Age*, March 15, 1926, p. 3.

41. *New York Times*, February 6, 1928, p. 2; *Waterbury Republican*, February 2, 1928, p. 1; *New York Amsterdam News*, February 8, 1928, p. 2.

42. *Baltimore Afro-American*, October 17, 1903, p. 1.

43. *New York Times*, January 24, 1884, p. 1. In an astonishing case the groom, a light-skinned black man, whom the community had always accepted as white, revealed his black ancestry upon applying for a marriage license to wed a white woman. The sentiments in the town turned against the man and opposed the marriage; within several days some residents mobilized against the union. According to the press, "As word spread, men came to his home." A group of local men, in Klan like fashion, "began digging up the couple's lawn and burned a cross ten feet high, which blazed in the darkness" (*New York Times*, November 7, 1925, p. 1).

44. *New York Times*, July 4, 1926, p. 2; in Fort Dodge the commissioner ordered that a woman intending to marry a black man be examined for insanity (Logan, *The Betrayal of the Negro*, p. 222).

45. *Pittsburgh Courier*, July 16, 1923, p. 1.

46. Just as white women who wished to marry black men were sometimes viewed as insane, the women's families, if they consented to the intermarriage, could also find themselves facing judges. In one important case, for example, Fred Hitchcock, who permitted his young daughter to marry Arthur Jones, was charged with breaking the law. Hitchcock was tried before a judge and jury and found guilty of violating public decency. He was sentenced to six months in jail and ordered to pay a fifty-dollar fine (*New York Age*, April 25, 1907, p. 1).

47. For discussions of the Mann Act, see Mark Thomas Connelly, *The Response to Prostitution in the Progressive Era* (Chapel Hill: University of North Carolina Press, 1980), pp. 57–59, 127–29; Daniel J. Leab, "Women and the Mann Act," *Amerikastuden/American Studies* 21 (1976): 55–65; William Seagle, "Twilight of the Mann Act," *American Bar Association Journal* 55 (1969): 641–47.

48. See *New York Times*, March 4, 1920, p. 3; for age of consent laws see Mary Ellen Odem, "Delinquent Daughters: The Sexual Regulation of Female Minors in the United States, 1880–1920," Ph.D. diss., University of California — Berkeley, 1989.

49. Ernest Porterfield, *Black and White Mixed Marriages: An Ethnographic Study of Black-White Families* (Chicago: Nelson-Hall, 1978), p. 26.

50. Porterfield, *Black and White Mixed Marriages*.

Epilogue

1. I gained this insight from an important conversation with Carl Degler regarding the Marxian tendency to essentialize class.

★

SELECTED BIBLIOGRAPHY

MANUSCRIPTS

Beineke Rare Book and Manuscript Library, Yale University
    Countee Cullen Papers
    Nancy Cunard Papers
    Rudolph Fisher Papers
    Langston Hughes Papers
    Harold Jackman Papers
    James Weldon Johnson Papers
    Claude McKay Papers
    Richard Bruce Nugent Papers
    Dorothy Peterson Papers
    Wallace Thurman Papers
    Carl Van Vechten Papers
Bureau of Social Hygiene Papers, Microfilm
Claude Barnett, National Negro Press Association Papers, Racial Definitions
    and
Lesbian Herstory Archives, New York City, Mabel Hampton Collection
Library of Congress, Manuscripts Division, Washington, D.C.
    National Association for the Advancement of Colored People, Manuscript
        Collection, Library of Congress

National Urban League Papers
New York Public Library, New York City
    Committee of Fourteen, Manuscripts
Schomburg Center for Research in Black Culture, New York Public
    Library, New York City
    Arthur Schomburg Papers
    Glenn Carrington Papers
    "Miscegenation," W. E. B. DuBois, Manuscript
Stanford University, Special Collections, Stanford, California
    David Goodman Croly Pamphlets
University of Chicago, Regenstein Special Collections, Chicago, Illinois
    Ernest Burgess Collection
    Committee of Fifteen, Manuscripts
    Julius Rosenwald Papers
University of Illinois—Chicago
    Chicago Woman's Aid Papers
    Juvenile Protective Association Papers
    Institute for Sex Education
    Dr. Ben Lewis Reitman Papers
Wisconsin Historical Society, Madison, Wisconsin
    Teasdale Vice Commission Collection
    Wisconsin Vice Commission, Manuscripts

UNPUBLISHED SECONDARY SOURCES

Adams, Bruce Payton. "The White Negro: The Image of the Passable Mulatto Character in Black Novels, 1853–1954," Ph.D. diss., University of Kansas, 1975.

Adams, Mary F. "Present Housing Conditions in South Chicago, South Dearborn, and Pullman," Master's thesis, University of Chicago, 1926.

Barnhart, Jacqueline Baker. "Working Women: Prostitution in San Francisco from the Gold Rush to 1900," Ph.D. diss., University of California at Santa Cruz, 1976.

Bernstein, Rachel Amelia. "Boarding House Keepers and Brothel Keepers in New York City, 1880–1910," Ph.D. diss., Rutgers University, 1984.

Berzon, Judith Rae. "Neither White Nor Black: The Mulatto Character in American Fiction," Ph.D. diss., New York University, 1974.

Brundage, William F. "Lynching in the New South: Georgia and Virginia, 1800–1930," Ph.D. diss., Harvard University, 1988.

Carlisle, Marcia. "Prostitutes and Their Reformers in Nineteenth-Century Philadelphia," Ph.D. diss., Rutgers University, 1982.

Cowgill, Theodore T. "The Employment Agencies of Chicago," master's thesis, University of Chicago, 1928.

Herbert, Leona Anne. "A Study of Ten Cases of Negro-White Marriages in the District of Columbia," master's thesis, The Catholic University of America, 1939.

★

Leashore, Bogart Raymond. "Interracial Households in 1850–1880 Detroit, Michigan," Ph.D. diss., University of Michigan, 1979.

Lemple, Leonard Richard. "The Mulatto in United States Race Relations: Changing Status and Attitudes, 1800–1940," Ph.D. diss., Syracuse University, 1979.

Little, Johnathan D. "Definition Through Difference: The Tradition of Black-White Miscegenation in American Fiction," Ph.D. diss., University of Wisconsin at Madison, 1989.

Lockard, Diana. "The Negro on the Stage in the Nineteen Twenties," master's thesis, Columbia University, 1960.

Lynn, Sister Annella Lynn. "Interracial Marriages in Washington, D.C., 1940–47," master's thesis, The Catholic University of America, 1953.

Maclean, Nancy K. "Behind the Mask of Chivalry: Gender, Race, and Class in the Making of the Ku Klux Klan of the 1920s in Georgia," Ph.D. diss., University of Wisconsin, 1989.

Mencke, John German. "Mulattoes and Race Mixture: American Attitudes and Images from Reconstruction to World War I," Ph.D. diss., University of North Carolina, 1978.

Moses, Earl Richard. "Community Factors in Negro Delinquency in Chicago," Ph.D. diss., University of Chicago, 1931.

Roberts, Robert Edward T. "Negro-White Marriages in Chicago," master's thesis, University of Chicago, 1939.

Rood, Alice Q. "Social Conditions among the Negroes on Federal Street between Forty-fifth Street and Fifty-third Street," master's thesis, University of Chicago, 1924.

Sprague, Greg. "On the 'Gay Side' of Town: The Nature and Structure of Male Homosexuality in Chicago, 1890–1935," unpublished manuscript in author's possesion.

Wagner, Roland Richard. "Virtue Against Vice: A Study of Moral Reformers and Prostitution in the Progressive Era," Ph.D. diss., University of Wisconsin at Madison, 1971.

Whiteaker, Larry Howard. "Moral Reform and Prostitution in New York City, 1830–1860," Ph.D. diss., Princeton University, 1977.

Wilson, Evelyn H. "Chicago Negro Families in Furnished Rooms," master's thesis, University of Chicago, 1929.

Young, Damon P. "Negro-White Contacts in the District of Columbia," master's thesis, Howard University, 1927.

NEWSPAPERS

Baltimore Afro-American, 1895–1924
Chicago Defender, 1910–30
Chicago Herald, 1917–19, 1922–24, 1926–28

Selected Bibliography

Chicago Whip, 1919–22
Crisis, 1911–40
Green Bay Gazette, 1920
New York Age, 1906–30
New York Amsterdam News, 1922–30
Opportunity, 1923–40
Pittsburgh Courier, 1911–30
New York Times, 1880–1960
Wisconsin State Journal, 1914–20

SELECTED OFFICIAL RECORDS

Atlanta Vice Commission, Report of the Vice Commission, 1922
Chicago Committee of Fifteen, Annual Reports, 1910–30
Chicago Commission on Race Relations, The Negro in Chicago, 1920
Chicago Vice Commission, The Social Evil in Chicago, 1913
Journal of Social Hygiene, 1917–30
New York Committee of Fourteen, Annual Reports, 1905–30
Report and Recommendation of Wisconsin Vice Committee, 1914
Report of the Vice Commission, Little Rock, Arkansas

SELECTED SECONDARY SOURCES

Books

Acton, William. Prostitution. 1857. Reprint, New York: Praeger, 1968.
Addams, Jane. A New Conscience and an Ancient Evil. New York: Macmillan, 1913.
Anderson, Nels. Hoboes: A Sociology of Homeless Men. Chicago: University of
    Chicago Press, 1922.
Ashbury, Herbert. The Gangs of New York: An Informal History of the Under-
    world. New York: Columbia University Press, 1928.
Becker, Howard S. Symbolic Interaction and Cultural Studies. Chicago: Univer-
    sity of Chicago Press, 1990.
Benson, Susan Porter. Counter Cultures: Saleswoman, Managers, and Custom-
    ers in American Department Stores, 1890–1940. Urbana: University of Illi-
    nois Press, 1986.
Bernstein, Iver. The New York City Draft Riots: Their Significance for American
    Society and Politics in the Era of Civil War. New York: Oxford University
    Press, 1988.
Boris, Eileen and Cynthia Daniels. Homework: Historical and Contemporary
    Perspectives on Paid Labor at Home. Urbana: University of Illinois Press,
    1989.
Bristow, Edward. Prostitution and Prejudice: The Jewish Fight Against White
    Slavery, 1870-1939. New York: Schocken, 1983.

★

Bulmer, Martin. *The Chicago School of Sociology: Institutionalization, Diversity, and the Rise of Sociological Research*. Chicago: University of Chicago Press, 1984.

Cashman, Sean Dennis. *Prohibition: The Lie of the Land*. New York: Free Press, 1981.

Champly, Henry. *White Women, Coloured Men*. London: John Long, 1936.

Chauncey, George. *Gay New York: Gender, Urban Culture, and the Making of the Gay Male World, 1890–1930*. New York: Basic Books, 1994.

Coben, Stanley. *Rebellion Against Victorianism: The Impetus for Cultural Change in 1920s America*. New York: Oxford University Press, 1991.

Committee of Fifteen. *The Social Evil, with Special References to Conditions Existing in the City of New York*, 1902.

Connelly, Mark Thomas. *The Response to Prostitution in the Progressive Era*. Chapel Hill: University of North Carolina Press, 1980.

Corbin, Alain. *Women for Hire: Prostitution and Sexuality in France after 1850*. Cambridge: Harvard University Press, 1990.

Cordasco, Francesco and Thomas Pitkin. *The White Slave Trade and the Immigrants: A Chapter in American Social History*. Detroit: Blaine Ethridge, 1981.

Cressey, Paul. *Taxi-Dance Halls*. Chicago: University of Chicago Press, 1932.

Cross, Gary. *A Social History of Leisure Since 1600*. State College, Pa.: Venture, 1990.

Cunningham, Hugh. *Leisure in the Industrial Revolution, 1780–1880*. London: Croom Helm, 1980.

Davenport, B. C. "The Mingling of the Races." In E. V. Cowdy, ed., *Human Biology and Racial Welfare*, chap. 23. New York: Paul B. Hoeber, 1930.

Degler, Carl. *Neither White Nor Black: Race Relations in Brazil and the American South*. 1971. Reprint, Madison: University of Wisconsin Press, 1987.

Denning, Michael. *Mechanic Accents: Dime Novels and Working-Class Culture in America*. London: Verso, 1987.

D'Emilio, John and Estelle B. Freedman. *Intimate Matters: A History of Sexuality in America*. New York: Harper & Row, 1988.

Drake, St. Clair and Horace Cayton. *Black Metropolis: A Study of Negro Life in a Northern City*. 2 vols. New York: Harcourt Brace, 1945.

Duberman, Martin, Martha Vicinus, and George Chauncey, eds. *Hidden from History: Reclaiming the Gay and Lesbian Past*. New York: New American Library, 1989.

Dudden, Faye E. *Serving Women: Household Service in Nineteenth-Century America*. Middletown, Conn.: Wesleyan University Press, 1983.

Duncan, Otis Dudley. *The Negro Population of Chicago: A Study of Residential Succession*. Chicago: University of Chicago Press, 1957.

Selected Bibliography

Duneier, Mitchell. *Slim's Table: Race, Respectability, and Masculinity.* Chicago: University of Chicago Press, 1992.

Ehrenreich, Barbara. *The Hearts of Men: American Dreams and the Flight from Commitment.* New York: Anchor, 1983.

Emery, Lynne Fauley. *Black Dance in the United States from 1619 to 1970.* Palo Alto, Calif.: National Press Books, 1972.

Erenberg, Lewis A. *Steppin' Out: New York Nightlife and the Transformation of American Culture, 1890–1930.* Westport, Conn: Greenwood, 1981.

Faderman, Lillian. *Odd Girls and Twilight Lovers: A History of Lesbian Life in Twentieth-Century America.* New York: Columbia University Press, 1991.

Ford, Charles Henry. *The Young and the Evil.* New York: Seahorse, 1930.

Foucault, Michel. *The History of Sexuality: An Introduction,* vol. 1. New York: Pantheon, 1980.

Fanon, Frantz. *Black Skin, White Masks.* New York: Grove Press, 1967.

Frazier, E. Franklin. *The Negro Family in Chicago.* Chicago: University of Chicago Press, 1933.

——. *The Negro in the United States.* New York: Macmillan, 1957.

Fredrickson, George F. *The Arrogance of Race: Historical Perspectives on Slavery, Racism, and Social Inequality.* Middletown, Conn. Wesleyan University Press, 1988.

Freedman, Estelle B. *Their Sisters' Keepers: Women's Prison Reform in America, 1830–1930.* Ann Arbor: University of Michigan Press, 1982.

Gatewood, Willard B. *Aristocrats of Color: The Black Elite, 1880–1920.* Bloomington: Indiana University Press, 1990.

Geoffrey, M. *Marriage Laws and Decisions in the United States.* New York: Russell Sage, 1929.

Gerlach, Larry. *Blazing Crosses in Zion: The Ku Klux Klan in Utah.* Logan: Utah State University Press, 1982.

Goldberg, Robert Alan. *Hooded Empire: The Ku Klux Klan in Colorado.* Urbana: University of Illinois Press, 1981.

Goodale, Thomas L. and Geoffrey Godbey. *The Evolution of Leisure: Historical and Philosophical Perspectives.* State College, Pa.: Venture, 1988.

Grossman, James R. *Land of Hope: Chicago, Black Southerners, and the Great Migration.* Chicago: University of Chicago Press, 1989.

Gusfield, Joseph R. *Symbolic Crusade: Status Politics and the American Temperance Movement.* Urbana: University of Illinois Press, 1974.

Hall, Jacquelyn Dowd. *Revolt Against Chivalry: Jessie Daniel Ames and the Women's Campaign Against Lynching.* New York: Columbia University Press, 1979.

Halsey, Margaret. *Color Blind: A White Woman Looks at the Negro.* New York: Simon and Schuster, 1944.

Hazzard-Gordon, Katrina. *Jookin': The Rise of Social Dance Formations in African-American Culture.* Philadelphia: Temple University Press, 1990.

★

Hearn, Jeff. *Men in the Public Eye*. London: Routledge, 1992.

Hebdige, Dick. *Subculture: The Meaning of Style*. London: Methuen, 1979.

Hill, Marilyn Wood. *Their Sisters' Keepers: Prostitution in New York City, 1830–1870*. Berkeley: University of California Press, 1993.

Hobson, Barbara Meil. *Uneasy Virtue: The Politics of Prostitution and the American Reform Tradition*. New York: Basic Books, 1987.

Huggins, Nathan. *The Harlem Renaissance*. New York: Oxford University Press, 1971.

Jackson, Kenneth T. *The Ku Klux Klan in the City, 1915–1930*. New York: Oxford University Press, 1967.

Johnson, Claudia. "That Guilty Third Tier: Prostitution in Nineteenth-Century American Theaters." In Daniel Walker Howe, ed., *Victorian America*, pp. 111–20. Philadelphia: University of Pennsylvania Press, 1976.

Johnson, James Weldon. *The Autobiography of an Ex-Colored Man*. New York: Knopf, 1917.

——. *Black Manhattan*. New York: Knopf, 1930.

Katz, Jonathan. *Gay American History: Lesbians and Gay Men in the U.S.A.* New York: Thomas Crowell, 1976.

——. *Gay/Lesbian Almanac*. New York: Harper & Row, 1983.

Katzman, David M. *Seven Days a Week: Women and Domestic Service in Industrializing America*. New York: Oxford University Press, 1978.

Kinney, James. *Amalgamation!: Race, Sex, and Rhetoric in the Nineteenth-Century American Novel*. Westport, Conn.: Greenwood, 1985.

Kusmer, Kenneth. *A Ghetto Takes Shape: Black Cleveland, 1870–1930*. Urbana: University of Illinois Press, 1976.

Lane, Roger. *Policing the City: Boston, 1822–1885*. New York: Oxford University Press, 1977.

——. *Roots of Violence in Black Philadelphia, 1860–1900*. Cambridge: Harvard University Press, 1986.

Lasch-Quinn, Elizabeth. *Black Neighbors: Race and the Limits of Reform in the American Settlement House Movement, 1890–1945*. Chapel Hill: University of North Carolina Press, 1993.

Locke, Alaine. *The New Negro: An Interpretation*. New York: A. and C. Boni, 1925.

Logan, Rayford. *The Betrayal of the Negro: From Rutherford B. Hayes to Woodrow Wilson*. New York: Collier, 1954.

Lott, Eric. *Love and Theft: Blackface Minstrelsy and the American Working Class*. New York: Oxford University Press, 1993.

Magnan, J. A. and James Walvin. *Manliness and Morality: Middle-Class Masculinity in Britain and America, 1800–1940*. New York: St. Martin's, 1987.

Majors, Richard and Janet Mancini Billson. *Cool Pose: The Dilemmas of Black Manhood in America*. New York: Lexington, 1992.

McKay, Claude. *Home to Harlem*. New York: Knopf, 1928.

Meyerowitz, Joanne. *Women Adrift: Independent Wage-Earning Women in Chicago, 1880–1930*. Chicago: University of Chicago Press, 1988.

Miner, Maude. *Slavery of Prostitution: A Plea for Emancipation*. New York: Macmillan, 1916.

Mowry, George E. *The Twenties: Fords, Flappers, and Fanatics*. Englewood Cliffs, N.J.: Prentice-Hall, 1963.

Muker, Richard. *Better Angel*. New York: Greenberg, 1933.

Myrdal, Gunnar. *An American Dilemma*. New York: Basic Books, 1945.

Niles, Blair. *Strange Brother*. 1931. Reprint, London: Gay Men Press, 1992.

O'Neill, Eugene. *Nine Plays by Eugene O'Neill*. New York: Modern Library, 1941.

O'Neill, William L. *Everyone Was Brave: The Rise and Fall of Feminism in America*. Chicago: Quadrangle, 1969.

Osofsky, Gilbert. *Harlem, The Making of a Ghetto: Negro New York, 1890–1930*. New York: Harper, 1965.

Ostransky, Leroy. *Jazz City: The Impact of Our Cities on the Development of Jazz*. Englewood Cliffs, N.J.: Prentice-Hall, 1978.

Ovington, Mary White. *Half a Man: The Status of the Negro in New York*. New York: Longmans, Green and Co., 1911.

Park, Robert. *The City*. Chicago: University of Chicago Press, 1924.

Peiss, Kathy. *Cheap Amusements: Working Women and Leisure in Turn-of-the-Century New York*. Philadelphia: Temple University Press, 1986.

——. *Passion and Power: Sexuality in History*. Philadelphia: Temple University Press, 1989.

Philpot, Thomas Lee. *The Slum and the Ghetto: Neighborhood Deterioration and Middle-Class Reform, 1880–1930*. New York: Oxford University Press, 1978.

Platt, Anthony M. *E. Franklin Frazier Reconsidered*. New Brunswick, N.J.: Rutgers University Press, 1993.

Porterfield, Ernest. *Black and White Mixed Marriages: An Ethnographic Study of Black-White Families*. Chicago: Nelson-Hall, 1978.

Posner, Richard A. *Sex and Reason*. Cambridge: Harvard University Press, 1992.

Rampersad, Arnold. *The Life of Langston Hughes: I, Too, Sing America*. Vol. 1. New York: Oxford University Press, 1986.

Roediger, David. *Wages of Whiteness: Race and the Making of the American Working Class*. London: Verso, 1991.

Rogers, Joel Augustus. *Sex and Race: The Old World*. Vol. 1. New York: Rogers, 1940.

——. *Sex and Race: A History of White, Negro, and Indian Miscegenation in the Two Americas*. Vol. 2. New York: J. A. Rogers, Publ., 1942.

——. *Nature Knows No Color Line*. New York: Rogers Press, 1952.

Rosen, Ruth. *The Lost Sisterhood: Prostitution in the Progressive Era*. Chicago, University of Chicago Press, 1982.

★

Rosenzweig, Roy. *Eight Hours for What We Will: Workers and Leisure in an Industrial City, 1870–1920.* Cambridge: Cambridge University Press, 1983.

Rotundo, Anthony. *American Manhood: Transformations in Masculinity from the Revolution to the Modern Era.* New York: Basic Books, 1993.

Ryan, Mary P. *Womanhood in America: From Colonial Times to the Present.* New York: New Viewpoints, 1976.

——. *Cradle of the Middle Class: Family and Women in Oneida County, New York, 1780–1860.* New York: Cambridge University Press, 1982.

Sanger, William. *History of Prostitution.* 1859. Reprint, New York: Arno, 1972.

Smith-Rosenberg, Carroll. *Disorderly Conduct: Visions of Gender in Victorian America.* New York: Alfred A. Knopf, 1985.

Spear, Allan. *Black Chicago: The Making of a Negro Ghetto, 1880–1920.* Chicago: University of Chicago Press, 1967.

Susman, Warren I. *Culture as History: The Transformation of American Society in the Twentieth Century.* New York: Pantheon, 1984.

Szarkowski, John, ed., *Bellocq Portraits: Storyville Portraits—Photographs from the New Orleans Red Light District, circa 1912.* New York: Museum of Modern Art, 1970.

Thurman, Wallace. *Fire!: Devoted to Younger Negro Artists.* Vol. 1. New York: Nendeln, Liechtenstein: Kraus, 1926.

——.*The Blacker the Berry.* New York: Collier, 1928.

——. *Infants of Spring.* 1932 reprint Boston: Northeastern University Press, 1992.

Van Vechten, Carl. *Nigger Heaven.* New York: Knopf, 1926.

Walkowitz, Judith R. *Prostitution and Victorian Society: Women, Class, and the State.* Cambridge: Cambridge University Press, 1980.

——. *City of Dreadful Delight: Narratives of Sexual Danger in Late-Victorian London.* Chicago: University of Chicago Press, 1992.

Weeks, Jeffrey. *Sex, Politics, and Society: The Regulation of Sexuality Since 1890.* Essex: Longman, 1981.

——. *Against Nature: Essays on History, Sexuality, and Identity.* London: Rivers Oram, 1991.

Westabrook, A. *Mongrel Virginians.* Baltimore: William and Wilkins, 1926.

White, Kevin. *The First Sexual Revolution: The Emergence of Male Heterosexuality in Modern America.* New York: New York University Press, 1993.

White, Luise. *The Comforts of Home: Prostitution in Colonial Nairobi.* Chicago: University of Chicago Press, 1990.

Williamson, Joel. *The New People: Miscegenation and Mulattoes in the United States.* New York: The Free Press, 1980.

Willoughby, Waterman. *Prostitution and Its Repression in New York City, 1900–1931.* New York: Columbia University Press, 1932.

Wilson, Samuel Paynter. *Chicago and Its Cesspools of Infamy.* Chicago: Samuel Painter, 1910.

Zorbaugh, Harvey. *The Gold Coast and the Slum*. Chicago: University of Chicago Press, 1930.

Journal Articles

Andrews, William L. "Miscegenation in the Late-Nineteenth-Century Novel." *Southern Humanities Review* 13, no. 1 (1979): 13–24.

Bowler, Alida C. "Social Hygiene in Racial Problems, the Filipinos." *Journal of Social Hygiene* 18 (November 1923): 452–56.

Burnham, John C. "American Historians and the Subject of Sex." *Societas: A Review of Social History* 2 (1974): 307–16.

———. "The Progressive Era Revolution in American Attitudes Toward Sex." *Journal of American History* 59 (1973): 885–907.

Butler, Johnnella E. and Marable Manning. "The New Negro and the Ideological Origins of the Integrationist Movement." *Journal of Ethnic Studies* 2, no. 4 (1975): 47–55.

Feldman, Egal. "Prostitution, the Alien Woman, and Progressive Imagination, 1910–1915." *American Quarterly* 19 (1967): 192–206.

Flynn, Joyce. "Melting Plots: Patterns of Racial and Ethnic Amalgamation in American Drama Before Eugene O'Neill." *American Quarterly* 38, no. 3 (1986): 417–38.

Freedman, Estelle B. "The New Woman: Changing Views of Women in the 1920s." *Journal of American History* 61 (June–September 1974): 372–93.

Gilmore, Al-Tony. "Jack Johnson and White Women: The National Impact." *Journal of Negro History* 58 (1973): 18–38.

Hirata, Lucie Cheng. "Free, Indentured, Enslaved: Chinese Prostitutes in Nineteenth-Century America." *Signs: Journal of Women in Culture and Society* 5, no. 1 (July 1980): 3–29.

Hofert, Sylvia D. "This 'One Great Evil,' " *American Historical Illustrated* 112, no. 2 (1977): 37–41.

Hooton, Albert. "When Races Intermarry." *The Nation* 127 (July–December 1928): 84–86.

Johnson, Michael P. " 'A Middle Ground': Free Mulattoes and the Friendly Moralist Society of Antebellum Charleston." *Southern Studies* 21, no. 3 (1982): 246–64.

Johnson, Wittington B. *Maryland Historical Magazine* 73, no. 3 (1978): 236–45.

Lewis, Roscoe E. "The Life of Priscilla Joyner." *Phylon* 20, no. 1 (1959): 71–81.

Mumford, Kevin J. " 'Lost Manhood' Found: Male Sexual Impotence and Victorian Culture in the United States." *Journal of the History of Sexuality* 3, no. 1 (July 1992): 33–57.

Nichols, Frank. "Social Hygiene and the Negro." *Journal of Social Hygiene* (October 1929).

Nye, Russell B. "Saturday Night at the Paradise Ballroom; or, Dance Halls in the Twenties." *Journal of Popular Culture* 7 (Summer 1973).

Park, Robert E. "The Mentality of Racial Hybrids." *Journal of Sociology* 36 ( ): 534–51.

Peel, Mark. "On the Margins: Lodgers and Boarders in Boston, 1860–1900." *Journal of American History* 72 (1986): 813–34.

Pivar, David. "Cleansing the Nation: The War on Prostitution, 1917–21." *Prologue* 12, no. 1 (Spring 1980): 29–40.

Reed, Ruth. "Negro Illegitimacy." *Journal of Social Hygiene* (February 1925).

Riegel, Robert. "Changing Attitudes Towards Prostitution, 1880–1920." *Journal of the History of Ideas* 29 (1968): 449–52.

Saks, Viola. "National Identity, Miscegenation, and Cultural Expressions: A Comparison Between the United States and Brazil." *Social Science Information* 22, no. 2 (1983): 165–68.

Schafer, Judith Kelleher. "New Orleans Slavery in 1850 as Seen in Advertisements." *Journal of Southern History* 47, no. 1 (1981): 33–56.

Schafer, Robert S. "White Persons Held to Racial Slavery in Antebellum Arkansas." *Arkansas Historical Quarterly* 44, no. 2 (1985): 134–55.

Siegel, Adrienne. "Brothels, Bets, and Bars: Popular Literature as a Guidebook to the Urban Underground, 1840–1870." *North Dakota Quarterly* 44 (1976): 6–22.

Smits, David D. " 'Abominable Mixture': Toward the Repudiation of Anglo-Indian Intermarriage in Seventeenth-Century Virginia." *Virginia Magazine of History and Biography* 95, no. 2 (1987): 157–92.

Sollors, Werner. " 'Never Was Born': The Mulatto, An American Tragedy?" *Massachusetts Review* 27, no. 2 (1986): 293–316.

Toplin, Robert Brent. "Between Black and White: Attitudes Toward Southern Mulattoes, 1830–1861." *Journal of Southern History* 45, no. 2 (1979): 185–200.

Wyman, Margaret. "The Rise of the Fallen Woman." *American Quarterly* 3 (1951): 167–76.

Zanger, Jules. "The 'Tragic Octoroon' in Pre–Civil War Fiction." *American Quarterly* 18, no. 1 (1966): 63–70.

Zellors, Parker R. "The Cradle of Variety: The Concert Saloon." *Educational Theatre Journal* 20 (1968): 578–86.

★

INDEX